American Critical Essays
on The Divine Comedy

AMERICAN CRITICAL ESSAYS ON

The Divine Comedy

Edited by ROBERT J. CLEMENTS

New York • New York University Press
London • University of London Press Limited
1967

© 1967 BY NEW YORK UNIVERSITY
LIBRARY OF CONGRESS CATALOG CARD NUMBER: 66–22220
MANUFACTURED IN THE UNITED STATES OF AMERICA

Dedicated to the memory
of Ernest Hatch Wilkins
by his fellow authors

THE Congresso Internazionale di Studi Danteschi of 1965, cele-
brated jointly in Florence, Verona, and Ravenna gave testimony
of the continuing and growing fame of Dante. A glance at the
historico-bibliographical volume, *Dante nel Mondo* (Florence,
Ohlschki, 1965), which appeared contemporaneously with the
first volume of the Acts of the Congress, shows the geographical
extent to which Dante retains his rank as one of any choice of
the half-dozen poets of all time, and not necessarily "sixth
among such great intelligence."

One fact emerging from the year's bibliographical re-
searches on Dante by Professor Marraro, updating those of Miss
La Piana, is the arrival of American scholars at the vanguard
of researchers on Dante. American Dante studies have come a
long way since the Trecento poet was first translated by a
Boston dentist and introduced here by such disparate com-
mentators as George Ticknor of Harvard and the notorious
Lorenzo da Ponte, refugee librettist and piecework instructor of
Italian at Columbia University. For all his picaresque ways, Da
Ponte held an edge over the New England school headed by
Longfellow, Emerson, and Norton. He did at least satisfy the
three qualifications required of a Dantist by Papini, being an
Italian, Catholic, and poet. Yet the New England school
founded in this country a fine tradition of Dante scholarship.
The world today holds in high esteem much of the prolific
investigation of Dante now being carried on in America.

It has thus seemed fitting that someone should bring together some of the finest examples of these American studies and essays on the *sommo poeta*, making them widely available in both clothbound and paperback forms. Some of the older scholars represented in these pages—Wilkins, Borgese, Tatlock, and Auerbach, for example—pick up the tradition early enough to form a continuum of sorts. Ernest Hatch Wilkins was for two brief years of his infancy a contemporary of Henry Wadsworth Longfellow, who died in 1882. In bringing together these essays all of which have appeared in the interval between the sixth centennial of Dante's death and the seventh of his birth, we have elasticized the adjective American, allowing it to denote the country where the author either was born or resided. Space restrictions made us exclude essays by Santayana and Pound, as well as several fine studies by scholars who are still in the "new life" of their careers.

I am grateful to my distinguished friends and colleagues or their executors for the privilege of assembling this varied florilegium. I owe thanks to the editors of the many journals and many presses who unanimously granted me reprint rights without cost as a contribution to the Dante Year, and to the sponsors of the VII Centenario della Nascita di Dante.

Italian and Latin passages have as a rule been translated into English. Where English versions were not provided in the original appearance of the essay, the familiar Wicksteed Englishings have been inserted.

Among others who have contributed to the successful appearance of this anthology are the members of the Graduate School of Arts and Science Committee on Research at New York University, Miss Mollie Comerford, most competent editorial assistant, and Professor Vittore Branca, Executive Secretary of the Associazione per gli Studi di Lingua e Letteratura Italiane, who has encouraged this and so many other American contributions to Italian letters.

> *E quant' io l'abbia in grado, mentre io vivo*
> *Convien che nella mia lingua si scerna.*
>
> R. J. C.

CONTENTS

                        ix

I. Introduction

Ernest Hatch Wilkins

1 · The Living Dante

I

The greatest of all poems bears the strangest of all titles: *Incipit Comedia Dantis Alagherii, florentini natione, non moribus*—"Here beginneth the Comedy of Dante Alighieri, a Florentine by birth, but not by character." These bitter words, penned by one who loved his native city with a passionate eagerness, proclaim indelibly the tragic intensity of Dante's life.

To that intensity witness is borne by his lyrics and his letters, by the very nature of his greater works, by the flashes of personal reference they contain, and by many of the legends that gathered swiftly around his memory. He was intense in his imaginative thought, which ranged relentlessly from his own immediate and central soul to the final spacelessness and timelessness of the Empyrean. He was intense in his emotions, whether of hope or fear, whether of love or hate. He was intense in mastering all the lore that entered the library of his mind, and in transmuting it into the processes of his own living. He was intense in the effort to achieve loyal poetic utterance: in the *Paradiso* he speaks of the Comedy as "the poem . . . that for many years hath kept me lean." He was intense in conviction, in action, and in the sufferings of his exile. He was intense in his faith in a God in whom power, wisdom, and love were fused in a radiance of supreme intensity.

No such soul could dwell apart. Into his own true self,

Reprinted from *Italica* (XXII, 2, 1945) by permission of the American Association of Teachers of Italian.

indeed, he must enfold all men, bound by the bond of love Nature herself creates—*lo vinco d'amor che fa natura*. And with all his might he toiled for the temporal and the eternal welfare of those with whom he shared that bond.

For their temporal welfare, he believed, it was necessary that the whole earth be brought into one single war-proof unity, a unity which he framed, inevitably, in terms of empire. This idea finds its most perfect statement in a passage in the *Convivio*, which is to be received with the realization that the imperial form is not essential to the thought:

> As an individual for his completeness requires the domestic companionship of the family, so a household for its completeness requires a neighborhood, since otherwise it would suffer many defects which would hinder the attainment of joy. And since a neighborhood cannot in all regards be self-sufficient, in order to satisfy all its wants there must needs be a city. Moreover a city, for the sake of its crafts and for self-defence, must needs have intercourse and brotherly relations with the neighboring cities, and for this reason the kingdom was instituted. But since the mind of man does not rest content with a limited possession of land, but always desires to acquire more, as we perceive by experience, disagreements and wars must needs arise between kingdom and kingdom. Which things are the tribulations of cities, and through cities of neighborhoods, and through neighborhoods of families, and through families of individuals, and thus the attainment of joy is hindered. Wherefore, in order to do away with these wars and their causes, it is necessary that the whole earth, and all that is given to the race of man to possess, should be a monarchy, that is to say, a single princedom, and should have a single prince, who possessing all things, and having nothing left to desire, may keep the kings confined within the borders of their kingdoms, so that peace may reign between them: in which peace the cities may have rest; in which rest the neighborhoods may love each other; in which love the households may satisfy all their wants; and when these are satisfied, man may attain joy, which is the end whereunto man was born.

Dante's life reached its highest peak of excitement when the Emperor Henry the Seventh entered Italy to assert the rights of empire and to receive the imperial crown; and Dante's style rose in its most soaring outbursts of vehement prophecy in the letters he wrote to herald Henry's coming. Henry's failure and death must have brought to Dante the most devastating distress he ever knew: yet his conviction and his faith remained unshaken.

Dante grasped the difference between time and eternity as few other men have grasped it. All men of his world envisaged life as consisting of two phases, the first to be lived upon this earth, the second to be lived either in Hell or in Paradise. All men of his world, also, would have said that the second phase was longer than the first; but to most of them the "longer" meant, in reality, only "somewhat longer," and while the experiences of life on earth were clear to them, the experiences of the other life were very vague. Dante's visualization of the matter was utterly different. For him, life on earth was, as it were, an infinitesimal point, and life after death a line infinite and sharply defined, a line, moreover, of utter bliss or utter woe. He believed that his fellow men, lacking such consciousness, were all too ready to take chances that would tend to exclude them from the joy of his realized and eternal Paradise, and to lead them irrevocably through the dread gate of his realized and eternal Hell. He was driven, therefore, by an irresistible compulsion, to set forth his vision for them all. The purpose of the Comedy, in his own words, is this: *removere viventes in hac vita de statu miserie, et perducere in statum felicitatis*—"to rescue those living in this life from a state of woe, and to lead them into a state of blessedness." The Comedy is a poem of many paradoxes; but its fundamental paradox lies in the fact that despite its poetic supremacy it is only secondarily a work of art: it is primarily an instrument of salvation.

There is cause for perpetual amazement in the fact that Dante, though he had this crystal-clear conception of the overwhelming difference between time and eternity, nevertheless asserted the possible value of this life, the value of the temporal blessedness, as he called it, more clearly than any other man of his time—as clearly, perhaps, as any man of any time. The great contrast, as he saw it, was not between a sorry vale of tears and a mystic glory, but between a life on this earth which in its own right was potentially a life of joy and an eternity far more joyous and more wonderful. His proclamation of the temporal blessedness is the noble proof and the mature expression of the intensity of his own living.

II

The writings of such a man must needs be profoundly full of life. In the oft-quoted words of one who drew much from Dante,

> Books . . . doe contain a potencie of life in them to be as active as that soule was whose progeny they are; nay, they do preserve as in a violl the purest efficacie and extraction of that living intellect that bred them.

The works of Dante do indeed contain in vital potency the activity of his creative soul. One can never dissociate them entirely from the inner life of their author; yet I should like to consider them now not as revelations of his own intensity, but as being in themselves enduring reservoirs of life. The lyrics are deep wells of life; the *Vita nuova* and the *Convivio* and the *Monarchia* are varied lakes of life; the Comedy is a great sea of life.

The lyrics are themselves of many kinds. Some, devoted to the voicing of reasoned praise, move from exquisite perceptions of beauty and gentleness to deeper perceptions of the lady as one through whom the divine goodness, shining, bestows blessedness. Others are delightful poems of love and friendship, or deeply moving poems of death foreseen in delirium or come to pass in overwhelming fact. Still others praise philosophy, or expound nobility, declaring it to be no matter of inheritance, but a gift of God. There are passing pictures of pilgrimage, of the hunt, of a group of ladies making holiday, pictures so finely etched that one exclaims: "This indeed is life seen, felt, preserved." And the rhythmic diction achieves many lines of echoing finality:

> *O voi che per la via d'Amor passate . . .*
>
> *Gentile è in donna ciò che in lei si trova,*
> *e bello è tanto quanto lei simiglia . . .*
>
> *Deh peregrini che pensosi andate*
> *forse di cosa che non v'è presente . . .*
>
> *Angelo clama in divino intelletto. . . .*

While the *Vita nuova* is essentially a collection of lyrics, there is plentiful life in the prose chapters that enclose them. Here first one feels the insistent purposefulness that pervades Dante's thought: the real purpose of the little book is to convince the reader that Dante, through his love for Beatrice, had been endowed with a divine commission for the writing of a great poetic treatise on the life after death. One learns here also that habit of Dante's mind that sees gathered in and around an actual person a wealth of more than individual significance. And one learns that the processes of scholarship are not incompatible with those of creative genius, but tend rather to give an architectonic clarity and vigor to chosen forms of expression. The *Vita nuova* has indeed beauty and gentleness and a slightly esoteric charm; but these qualities— toned in Rossetti's version to an undue preciousness—clothe an inner strength and a variety of authentic human report of which one becomes increasingly conscious as the book becomes more familiar. The *dramatis personae* are many; and the action takes place in the streets, in the churches, in the homes of a real city, or *per uno cammino lungo lo quale sen gia uno rivo chiaro molto.*

The *Convivio* is an incomplete encyclopedia, strangely but thoughtfully ordered, and planned to include in its range everything worthy of humane discussion. One finds here a controlling sense of the public responsibility that results from the possession of special intellectual gifts and opportunities; and one is stirred by the courage of this universal mind that deliberately and very eagerly takes all knowledge to be its province. Particular discussions range far and wide. The main themes of the finished portions of the work are the character and the praise of philosophy, and the nature of nobility.

The *Monarchia* is a political treatise, intended to prove that the existence of a universal empire is necessary for the well-being of mankind; that the Roman Empire (continued in the Empire of Dante's own day) was divinely ordained; and that the emperor and the pope are in reality coordinate, the guidance of the emperor being essential for the achievement of blessedness in this life just as the guidance of the pope is essential for the achievement of blessedness in the life after death. Ardent conviction underlies the whole process of the thought, burning now and then into a clear eloquence. The story of the Roman Empire is for Dante the story of a succession of heroic figures, personal and vivid in his evocation. The sense of the responsibility that comes with special gifts is strong again, and the dominance of purpose: the ultimate goal, Dante says, determines even the initial direction of any significant activity. The concept of the inherent and needful unity of mankind pervades the book: *genus humanum maxime Deo adsimilatur quando maxime est unum.* The courageous assertion that the emperor and the pope are coordinate gives a militant urgency to the closing chapters, and the climax carries Dante's clearest statement of his noble doctrine of the twofold blessedness: the blessedness of this life and the blessedness of the life eternal.

The Comedy lives with all the vitalities manifest in the earlier works, and deepens and extends them. No other great poem was ever so completely determined by a dominant sense of purpose; no other poet ever spent himself so utterly in the effort to fulfill his ordained responsibility; no writer ever sought more valiantly to gather and to set forth all the true treasures of human thought and human experience; no drama was ever enacted in a setting of more convincing vividness, or amid sounds of more convincing resonance. Life pulses through the whole organism of the Comedy, pervades its thought, glows in the hosts of individual spirits who people it, sings in the challenge, the grace, the power of the *terza rima.*

The Comedy is indeed an organism, firm in its central structure but as various and as individual in its forms and features as any strong organic creation could possibly be.

Protean in its phases, ranging in its keen consciousness from Hell to Paradise, it possesses nevertheless a mastering unity—a unity engendered by growth from a controlling purpose, but re-enforced by every architectonic resource at the command of the poet's genius. There is a perfect correspondence between the essential process of the poem and Dante's scheme of human life. As man is led, under the guidance of Philosophy, to the Temporal Blessedness, so, in the poem, Dante is led by Vergil to the Earthly Paradise. As man is led, under the guidance of Revelation, to the Eternal Blessedness, so Dante is led by Beatrice to the Empyrean. Dante holds the entire poem in mind at all times, and strives to compel the reader to do so. Hell is linked to Purgatory, and Purgatory to Paradise, by passages of deliberate parallelism, as unmistakable as the contrast between Charon's crossing of the Acheron and the angelic voyage that ends on Easter morning on the shores of Purgatory, or as subtle as the failures of Dante the traveler to recognize Forese Donati in Purgatory, and his sister in Paradise, because of their changes in countenance—recognition coming when they speak. The devices of anticipation unfulfilled and of reminiscence adding to the record of previous experience are so used, also, as to strengthen the reader's sense both of unity and of reality.

In greater measure than any other poet Dante wields the unifying power of surveyance. He achieves consciousness of the simultaneous lights and shadows of the whole round earth:

> On Golgotha the rays of the dawn were shining; the Spanish strait lay in the depth of night; the waves of the Ganges burned in the noon-tide; and from the mount of Purgatory the day was dying.

Looking downward from the Gemini he surveys heaven and earth alike, seeing in the center of the universal scene "the little threshing-floor we grow so fierce about." With equal clarity he can survey the occupations and the characters of men, or can review swiftly the whole course of his own poem. So Dante the traveler speaks to Cacciaguida, in the heaven of Mars, of things he has heard

> Down through the world of eternal woe, up over the mountain from whose fair summit my Lady's eyes have lifted me, and thence through heaven from star to star.

There are areas of Dante's thought that have lost significance for us: like any other organism, the Comedy is marked by death as well as life. Yet the obsoletisms serve, in the sweep of the poem, to establish in even clearer eminence the masses of poetry and of thought that are still vital. And there are passages even of purely theological discourse, such as the canto that sets forth the doctrine of the redemption, in which the triumphant surge of poetry accompanies the highest reaches of intellectual austerity. The wonder is not that something of Dante's thought should have died, but that so much of it, so vastly much, should be living still. He possessed wisdom as well as knowledge, and he so uttered his wisdom that one who learns from him gains a greater understanding of this life of ours, greater insight, greater courage, greater concentration, a more compelling and a more satisfying sense of that bond wherewith every man is bound to every other man.

The Comedy is an assemblage of an amazing number of persons, drawn from all the regions and all the centuries of human history. Some of them take their turns as protagonists, others stand forth briefly in swift and revealing converse with the traveler and his guide, or with each other—converse now friendly, now pleading, now hostile—others appear in single lines or flashing characterization. To become familiar with the Comedy is to attain acquaintance with this throng of persons, persons so personal that they become living companions in one's thought.

They manifest an extraordinary variety of look and character and experience. Neither Hell nor Paradise can suppress them. They are complex, as living beings are complex. Damnation results not from ignobility but from unrepented sin: there are noble spirits, therefore, among the denizens of the valley of eternal woe. Salvation results not from sinlessness, but from the attainment of harmony with God at the moment of death: in Purgatory, therefore, before the draught of Lethe, there is memory of wrong. And the thunder of righteous indignation may resound in Paradise itself. Ulysses, Peter Damian, Bertran de Born, Sordello, Pier della Vigna, Farinata, Cavalcante, Paolo and Francesca, Ugolino, Manfred, Pia de' Tolomei: these and a host of others have through Dante an indestructible reality of life, and remain ready to converse with us as they conversed with him.

The fine rhythmic diction of the lyrics has developed into a fully mature beauty, even into majesty—as in the opening and the closing lines of the *Paradiso*:

> The all-mover's glory penetrates through the universe,
> and regloweth in one region more, and less in another.

But already my desire and will were rolled—even as a
wheel that moveth equally—by the Love that moves the sun
and the other stars.

III

Dante lived in the very first century of Italian literature;
and it was therefore inevitable that his life should enter per-
sistently into the lives of a host of later Italian writers. Times
and persons have varied greatly in their responsiveness to his
influence; but few Italian men of letters have been unaffected
by their towering predecessor. There even exists a curious multi-
volume collection of poems about him, entitled *Poesie di mille
autori intorno a Dante Alighieri.*

Petrarch, who grew to manhood during the last years of
Dante's life, sought deliberately to avoid the influence of the
elder poet; but despite their deep dissimilarities there are occasional Dantean elements in Petrarch's lyric verse and in his
thought, and the *Triumphs* were his ineffectual attempt to
outdo the Comedy. Petrarch's own influence prevailed over
that of Dante in the Renaissance, as it has prevailed at other
times with persons who find more satisfaction in an urbane and
undisturbing beauty than amid the fires of a supreme creative
energy. Yet it was within the Renaissance that the Comedy was
first called "Divine."

Among the greater men of spirit akin to that of Dante, and
stirred by him, are Michelangelo, Leopardi, and Carducci. Let
the sculptor-poet speak for all three, and for many more, in
the familiar sonnet rendered thus by John Addington Symonds:

> From heaven his spirit came, and robed in clay,
>   The realms of justice and of mercy trod:
>   Then rose a living man to gaze on God,
>   That he might make the truth as clear as day.
> For that pure star, that brightened with his ray
>   The undeserving nest where I was born,
>   The whole wide world would be a prize to scorn;
>   None but his Maker can due guerdon pay.
> I speak of Dante, whose high work remains
>   Unknown, unhonoured by that thankless brood,
>   Who only to just men deny their wage.
> Were I but he! Born for like lingering pains,
>   Against his exile coupled with his good
>   I'd gladly change the world's best heritage!

IV

The influence of Dante, reaching across the mountains and the seas, has been strong in many lands. Translations of the Comedy have multiplied in many languages; and writers in many portions of his "little threshing floor" have found treasure in his thoughts and words.

For England, the two substantial volumes of Paget Toynbee's *Dante in English Literature* assemble the material very completely, with quotations from some five hundred writers who show some knowledge of Dante.

Chaucer, who was familiar with both verse and prose of

> the wyse poete of Florence
> That highte Dant,

revives for his own purposes many Dantean passages and ideas; has his Monk tell at length the story of Ugolino; and places the prayer of St. Bernard, very perfectly rendered, as prologue to the Second Nun's Tale.

Paradise Lost "preserves as in a violl" much that Milton learned from Dante, from whom also he derived his "smooth enamelled green," his "odorous breath of morn," his "grisly legions that troop/Under the sooty flag of Acheron," his "milder shades of Purgatory," and the St. Peter of his *Lycidas*.

Gray knew Dante well, translated again the story of Ugolino, and found in the evening bell

> *che paia il giorno pianger che si more*

his inspiration for

> The curfew tolls the knell of parting day.

The impress of the *Purgatorio* is strong upon the *Epipsychidion:*

> True Love in this differs from gold and clay, . . .
> That to divide is not to take away, . . .
>
> If you divide pleasure and love and thought,
> Each part exceeds the whole; and we know not
> How much, while any yet remains unshared,
> Of pleasure may be gain'd, of sorrow spared:

This truth is that deep well, whence sages draw
The unenvied light of hope; the eternal law
By which those live, to whom this world of life
Is as a garden ravaged, and whose strife
Tills for the promise of a fairer birth
The wilderness of this Elysian earth.

So, also, one might quote from Byron, from Keats, and from many a later English poet.

In our own land—the land Ulysses never found—knowledge and love of Dante, for the last hundred years, have never failed. Scholars and poets have translated, have taught, have interpreted, have gone on to new creation. Those who have lived most closely with Dante have found no truer poetic voicing of what they have felt than the two sonnets prefixed by Longfellow to his translation of the Comedy. The second ends with a fine realization of the intensity of Dante's own living and of its embodiment in his poem:

Ah! from what agonies of heart and brain,
What exultations trampling on despair,
What tenderness, what tears, what hate of wrong,
What passionate outcry of a soul in pain,
Uprose this poem of the earth and air,
This mediaeval miracle of song!

But the Comedy is much more than a medieval miracle. The other sonnet, in which the Comedy is represented as a cathedral, ends with these still nobler lines:

So, as I enter here from day to day,
And leave my burden at this minster gate,
Kneeling in prayer, and not ashamed to pray,
The tumult of the time disconsolate
To inarticulate murmurs dies away,
While the eternal ages watch and wait.

v

We, too, are living amid the tumult of a time disconsolate
—a time more tragic, even, than the tragic time of Dante.

It is a time that tries not only the souls, but all the works of men. There are institutions, there are monuments, there are poems that seem to have lost significance, to have become so

pallid as to invite forgetfulness, if not oblivion. Not so the
Comedy. It stands amid the universal wrack, lofty and four-
square,

> come torre ferma che non crolla
> già mai la cima per soffiar de' venti.

It stands vibrant with life. It stands prophetic still of ultimate unity, uncompromising in its insistence upon purposefulness, upon completeness, upon the responsibility that comes
with every good gift. It stands as a strong shelter, wherein one
may find the companionship of a spirit penetrant, luminous,
loving, brave, and altogether noble.

If Dante had been living at this hour . . . But Dante *is*
living at this hour—as he will continue to live through watching ages, which will yet see the fulfillment of his prophecy of
peace.

II. *Form and Composition*

Allan H. Gilbert

2 · Dante's Hundred Cantos

IS ANY POEM more regular than Dante's *Commedia*, with its hundred cantos, 33 for *Purgatorio* and *Paradiso* and 34 for *Inferno*? Such symmetry has led even eminent writers to say that the *Inferno* also really has 33 cantos and that the hundredth is introductory to the whole. Yet as everybody knows, the end of the second canto announces that the rescued man is willing to follow his guide, and only at the beginning of canto three does Hellgate appear. So Dante's plan is less rigid than the one his disciples—outdoing the master in their demand for symmetry—permit him.

The cantos Dante allowed to vary in length. Two are of but 115 lines; one reaches 160; most of them depart little from the norm of 142.33 lines. The *Inferno* runs to 4720 verses; the *Purgatorio* is 35 lines longer, the *Paradiso* only three lines longer still, or 4758 verses in all. Dante did not learn such uniformity from his chief sources. The twelve books of the *Aeneid* vary from 705 to 952 lines. Not much different is the variation in Lucan's *Pharsalia* and Statius' *Thebaid*. If Dante were proportioning his space to the importance of his thoughts, could he have attained such regularity? Can we attribute such even length to love for symmetry, without respect to content?

Since Canto 3 of the *Inferno* offers the neutral part of Hell, the first circle of that realm is entered by the travelers in Canto 4. Similarly Canto 1 of the *Paradiso* presents Dante as ascend-

Reprinted from *Italica* (XL, 2, 1963) by permission of the American Association of Teachers of Italian.

ing from the earth, though he enters the first Heaven in Canto
2. The *Purgatorio*'s introduction may be called hypertrophied.
Nine cantos relate the adventures of guide and guided, before
they pass through the gate of Purgatory, which makes the lower
slopes more distinct from the upper than is the neutral part of
Hell from the rest; Acheron is within Hellgate.

The last seven cantos of the *Purgatorio* have their distinc-
tive quality. Once the journey through Hell has begun, it continues throughout the *cantica*. Not until the end of Canto 34
does Vergil release his grasp on Lucifer's shaggy pelt. At the
end of the *Paradiso*, the visitor is still in Heaven. But Purgatory's climbers complete its terraces and enter the Earthly
Paradise in Canto 28. The Earthly Paradise is obviously purgatorial only in the drafts from Lethe and Eunoe; even they are
seals of finished purging rather than needful to cleansing. On
the terraces, the vices have one by one been conquered. Though
probably Statius drank from Eunoe, Dante does not affirm it.
Both before and after the draft the narrator speaks only in the
singular:

> I returned from the holy waters... pure and fit to rise to the
> stars (*Purg.* 33. 142).

Was Statius' suffering on the terraces enough to fit him for
Heaven? Eunoe is not mentioned before *Purgatorio* 28. 131.
Lethe is mentioned in the *Inferno* as for bathing rather than
drinking, to be found

> where the souls go to be washed when sin repented is
> removed (*Inf.* 14, 137).

Yet after utmost allowance to Lethe and Eunoe as com-
pleting Purgatory's functions, but little of the last seven cantos
is evidently purgatorial. In these cantos is the beauty of the
Garden, Dante and Beatrice's story developed from the *Vita
Nuova*, the allegorical procession, the chariot and the sym-
bolical tree. These are slightly prepared for in preceding cantos.
Beatrice, we have been told, will assist Dante in Heaven. Vergil
promises a sight of her on the summit of the mountain, without
mentioning the Earthly Paradise (*Purg.* 6. 47). The Garden,
then, is put before unprepared readers at the end of Canto 27
of the *Purgatorio*. Beatrice is known from Canto 2 of the *In-*

ferno, where she appears rather as a messenger than a principal. For the development of the *Vita Nuova* in the Earthly Paradise, a reader of the *Commedia* only has no preparation. Though the Beatrice of the Earthly Paradise is not altogether the Beatrice of the early work, Dante goes far in assuming that a reader comes to the *Purgatorio* from the *Vita Nuova*. When speaking of ten years' thirst he requires knowledge of the early work's date (32. 2). Yet he does give enough of its story to make the *Commedia* readable without its predecessor. Early commentators were not familiar with the youthful narrative. Boccaccio and Benvenuto da Imola, knowing the legend of Beatrice Portinari, so write that they could not have studied Dante's account of his love.

The Biblical procession in the Garden, with the chariot and the tree of knowledge, is an interlude in the narrative. It is not prepared for by preceding verses and appears but once further on in the poem (*Par. 20. 128*).

The main part of Purgatory, the seven terraces, thus occupies 17 or 18 cantos, or somewhat more than half of the total 33. The central part of the mountain, with its seven encircling ledges, harmonizes with the circles of the *Inferno*, especially in Malebolge, and with the ten spheres of the *Paradiso*. The four divisions of Antepurgatory are not described as circles. The seven terraces are fewer in number than those of the primary divisions of the other *cantiche*, and little discursive matter is used; the passages on Statius are the most prominent. An extreme hypothesis is that Dante finished a *Purgatorio* early in his period of composition. To give a detail, Professor Grandgent makes the reference to Manto, daughter of Teresias, in *Inferno* 20. 55, later than that in *Purgatorio* 22. 113. If Dante early wrote a short *Purgatorio*, he was forced, when he decided upon a hundred cantos, to lengthen it. His solution was Antepurgatory and the Earthly Paradise, some fifteen cantos. On the other hand, maybe he planned from the beginning eighteen cantos for the seven terraces, gaining from a long introduction and conclusion both variety and the requisite length. In either case, any supplementary character allowed to the first nine and the last six or seven cantos still reflects the plan for 33 limited cantos. The cantos at beginning and end are not therefore inferior or superior; they are to be judged without respect to their origin.

Yet to see an artist at work is pleasant and even helpful. The first hint of the *Comedy* is often seen at the end of the *Vita Nuova*, where Dante as artist promises to write of Beatrice. If we take this promise as prosaic rather than as dramatic and imaginative, Earthly Paradise and *Paradiso* are facts issuing from it. Yet they do not prove that in 1290 Dante was soberly planning the *Commedia* we have. Legend says that the poet going into exile abandoned in Florence the first seven cantos of the *Inferno* in manuscript. The story seems to depend in part on the transition at the beginning of Canto 8, which perhaps signifies the reverse: immediate continuance rather than suspension. It also requires Dante to write from the beginning cantos much as they now stand. Yet such improbability need not diminish likelihood that Dante in his early thirties, like Ariosto in his, was engaged on the poem that for years made him thin (*Par.* 25. 3). If his words "many years" are to be prosaically understood, they hardly put the beginning of the *Comedy* later than 1300.

The reports about cantos written before exile and about others discovered by Dante's executors after his death assume that he began with *Inferno*, Canto 1, line 1 and wrote steadily on to *Paradiso*, Canto 33, line 145, thus producing, however in need of revision, about what we now read. But mere statement exposes the improbability of such a simple procedure. Poems that make authors thin for years are not facile constructions. Did not Dante's plan shift over the years, so that the poem gradually took its present form, after sections had been discarded and surviving ones more than once rearranged?

Was some form of the *Paradiso* first brought to temporary completion? At least the *Vita Nuova*'s promise of a poem praising Beatrice among the angels is an important hint. Dante's verse correspondence with Giovanni del Virgilio has been read by scholars assuming that the *Inferno* was first completed and circulated, next the *Purgatorio*, and only then the *Paradiso* begun. When the *Eclogues* are read without such preconception, do they confirm such clarity of progress? Shall we insist that before Dante wrote a word of his poem he formed an outline so firm that it determined the details of a product twenty years later? That product is made up of 100 approximately equal cantos arranged in three *cantiche* varying at the most by 1/125 of their total.

The excellence of the *Paradiso* has sometimes been belittled, as by De Sanctis' blunt words; even proponents may appear apologists. Does dissatisfaction follow early composition of parts, at a time when the author's powers were short of maturity? In the process of revision, nevertheless, some portions of the *Paradiso* may have been written in the fullness of Dante's strength. Other parts may be of early composition, even for some other purpose, but of late insertion. Yet passages put on paper when Dante was fifty years of age may show the pressure of adapting verses to arbitrary length. No single word in the *Commedia* is hastily to be assumed as either early or late.

With this in mind, let us consider Beatrice. A recent commentator has been somewhat disturbed by her diverse qualities. We read of Beatrice whose beauty grows greater as her lover beholds her rise from Heaven to Heaven, and of Beatrice who delivers lectures befitting a learned man grounded in Plato. In pedagogical contexts, Beatrice addresses her pupil as Brother (*Par.* 4. 100; 7. 58, 130). Her long didactic passages, such as those on vows and moon spots, are not distributed throughout the *Paradiso*. They bulk large in the first seven cantos. Of these cantos, totaling fewer than a thousand lines, the sixth is wholly Justinian's and most of the third Piccarda's. Of 719 remaining lines, 440—nearly 2/3—are given to set speeches by Beatrice. With Canto 8, she abruptly ceases such lecturing. She does not resume it until Canto 27, with 43 lines beginning "The nature of the world." In Canto 28 she occupies less than half, but she almost fills Canto 29 with scholastic subject matter and invective against popularity-seeking preachers. In the thirtieth canto she is again merely guide, except for a brief denunciation of simoniac popes. Thus, as the lady developed from the *Vita Nuova*, she is the traveler's supervisor and not a lecturer in Cantos 8–26. Who can prove that Dante did not from the beginning plan so strange a distribution of Beatrice's speeches? Probability nevertheless suggests that composition was far advanced before she appeared as learned expositor, and that her speeches were inserted to raise the *Paradiso* to its required length. Maybe they were not composed for the gentle lady but came out of Dante's desk, the fragments of an abandoned philosophical poem in which a learned man spoke to the "Brother" now addressed by Beatrice.

Other anomalies of construction appear. In the Starry Sphere, the pilgrim is examined on faith, hope, and charity. This heaven receives the most space of any, five cantos. After the "good Christian's" test is concluded, he beholds a light encompassing Adam. The theological importance of the Fall of Man, touched in the Earthly Paradise, raises expectation of doctrinal exegesis, but instead appears curious information on Adam's language and the length of his stay in Eden (*Par.* 26. 109). At the end of the canto he ceases speaking, and Canto 27 begins with angelic rejoicing, continuing a similar scene broken off in the middle of the preceding canto (26. 69), when Adam came forward. After the heavenly song is concluded, Saint Peter again addresses the visitor. Thus the sixty verses devoted to Adam seem a stop-gap, bringing the canto to its inexorable length. Not that the lines on Adam are uninteresting: the comparison of the first man within his robe of light to a "pig in a poke" justifies their insertion.

Cantos need not be taken as absolute units throughout Dante's procedure. The section on the Eighth Heaven, just mentioned, appears written as a unit of about 700 lines, without division into cantos. For example, at the end of Canto 25 the traveler loses his power to see. The next canto begins:

While I was feeling afraid because my sight was gone. . . .

Though the course of the narrative is interrupted by Adam, it is resumed with the first line of the next canto, the twenty-seventh. In the middle of that canto comes the transition to the following heaven. Such medial conclusions and inception of new topics, as if to deny the structural importance of cantos, are frequent. But though the narrative of the Starry Heaven flows on without marking bounds, some respect is paid to the initial lines of cantos. Canto 23, the second on the Heaven of the Stars, begins with a simile of nine lines to express the action of Beatrice, that is, the comparison of the bird on the nest awaiting the sun. The second canto following, the twenty-fifth, begins with a well-known personal passage:

> If ever it happens that the inspired poem—on which heaven and earth have labored, so that for many years it has made me thin—if that poem should overcome the cruelty that locks me out of the fair sheepfold where I slept as a lamb, hostile to the wolves who make war upon it, with other voice, with other fleece shall I return as poet, and at the font of my baptism shall take the wreath; since in the faith that makes souls known to God I there entered, and then Peter for it so encircled my brow (25. 1).

The connection of the Florentine baptistery with events in this heaven is not immediate. Thus two cantos are announced as new sections by formal introductions. Even now the two cantos are both of 139 lines only, while the average for the *Paradiso* is above 144. We may fancy that Dante, having written on the Eighth Heaven some 700 lines (or if we omit Adam, some 640), divided them into cantos, selecting the best places for his cuts. Cantos 23 and 25 were short, 130 lines or fewer, so he provided each with introductory comparisons, nine lines for one, twelve for the other. Additions at the beginning of a canto cause least disturbance of rime. A number of the famous similes of the poem begin cantos, such as the Venetian navy yard and the players at *zara* (*Inf.* 21; *Purg.* 6). Doubtless other comparisons filling one or more tercets were inserted as the author strove for the length demanded. So Ariosto's manuscripts show similes an octave long thrust into otherwise complete cantos, though his intercalations were not forced by predetermined numbers.

In the *Inferno* Cantos 3–10 and a bit of 11 serve for the first six circles. Twenty-three cantos then present the remaining three circles. These three are compounded: three parts to the seventh circle, ten to the eighth, four to the ninth, or seventeen in all. The average space given to each of these seventeen is almost that allowed for each of the circles above. Was Dante's early *Inferno* shorter than the present one, with lower circles on the scale of those above? Such a brief project would have preceded the decision on a hundred cantos of the present length. That decision required the addition or expansion of Malebolge to bring the *Inferno* up to thirty-four cantos. Yet if Heaven had

ten parts and Purgatory seven, symmetry rejected a Hell of
twenty-three. Nine, so important in the *Vita Nuova*, was inevitable. Eleven or eight do not correspond with the round ten
and the perfect seven. Thus an unrevised form of Cantos 3–8,
whether or not divided as at present, would precede any plan
for 100 cantos. Rather than completely recast this material, the
poet undertook to subdivide the last three circles, giving any of
the ten rounds of Malebolge almost as many lines, on the
average, as any of the upper circles. So outwardly but not
genuinely the nine circles of Hell harmonize with the seven
terraces of Purgatory and the ten spheres of Heaven. Here, as
often, Dante wishes some variety within his symmetry. The
part of Hell closely fitting the symmetrical plan for circling
parts is Malebolge alone, as clear as the terraces of Purgatory.
Yet Malebolge is the poet's creation, not after a familiar model,
such as the medieval scientist's ten spheres of Heaven, or the
medieval ethicist's formula of the seven capital vices.

Such variation in the diagram of Hell suggests a slow evo-
lution of its design, beginning soon after the *Vita Nuova* and
extending throughout the long delight of composition—emaci-
ating though it be pronounced. When the companions enter
Hell they go through a gate with no suggestion of descent.
Soon they arrive at the abyss of pain. Of their further downward path Toynbee writes:

> Circle 6 appears not to be any lower than Circle 5, the descent
> hitherto having been very gradual, the only changes of level
> mentioned being between the first and second circles (*Inf.*
> 5. 1) and between the third and fourth (*Inf.* 6. 114).

Actually a descent between four and five is twice mentioned
(7. 97. 105). Yet the narrator speaks of no slope between Circles
2 and 3 and between 5 and 6. Toynbee's oversight shows that
to an experienced Dantist the declivity was not impressive.
Grandgent remarks of upper Hell that "Dante likes to pass
lightly over the transitions" between circles (Edition, Canto 6,
Arg.). In the early cantos the word *circle* so often appears as
to establish Dante's final intention, though the meaning may
sometimes approach *district* (4. 24; 5. 1; 6. 7; 7. 44, 100). But
in spite of the word, the circles above Phlegethon are little
evident. In the six early circles and the latter parts of the

seventh are spaces for crowds of shades, for a *castello*, a forest,
a swamp, a desert, a city. In contrast, two of the *bolge* of the
Eighth Circle are called narrow (19. 42; 23. 84), and all of them
are compared with the moats ringing castles, crossed by little
bridges (18. 11, 15). The Fifth is of such slight width that the
devils striving to rescue Alichino and Calcabrina from the
pitchy trench extend from both sides their hooks to be grasped
by their "cooked" companions (22. 149). In Purgatory the
ledge of pride is about seventeen feet wide (*Purg.* 10. 24). But
in Hell, above the round course of the River of Blood, the
circles—unless we except that for the misers and wasters—are
not functional. The effect is one of normal earthly topography,
as in other visits to the lower world, especially that of Aeneas
in the sixth *Aeneid*. The first quarter of the *Inferno* may be
viewed as a Vergilian visit to the realm of shades, revised with
references to circles after the rounds of Malebolge, in harmony
with the terraces of Purgatory, had been devised. Thus an early
Inferno was adapted to a plan for a hundred cantos.

The *Comedy* we read may be considered a fusion and
development of two poems, one on *Beatrice angelicata*, the
dream of a visit to Heaven, the other a progress through the
world of the dead guided by the author of *Aeneid* 6. The mature
genius, the experienced humanity of Malebolge smack of late
composition. Yet in Dante's long pilgrimage toward his hundred
cantos he was so assiduous that while any portion of the
Comedy may offer youthful endeavor, equally in any canto
may stand verses from the artist's maturity.

J. S. P. Tatlock

3 · *Dante's* Terza Rima

Terza rima is a series of threes, the two outer lines of each riming with each other, the inner line riming with the two outer lines of the next three; in homely terms, like a pile of paper cones set into each other. The first rime in a canto and the last therefore occur only twice, but all the rest three times; none is dropped before a new rime is begun, or, except at the beginning and end of a canto, is confined to a single *terzina*. A consequence of this structure is that, while (if the sense permits) one or more *terzine* may be cut off at the beginning or end of a canto without detection of the loss, this is impossible anywhere else; the alternation of rimes and the linking with the preceding and the following *terzine* would be upset. Accordingly omission of lines or passages occurs in the manuscripts with notable rarity.[1] This result of the verse form no doubt is well known to some, but, so far as I find, it has never been mentioned in print.

Another peculiarity makes it almost as difficult to add (except at the beginning or end), for at no point could the sequence of rimes be broken by an insertion without leaving one, or two, of the rime-words on each side of the insertion, and therefore without repeating the rime. But a rime is almost never repeated in a canto; if words in *-ino* or *-ele* or *-ove* end lines in adjoining *terzine*, or in the first or last *terzina*, in that canto the rime almost never reappears—among nearly five thousand

Reprinted from *PMLA* (LI, 1936) by permission of the Modern Language Association of America.

rimes only eleven times, in but nine out of a hundred cantos.[2] Though rarely mentioned in print, this rule is sufficiently well known, was so early noticed that it was followed at once by Dante's followers in *terza rima*, and may be verified by fifteen minutes with a *rimario*. But more than this, the eleven existing recurrences are on an average at intervals of nearly 100 lines, never less than 65 except once (*Purg.*, xxix, 3 and 26), where *-ata* recurs after only 23 lines; therefore the recurrences are as little noticeable as possible.[3] Now the cantos vary in length only between 100 ll. (*Purg.*, xxxii) and 115 (*Inf.*, vi. xi), and only three are under 130; seventy-one of the hundred vary by only 12 lines, and the extreme variation is only 45.[4] Any spurious interpolation, therefore, however skillful an imitation, if long enough for the recurrent rime to be inconspicuous, would swell almost any canto to an unacceptable length. A highly interesting corollary is that no more easily could Dante himself have made later insertions without extensive recasting, a fact which conveys a vivid sense of how carefully he planned each canto before its incarnation in words, and which would throw doubt on any suggestion of such revision. But the chief point now is that, except at the beginning or end of a canto, no passage could be added without probable detection.

That the beginnings and endings of cantos are practically the only possible places for addition has been pointed out, among many contributions, by Dr. H. D. Austin,[5] also that the especial destiny of construction and expression there may be due to a conscious effort to protect them. To this I add that other matters give a suddenness or finality to the first and last *terzina* of a canto. Both, though usually without close connection with the next canto, are apt to be dramatic and striking for literary reasons, but this does not preclude desire for protection. The first *terzina* is nearly always indispensable to the sense of what follows; the ending is nearly always a unified quatrain, the last line closely knit to what precedes (as the line following a *terzina* elsewhere usually is not), and the quatrain is usually indispensable to the preceding sense. Therefore the only vulnerable points are *de facto* less vulnerable than might be expected. If Dante deliberately planned to head off omissions and additions, he could hardly have done it more effectively.

True, he might have distinguished beginnings and endings in
some more marked way, as by final couplets (like Shelley with
his *terzine* in the *Ode to the West Wind*), but these would
have marred the even flow of the poem, and probably any
reader of Shelley will feel why Dante in a narrative did not do
likewise. Against substitution of spurious for genuine lines of
course he had no defense; against internal omission he was completely protected, and against internal additions almost completely.

Now, one happy result of all this is that Dante's text is
freer from important question than that of any other con-
spicuous poet before the invention of printing—even of some
since. There are doubtful words, of course, and some clear alter-
ations; some dozens of lines or passages dropped, transposed, or
repeated in certain manuscripts, and of course easily corrected;[6]
but so far as I find only one passage certainly added. In *Inf.*,
xxxiii, between ll. 90 and 91, two manuscripts insert a malicious
episode of eighteen lines at the expense of someone of Lucca,
involving the recurrence of the *-ata* rime within 17 lines; wholly
unparalleled, as Witte pointed out [7] in indicating the spurious-
ness. As to losses, none so far as I discover has been plausibly
suggested.

No such scheme is known before his day. He is agreed by
almost all, with varying positiveness, to have invented *terza
rima*, and no one disputes the fact that no earlier use of it is
known.[8] But few things are invented *ex vacuo*. Among thirteenth-century Italian and Provençal lyric forms there are two
or three which as precedents readily pierce toward the seat of
conviction.[9] Vaguer and more casual analogies are not now
worth collecting. That oftenest mentioned is the *serventese*;
enough to discuss the Italian, disregarding the similar Provençal
sirventés. This "duty-poem" is lyric, though a narrative could
be mentioned; rarely on love, it is political, moral, satirical, or
the like. Dante himself had written one, as he tells us in the
Vita Nuova (§ 6), in what form no one can say. But one of the
common forms is in four-line stanzas, three hendecasyllables
riming together and one five-syllable line ending with a fresh
rime and a pause, which fresh rime is carried on by the three
hendecasyllables of the next stanza. The form therefore is

AAAb.BBBc.CCCd. . . ; and the shortness and different movement of the fourth line give the stanzas much the effect of Latin sapphics. The following will serve as a specimen: [10]

Placente vixo, adorno,	——*doloroso*	——*lo meo volere,*
angelicato,	*afano*	
Per de novo sono	——*per Isota*	——*de vedere,*
recomandato:	*Tristano,*	
Mercé, s'eo t'amo, fia	——*quando m'e*	——*poixi avere*
miritato	*luntano*	*Me lasarisi.*
Amore soprano.	*Lo to vedere*	

Obviously no trait in this resembles *terza rima* except that the units are linked; it would be hard to drop any short part without the loss being instantly perceptible. Passages could easily be added, however, for there is no avoidance of linking in a longish poem, but not Dante's manner of linking. And it is hard to see here any closer linking than, e.g., in the *sestina*, in which the final word in the last line of a stanza is final in the first line of the next.[11]

Another origin sometimes suggested is the *ritornello* (or its variant, the *stornello*), a single stanza, sometimes of three lines, of which one form, perhaps the oldest, is of hendecasyllables riming *aba*; [12] clearly *terza rima* is a string of these in which the inner end-word of the first dictates the outer rimes of the next, and the usual pause in Dante at the end of each *terzina* shows that this in his mind was the unit. The chief grounds for doubt of this origin are that the ritornello is not known to antedate Dante, and is not commonly found before the seventeenth century,[13] and that it is a mere three-line *quasi*-epigram, with its own technique, so far as I find rarely strung with others into a longer lyric,[14] to say nothing of narrative.

A much more likely origin, making the question as to the mere *ritornello* unimportant, is one form of the sestet of the thirteenth-century Italian sonnet, in which it consists simply of two such *terzine*, a strong pause between them almost always marking each as a unit, and of course with linking of the two by the rimes, very often in a way almost identical with *terza rima*. What is specifically significant is that Dante himself had often used this form, well exemplified by a skeleton of the sestet from the twelfth sonnet in the *Vita Nuova*:

——*tanta pietate,*   ——*c'hanno pianto,*
——*qui meco alquanto,*   ——*si sfigurate,*
——*nol mi celate:*   ——*vederne tanto.*

It is easy to see that if the fifth line introduced a fresh rime to lead onward, there would be here two *terzine* like those of the *Commedia*. Just this form of sestet is used in two sonnets in the *Vita Nuova*, and in 11 more (including only one without a strong pause in the midst) among Dante's fifty-six or so of regular sonnets; and five more have the sestet of two such *terzine*, but rimed *abaaba*.[15] Among his predecessors and contemporaries a remarkable number of sestets have the first, or almost *terza rima*, structure; indeed, to judge from such collections as those of Ulrich and E. Monaci,[16] this was the commonest early form, almost always with a strong pause in the middle; I find this form in no less than forty out of some seventy or so by Guido Guinicelli and various others.[17] It is worth noting also that every regular sonnet ever written is fully protected throughout from omission and addition, and might well suggest the same trait in a longer poem. But the main point is that in the sestet Dante had himself often written just this germinal form for his own *terzine*, just as Chaucer took over from Machault the lyric seven-line stanza for narration. To the hasty eye of a reader the *serventese*-form with its simple linking may seem the likeliest precedent; but for one who had been wrestling intimately with the technique the sestet-form was more essentially like. Both perhaps contributed.

An examination of these and other early forms of linked riming verse makes several things clear. The linking and recurring rime contributes to melody, through the fact that the recurrence is in a way sensuously unexpected; pragmatically one may find that in stanzas which strike most readers as specially melodious, such as in English those of Spenser and Fitzgerald, there is some element of the unexpected. Another reason for the linking in the *serventese* and *sestina* is (to say nothing of the structural) undoubtedly mnemonic. Lyric poetry was primarily to be sung or recited, and at each pause a suggestion to the ear for the next line would be a very present help in trouble.[18] But no suggestion is perceptible in any of these Italian verse forms that the linking was in any degree designed to prevent corruptions in copying.

Now as to the function and effect of the rime scheme of Dante's *terza rima*. The mnemonic function is unimportant, for it is certain that he designed his poem to be read, not recited from memory; [19] further, the scheme is too intricate to help the memory unless after a pondering pause. As to melody, the entire flow is highly individual, sinewy, close-knit; but it is not clear how far the peculiar linking would have been intended to serve the interests of sensuous pleasure. The continuity of the flowing narrative is undoubtedly served by the linking; yet other great narrative poets have been pleased with forms which firmly emphasize the closure of the stanzas—needless to mention Chaucer, Spenser, Italians from Boccaccio to Tasso. The strong tendency throughout the *Commedia* to divide into threes, to stop each *terzina* with a marked pause, instead of markedly varying the linking of sense, also argues against any continual study of fluidity. Desire for fluidity is assuredly not the reason for certain traits which we noticed at the beginnings and endings of cantos, nor for Dante's general conscientious avoidance of recurring rimes; and it is doubtful if this last can be ascribed merely to his denying himself what was cheap and easy. It is doubtful whether melody, continuity, or strictness any more than mnemonic convenience accounts fully for the verse and structure of the cantos.

That Dante foresaw what has actually come about, the protection of his poem from the inroads of time, agrees with all we know of him and with the literary conditions of his day. I have written elsewhere of the gloomy prospect confronting a finished poet before the days of printing; the errors due to copyists' dullness, heedlessness, and self-assertion, and the sometimes worse mending of them by other copyists, all of which the poet would foresee. Chaucer expressed such solicitude no less than four times; similarly the English Orm, the Spaniard Don Juan Manuel, St. Anselm, one or two early Irish texts, and even St. John the Divine.[20] Chaucer and the others are not always thinking especially of additions and omissions; and Chaucer, content on a less lofty plane than Dante, expressed his concern with diverting frankness. But though Dante's personality was less expansive, no doubt he felt the same. Needless to argue to any student of him that he was not one of those who suffer fools gladly and shrug their shoulders philosophically when they think of even irremediable ills.

Further, he makes no secret of his high esteem for his poem. Any seeming humility appears solely in the title *Commedia*, undoubtedly due to discretion and good taste, with possibly a dash of dour bitterness. No important long poem in the *lingua volgare* had preceded his, and he is reported to have originally considered writing his in Latin. Further, even among vernacular poetry, the canzone, sonnet, and the like were aristocratic, narrative and visions were popular. For these reasons, to an innovator in language, whatever his convictions, an air of modesty might well seem prudent, and to his contemporaries fitting. "*Commedia*" is antithetical therefore to "*l'alta mia tragedia*," Vergil's phrase for the *Aeneid* (*Inf.*, xx, 113); while the style of *tragoedia* is lofty, as to that of *comoedia* "remissus est modus et humilis, quia loquutio vulgaris, in qua et mulierculae communicant." [21] When in this tenth epistle he mentions the heading of his poem as "Incipit Comoedia Dantis Alagherii Florentini natione non moribus," the bitterness of the last words may be thought to suffuse the whole. That his early admirers thought the word too modest is no doubt why they persisted in prefixing *Divina*; [22] and that it is only with his greatest work that he shows modesty indicates that it was not even here his fundamental feeling. This last is what appears in the same epistle, where he speaks of "Comoediae sublimem canticam quae decoratur titulo Paradisi," and where in the *Paradiso* he calls the poem "sacrato poema," "poema sacro"; [23] in the Middle Ages to use *poema* of a vernacular work was almost arrogant.[24] Not only the tenth epistle but various passages in the *Commedia* show his admiration: "Lo bello stile che m'ha fatto onore"; he swears by his own pages, "S'elle non sien di lunga grazia vote"; and maintains his matter with greater art because, "Lettor, tu vedi ben com' io innalzo/La mia materia." [25] The toil which kept him lean for many a year (*Par.*, xxv, 3) has allowed few oversights and no negligence. Assuredly he knew that the poem amply fulfills his hope that he should live to say of Beatrice

what was never said of any woman. Like indications of esteem
for his own works are the expositions (read by moderns with
mingled feelings) of the meaning of the lyrics in the *Vita Nuova*
and the *Convivio*; and his explanation that he wrote the latter
in the vulgar tongue (I, 10) out of *gelosia*, trusting himself
more than another, lest had he used Latin some illiterate person
should translate it, and make it ugly. A couple of anecdotes related by Franco Sacchetti (c.1330–c.1400) [26] point the same way.
Because a characteristic anecdote is picturesque it is not necessarily false, but at any rate these anecdotes show Dante's amusing reputation for purism about his own works. The poet,
hearing a smith singing some of his verses, threw away the
smith's tools; asked why, he replied, "If I am not to spoil your
goods, do not spoil mine." Likewise, hearing a teamster singing
his verses, beating his animal and crying "Arri!," Dante is said
to have struck him saying, "I did not put in 'Arri'!" No great
poet avowed for his own work such esteem as Dante has.

With the endless variety and appeal of his matter, perhaps
it is no wonder that even the most important of his verse forms
has received so little consideration. The foregoing makes no
claim to be exhaustive or definitive. It must always be impossible to prove this or that the only origin of the *terza rima*;
any of the existing precedents would be enough to produce the
click of creation. But the likeliest thing hitherto mentioned
seems to be one of the commonest early forms of sonnet-sestet,
considering Dante's frequent writing it, the all but identity of
form, and the strong tendency in both to pause at the end of
each *terzina*. As to the protection of the verse from insertions
or omissions, in which *terza rima* is so like this form of sestet,
the idea may well come from it. At all events it is incredible
that Dante, with his experience in many forms of verse and in
the vagaries of copyists, with his general awareness and with
his straining after perfection, was unaware of this feature of his
own verse. By his uncompromising views and intense partisan-
ship, the ecclesiastical thin ice on which he moved, his severity
toward personal, political, and clerical enemies, he invited al-
terations and must have known he did; and in regard to church
matters sometimes got them.[27] At the very least one must agree
that the excellent state of the text in large matters is due *de*

facto in great degree to the close-knit rime and structure. And any Dantist will agree that, with his peculiar personality and intellect, scarcely any forethought or subtlety well supported by evidence is too great to be attributed to him.

Notes

1 E. Moore, *Textual Criticism of the D. C.* (Cambridge, 1889), pp. 686–687.

2 See L. G. Blanc, *Gramm. d. ital. Spr.* (Halle, 1844), p. 781; C. F. Schneider, *Ueber d. Reim in D's D. C.* (Bonn, 1869), p. 2.

3 There is a curious parallel in Chaucer; when he uses a dubious rime in his *ababbcc* stanza in the *Man of Law's Tale* he tries to put the words as far apart as he can, in the second and fifth lines. On what follows see figures in N. Zingarelli, *Vita di Dante* (Milan, 1914), p. 114.

4 How deliberately the size of the several members of the *Commedia* was planned is shown at the end of the *Purgatorio*—

> *Ma perchè piene son tutte le carte*
> *Ordite a questa Cantica seconda, . . .*

5 *Romantic Review*, XXIII, 38–40, with the suggestion that the grim lines *Inf.*, XX, 1–3, are a spurious addition. To him and Dr. Rudolph Altrocchi I am grateful for suggestions and cautions.—I add that nowhere could a whole canto have been inserted without disturbing the numerical symmetry of the poem.

6 Moore, *Textual Crit.*, pp. xviii, 686–687.

7 Moore, pp. 706–711, esp. 709.

8 Among many critics see Schneider, *op. cit.*, p. 4.

9 On the Provençal, Gröber's *Grundriss d. rom. Ph.*, II, ii, and *Grundr. d. Lit.*; F. Witthoeft, *Sirventes Joglaresc*, in *Ausg. u. Abh.*, 88 (Marburg, 1891); K. Bartsch in *Jahrbuch f. rom. u. engl. Philol.*, I, esp. 178–182. The sapphic *serventese* appears in French as late as about 1400; see *Collection des Chron. Nat. Franç.*, XXIII, 323–405, in Buchon's Froissart.

10 E. Monaci, *Crestomazia Ital. dei Primi Sec.* (Città di Castello, 1889), I, 295–296 (thirteenth century); another sapphic *serventese* in Monaci, pp. 406–411 (one of the oldest—a narrative), and one in *Scelta di Curiosità*, XI (Bologna, 1865), pp. 11–24. See N. Zingarelli, *Vita . . . di Dante* (Milan, 1931), pp. 772–773, who points out that *terza rima* in essence is formed on the principle of the sestet, or the canzone.

11 Here and later I use E. Moore's *Opere di Dante*, re-edited by Toynbee (Oxford, 1924); two such anonymous *sestine* in this form are on pp. 182c and 182d, and see Blanc, *op. cit.*, pp. 765–766.

12 The first suggestion of this origin seems to have been made by H. Schuchardt, *Ritornello u. Terzine* (Halle, 1874), pp. 122–133, also 3, 6, 17, and apparently by V. Imbriani. See also M. Barbi in *Studi . . . dedicati a Pio Rajna* (Milan, 1911), p. 97. The subject seems confused.

13 Schuchardt, p. 122; Barbi, *loc. cit.*, pp. 97–98.

14 Schuchardt (pp. 133–34) gives one fourteenth century case of six *ritornelli* strung together, without interlinking; later cases pp. 17, 134, and

in O. Marcoaldi's collection of nineteenth-century Umbrian folk-poetry (p. 60), etc.

15 The sonnets in these two groups are those numbered, in the Moore-Toynbee *Opere*, 54, 26 *, 29, 30, 33 *, 36, 41, 47 *, 49, 51 *, 51, V. N. 12 and 13; 43, 46, 44, 49 *, and V. N. 1. Poems of over fourteen lines called sonnets are disregarded (but show how he experimented with other forms than the *terzina*), and also dubious and spurious ones, in the Moore-Toynbee edition; but of these quite a number are of the first sort above.—A minor American poet has lately realized the kinship between the two forms of verse, and published a volume *Terza-Rima Sonnets*, each having four *terzine* with a final couplet resuming one of the earlier rimes.

16 *Altital. Lesebuch* (Halle, 1886), pp. 88–92, 101; *Crestomazia*, I, 193–310. I disregard a half dozen or more sonnets in which all the six rimes are the same word. One or two sonnets in the two books may be identical. Among the early Sicilian poets about a third of the sonnets have this scheme, almost all the rest *abcabc* (Langley in *PMLA*, XXVIII, 518, 520).

17 The same scheme exists in the first six lines of *ottava rima*, used in popular poetry, some believe (Volpi, *Il Trecento*, p. 188), earlier than Boccaccio, the first literary poet to use it.—I do not know, nor seemingly do others, the origin, history, and exact significance of the phrases *terza, ottava rima*, instead of *rima di tre, di otto*, which seem more idiomatic for the present sense. But the "third rhyme," *la terza rima*, is exactly what and only what distinguishes this verse from the common early form of sestet. For want of evidence I do not pursue this subject.

18 Melodic and mnemonic repetitions of rimes and other words at ends and beginnings of adjacent stanzas are far from being confined to Romance poetry, and are a marked feature of certain English poems, narrative and especially lyric, and especially in the fourteenth century in northerly England. Such are the *Song of Husbandmen* in T. Wright, *Polit. Songs*, Camd. Soc. (1839), pp. 149–152, *Pearl, Awntyrs of Arthure*, a legend of the B. V. M. in C. Horstmann, *Altengl. Leg.*, N. F. (Heilbronn, 1881), pp. 499–502, several lyrics by Lawrence Minot. On these and others see J. E. Wells, *Manual of the Writings in Mid. Engl.* (New Haven, 1916), index. No doubt the repetitions are for melodic, mnemonic, and sometimes structural purposes; whether ever to prevent losses is hard to say.—This is by no means the only case of reappearance in the far north of very special usages of the far south. I would specially mention the use by Burns in *To a Louse, To a Mouse, To a Mountain Daisy*, and many others, of a very peculiar and quaint stanza not uncommon in medieval Provençal; see C. A. F. Mahn, *Werke d. Troubadours* (Berlin, 1846), I, 3, etc., and C. Appel, *Prov. Chrest.* (Leipzig, 1920), p. 80. Some of these reappearances of forms may be coincidences, but not all; the explanation I do not know.—Adjacent final-initial repetitions occur in Welsh poems, of date unknown to me, but some professedly early; see *Iolo MSS* (Llandovery, repr. Liverpool, 1888), pp. 240–242, 246–247, 250–251, 313, 645, 650, 693. Rimes linking stanzas occur in middle Breton, as Loth shows (*Métr. Galloise*, II, ii, 188–189, in d'Arbois de Jubainville, *Cours de Litt. Celt.*, xi); and the other repetitions as early as ninth- or tenth-century Irish (D. Hyde, *Lit. Hist. of Irel.*, pp. 413–414), in a poem ascribed to Angus the Culdee.—The alphabetical poems, stanzas opening with successive letters, not uncommon in medieval Latin,

French, and English, may be mnemonic as well as *tours de force*.—Of course none of this is much like Dante's scheme.

19 *Inf.*, xx, 19, xxii, 118; *Purg.*, ix, 70, xxxiii, 136–141; *Par.*, xxii, 106.
20 M. P., XVIII, 625–626; *PMLA*, L, 105, and *passim*.

21 *Epist.* x, 10; *De Vulg. Eloq.*, II, 4; *commedia* used of Dante's poem in *Inf.*, xvi, 128, xxi, 2, and in *Epist.* x, 6, 13.

22 On the history of the *Divina*, see Rajna, *Bull. della Soc. Dant. Ital.*, n. s., XXII, 107–115, 255–258; also III, 9–10.

23 xxiii, 62, XXV, 1 ff. But in the sublime heavens *commedia* would be out of place. There is significance in his ways of speaking of the poem in the several parts of it.

24 M. P., XVIII, 631–632. In *De Vulg. Eloq.*, ii, 4, he defends the use of *poetae* for some vernacular writers—but in contrast with *magni poetae*.

25 *Inf.*, I, 87, XVI, 129; *Purg.*, IX, 70–71; etc.

26 Novelle 114 and 115, mentioned to me by Dr. J. B. Fletcher, and quoted in various books on the Dante-tradition, such as G. Papini's (Lanciano, 1910), pp. 25–27.

27 Moore, *Text Crit.*, pp. xviii f.

Erich Auerbach

4 · Dante's Addresses to the Reader

THERE ARE some twenty passages in the *Commedia*[1] where
Dante, interrupting the narrative, addresses his reader: urging
him either to share in the poet's experiences and feelings, or to
give credence to some miraculous occurrence, or to understand
some peculiarity of content or style, or to intensify his attention in order to get the true meaning, or even to discontinue
his reading if he is not duly prepared to follow. Most of the
passages concerned are highly dramatic, expressing, toward
the reader, at the same time the intimacy of a brother and the
superiority of a teaching prophet. Professor Hermann Gmelin,
who has listed and discussed them in a recently published
paper,[2] is certainly right in saying that the addresses to the
reader are one of Dante's most significant style patterns, and
that they show a new relationship between reader and poet.

Indeed, it is difficult to find anything similar in earlier
European literature. Formal address to the reader was never
used in classical epic poetry, such as Vergil's or Lucan's. Elsewhere, it was not unknown, but almost never reached the level
of dignity and intensity present in Dante. Ovid addresses his
reader fairly often, mostly in the *Tristia*,[3] apologizing, asking
for pity, or thanking the reader for his favor which promises the
poet eternal glory. These addresses are still more frequent in
Martial's *Epigrams*;[4] Martial creates an atmosphere of witty
and polite intimacy between the public and himself. There are,

indeed, a few passages on his literary fame which have an accent of earnestness and solemnity;[5] but everywhere he considers the reader as his patron, and his attitude is that of a man whose main object is to win the reader's favor. There are some casual addresses in Apuleius' *Metamorphoses*[6] and in Phaedrus;[7] that is all, as far as I know. One may perhaps add certain funeral inscriptions such as the famous epitaph of a housewife: "hospes quod deico, paullum est, asta et pellege. . . ."[8] All these examples have little in common with Dante's style.

In the Middle Ages, addresses to the reader, or to the listener, were rather frequent in poetry, both Latin and vernacular. But there, too, the form was mostly used somewhat casually and without much emphasis: asking for attention, announcing the content, apologizing for deficiencies, sometimes moralizing or asking the reader to pray for the writer. Examples from medieval Latin poetry can easily be found in the anthologies or in Raby's *History of Secular Latin Poetry in the Middle Ages*.[9] As for vernacular poetry, Gmelin has quoted (pp. 130–131) some introductory passages from Chrétien de Troyes' *Cligès* and *Ivain*, and from the *Chanson d'Aspremont* ("Plaist vos oïr bone cançun vallant . . ."). Such addresses are very frequent in the Chansons de geste,[9a] as they are in ancient Germanic poetry. One may add the beginning of the *Passion* of Clermont-Ferrand, or of *Aucassin et Nicolette*. In this latter poem, there is also the recurrent formula *si com vos avés oï et entendu*. Observe, finally, that the first chronicler in vernacular prose, Villehardouin, constantly addresses his narrative to the reader, using phrases such as: *Or oiez . . .* or *Lor veïssiez. . . .* Most of these forms are not very emphatic; they help give to Villehardouin's prose that air of solemn story-telling which is one of its charms. The tradition continued with many later chroniclers in the vernacular; it may have some importance for our problem, since Villehardouin was, like Dante, a man who tells the story of a journey to those who have remained at home.[10]

There appears in the Middle Ages another type of address to the reader, less casual and more urgent: the religious appeal. It is, obviously, nearer to Dante's style than anything we have hitherto encountered. For if Dante's sublimity is Vergilian, his urgency is Augustinian.[11] Most of the medieval examples are not addressed to the reader as such, but to mankind in general, or to the hearers of a sermon. They are very numerous; typical specimens are Bernard of Morlaix's *De contemptu mundi* or Alexander Neckham's *De vita monachorum*. Similar forms occur also in the vernaculars. One may recall the beginning of Marcabru's crusade-song, basically nothing but the usual call for attention; however, the subject confers upon it much greater intensity:

> Pax in nomine Domini!
> Fetz Marcabrus lo vers e'l so.
> Auiatz que di!

Before ending this rapid inventory, let me say a few words regarding ancient and medieval theories of rhetoric. The theorists have never described or listed the address to the reader as a special figure of speech. That is quite understandable. Since the ancient orator always addresses a definite public—either a political body or the judges in a trial—the problem arises only in certain special cases, if, with an extraordinary rhetorical movement, he should address someone else, *a persona iudicis auersus*, as Quintilian says. He may, in such a moment, call on somebody who is present, e.g. on his opponent, as did Demosthenes with Aeschines, or Cicero with Catiline—or on someone absent, e.g., the gods, or any person, living or dead—or even an object, an allegorical personification—anything suitable to create an emotional effect. This rhetorical figure is called apostrophe,[12] and it very often has the character of a solemn and dramatic invocation,[13] which interrupts a comparatively calmer exposition of the facts. The classical apostrophe no doubt exercised a deep influence on Dante's style; it was in his mind and in his ears. But it is not identical with the address to the reader; this address constitutes a special and independent development of the apostrophe.

Nor did the medieval theorists mention the address to the reader as a special figure of speech, for they did nothing but imitate or adapt their precursors in Antiquity to their needs and to their horizon. They do describe the apostrophe; one of the most important, Geoffroi de Vinsauf, devoted some two hundred verses to such a description.[14] He considers the apos-

trophe as a means of amplification and uses it for moral purposes: his examples are meant to serve as an admonition against
pride and insolence, as an encouragement in adversity, as a cau-
tion against the instability of fortune, etc. They are highly,
indeed pedantically, rhetorical; the purpose of "amplification"
is unpleasantly evident throughout. But they are put in the
second person, and thus directly addressed to the persons or
groups or countries which are supposed to invite criticism or
admonition (Geoffroi uses the word *castigare*). In this respect
they closely resemble "addresses to the reader."

Dante's address to the reader is a new creation, although
some of its features appear in earlier texts. For its level of style,
i.e., its dignity and intensity, it is nearest to the apostrophe of
the ancients—which, however, was seldom addressed to the
reader. The compositional schema of Dante's addresses recalls
the classical apostrophe, especially the apostrophe of prayer and
invocation ("Musa, mihi causas memora . . ."). In both cases
the basic elements are a vocative and an imperative (*Ricorditi,
lettor*, or *Aguzza qui, lettor*). Both may be paraphrased and, in
some instances, replaced by other forms. The most frequent
paraphrase of the vocative is the solemn invocation known
from classical poetry: *O voi che . . .* , or its humbler variant,
the simple relative clause: (*Immagini*) *chi bene intender cupe*
(much as in the Old French introductions *Qui vorroit bons vers
oïr*). The vocative is an essential element of the address to the
reader as well as of the apostrophe in general; the imperative
is not essential. The ancient invocational apostrophe can be
complete without any verbal addition (μὰ τοὺς Μαραθῶνι
προκινδυνεύσαντας . . .). The address to the reader may be
introduced into any discourse or statement whatsoever. There
are passages in Dante where the imperative is paraphrased by a
rhetorical question or by some other expression of the poet's
intention, as in the following verses from the *Vita Nuova*:

> Donne ch'avete intelletto d'amore,
> i' vo' con voi de la mia donna dire, . . .

Others are even without any imperative intention at all (*Inf.*
XXV, 46: "Se tu se' or, lettore, a creder lento"; *Purg.* XXXIII,
136: "S'io avessi, lettor, più lungo spazio . . ."; *Par.* XXII,

106 ff.: "S'io torni mai, lettor . . ."). But these passages too possess the specific intensity of Dante's addresses.

There are two passages in the *Commedia* where Dante uses the noblest and most suggestive pattern, the *O voi che* form with the imperative: one in *Inf.* IX: "O voi ch'avete li intelletti sani," and the other in *Par.* II: "O voi che siete in piccioletta barca . . . / Voi altri pochi che drizzaste il collo. . . ." It is definitely a classical pattern; Dante knew many passages (apostrophes, not addresses to the reader) from classical Latin poets which may have inspired him. There are frequent examples in earlier medieval Latin poetry also (see fn. 9), but Dante's Italian verses have much more of the antique flavor and of what was then called "the sublime" than any medieval Latin passage I happen to know. Dante had used this form long before he wrote the *Commedia*, at the time of his youthful Florentine poetry. The earliest example seems to be the second sonnet of the *Vita Nuova* (7). It is not addressed to the reader (no readers are mentioned in the *Vita Nuova*; the corresponding addresses in this work are either the *Donne amorose* or, more generally, the *fedeli d'amore*, and, on one occasion, the pilgrims who pass through the city of Florence). This second sonnet begins as follows:

> *O voi che per la via d'Amor passate,*
> *attendete e guardate*
> *s' elli è dolore alcun, quanto 'l mio, grave.*

This is, obviously, not a classical inspiration, but a paraphrase, or even a translation, of a passage from the *Lamentations of Jeremiah* (1: 12): "O vos omnes qui transitis per viam, attendite et videte, si est dolor sicut dolor meus." Indeed, Dante has in some way diverted its meaning from the prophet's original intention; he does not address everyone who happens to pass, but only those who pass by the rather esoteric way of love: the *fedeli d'amore*. But a little later, in the final chapters after the death of Beatrice (29 and ff.), when he again quotes the *Lamentations* ("Quomodo sedet sola civitas. . . ."), the development leads to a new address and apostrophe, this time directed to a much larger group of persons: "Deh peregrini che pensosi andate . . ." (Sonnet 24, ch. xli). And after many

years, or even decades, he again several times chose to quote the
motives of the first chapter of the *Lamentations*: in the apostrophe to Italy, *Purg.* VI, 78 ff. ("non donna di provincie, ma
bordello"), and in the Latin *Epistola* VIII written in 1314 to
the Italian cardinals. In the meantime, his horizon had widened;
he had long since ceased to address his verses to an esoteric
minority. The range of his ideas now comprehended the whole
world, physical, moral, and political; and he addressed himself
to all Christians. The "lettore" in the *Commedia* is every Christian who happens to read his poem, just as the passage in the
Lamentations was addressed to everyone who happened to
pass through the streets of Jerusalem. Dante had reached a
point where he conceived his own function much more as that
of a *vas d'elezione*, a chosen vessel, than as that of a writer
soliciting the favor of a literary public. Indeed, from the very
beginning, he never had the attitude of such a writer. Although
he expects glory and immortality, he does not strive for it by
trying consciously to please the reader; he is too sure of his
poetic power, too full of the revelations embodied in his message. Already in the *Vita Nuova*, his charm is a kind of magic
coercion; even though much of this work is an expression of
grief and lamentation, his voice very often sounds no less commanding than imploring; calling up those who have *intelletto
d'amore*, and ordering them into the magic circle of his verses
(recall also the Casella episode in *Purg.* I).

But only in the *Commedia* does the accent of authoritative
leadership and urgency reach its full strength—and it is there
linked to the expression of brotherly solidarity with the reader.
The *Fauete linguis* of Horace, the "musarum sacerdos" (*Carm.*
I, 3), may be comparable to Dante's addresses for its authoritative sublimity—still, it remains quite different. It lacks Dante's
actual urgency; Dante is much nearer to the reader; his appeal
is that of a brother urging his fellow brother, the reader, to use
his own spontaneous effort in order to share the poet's experience and to *prender frutto* of the poet's teaching. "O voi
ch'avete li intelletti sani, / mirate. . . ." It is as sublime as any
ancient apostrophe, but has a distinctly more active function:
incisive, straightforward, upon occasion almost violent, yet inspired by charity; a mobilization of the reader's forces. To be

sure, the imperative echoes Vergilian apostrophes, but these were not addressed to the reader; Vergil did not, as Dante does, interrupt an extremely tense situation by an adjuration, the content of which, in spite of its urgency, is an act of teaching. Inciting emotions and teaching were separated in ancient theory and very seldom combined in practice.[15] Dante's *mirate* presupposes the Christian *uigilate*; it presupposes a doctrine centered around the memory and the expectation of events. It occurs at a moment of present danger, immediately before the intervention of Grace—just as another passage, comparable in many respects, though lacking the figure *O vos qui:* "Aguzza qui, lettor, ben li occhi al vero" (*Purg.* VIII).[16]

Other addresses to the reader are less dramatic, but almost all contain an appeal to his own activity. Very often, the imperative is *pensa* ("pensa per te stesso"; "pensa oramai per te, s'hai fior d'ingegno");[17] in other passages it is *ricorditi, leggi, immagini chi bene intender cupe, per te ti ciba,* and so on. The pedagogical urgency is sometimes very strong, as in one passage just mentioned (*Inf.* XX, 19 ff.):

> Reader, so God grant thee to take profit of thy reading, now think for thyself. . . .

or in the following encouragement to the reader confronted by an example of very severe and deterrent punishment in the *Purgatorio* (X, 106 ff.):

> I would not, reader, that thou be scared from a good purpose through hearing how God wills that the debt be paid.
> Heed not the form of the pain; think what followeth, think that at worst beyond the great judgment it cannot go.

The most telling example of the pedagogical attitude is probably the passage on the movement of the celestial spheres, *Par.* X, 7 ff.:

> Then, reader, raise with me thy sight to the exalted wheels, . . .[18]

with its continuation:

> Now stay thee, reader, on thy bench, back thinking on this foretaste, wouldst thou have good joyance ere that thou be weary.
> I have set before thee; now feed thou thyself. . . .

There is, of course, a great variety of style in the addresses. They include the levels of horrible sublimity, of gloomy humor ("O tu che leggi, udirai nuovo ludo," *Inf.* XXII, 118), of invocation (*Inf.* XVI, 127 ff.; *Par.* XXII, 106 ff.), of friendly advice, and many other intonations. Note one passage, among the most charming, possibly involving a shade of playful humor (though I have my doubts; friendly irony is a very infrequent phenomenon in Dante). It occurs in *Par.* V, 100 ff., when in the heaven of Mercury the souls gather around Beatrice and Dante, just as fishes in a quiet and limpid pond gather around something which may be food—exclaiming: "Here is someone who will increase our fervor." At this juncture Dante interrupts:

> Think, reader, if what I now begin proceeded not, how
> thou would'st feel an anguished dearth of knowing more,
> and by thyself thou shalt perceive . . .

Obviously, the originality of Dante's addresses to the reader is a symptom of a new relationship between both, one which is based on Dante's conception of his own role and function as a poet. With the utmost explicitness and consistency, he maintains the attitude of a man who, by special grace, after Aeneas and Paul, has been admitted to see the other world, and has been entrusted with a mission as important as theirs: to reveal to mankind God's eternal order and, accordingly, to teach his fellow men what is wrong in the structure of human life at this special moment of history. The imperial power, ordained to unite and to govern human society, is despised and almost destroyed; the papacy has forgotten its spiritual function; by transgressing its boundaries, by pursuing worldly ambitions and worldly avarice, it has ruined itself and has corrupted the entire human family. Dante goes so far as to describe this disorder as a second fall of man. True, such ideas were not unheard of: similar motifs had occurred at least since the time of the Investiture conflict.[19] Yet a great poem in the vernacular with such a content and such an attitude of the writer was entirely new. It implied, indeed, it necessitated a kind of relation to the reader similar to a prophet's to his hearers: authoritative, urgent, and, at the same time, inspired by Christian charity; trying, at every moment, to keep his hold upon the reader, and to let him share, as concretely and intensely as possible, in the whole experience reported in the poem. The form of the addresses, indeed, is often similar to that of classical apostrophes; but whenever Dante adapted such a classical form in addressing his reader, he would Christianize it.

Yet there is a limit to Dante's attempt to carry the reader along with him on the journey: the reader of the poem never becomes an actual companion of the journey. Dante alone, among the living, has been in Hell, in Purgatory, and in Heaven. One passage, an address to the reader, may seem to cast doubt on this claim. It is the most sublime of all, the beginning of *Par.* II, 1–15: "O voi che siete in piccioletta barca. . . ." It is extremely tempting to interpret this apostrophe as addressed not to readers of a book, but to actual followers on a journey. If one isolates these fifteen verses from the remainder of the poem, such an interpretation would not be difficult. It would imply the explanation of *qui* (vs. 11–12: ". . . al pan de li angeli, del quale / vivesi qui ma non sen vien satollo") not as "here on earth," but as "here in heaven." That makes sense since many authoritative texts, from Augustine to Peter Damiani and Richard of St. Victor,[20] describe the beatitude of the blessed as an *insatiabilis satietas*, where the celestial manna is given *ad plenitudinem, sed numquam ad satietatem*. One could even go on to demonstrate that only in Heaven one lives really on the bread of Divine Wisdom which is *per se uiuificatiuus*. . . .[21] Yet all this would be misleading. The traditional explanation of *qui* as "here on earth" is correct; Dante's readers are summoned to interrupt (or to continue) the reading of a book, not a journey through Heaven. For it is not even certain whether, at the moment of this address, Beatrice and Dante have already entered Heaven. Furthermore, Dante, as the narrator, invariably uses *qui* for "here on earth." [22] Finally, just a short time ago (in Canto I, 4 ff.) he has said that he has been in Heaven ("nel ciel . . . fu io") and is now going to report his experiences:

Whatever of the holy realm I had the power to treasure in my memory, shall now be matter of my song.

At this point, as always, he remains the man who has returned from the other world and records what he has seen, so that others may read it.

Dante was the writer of a book, and the *vas d'elezione* of a revelation which he had to report in that book. Hence, the book had to combine didactics and poetic fascination; a forceful charming of the soul which particularly suited his revelation, since this was shaped as a sequence of events, as a journey through the other world, highly emotional in all its parts, and linked at every moment to the most urgent problems of contemporary life. The *Commedia* is a special development of the tradition of the Gospels, which also were a revelation of a doctrine centered around an historical event. As the announcer of a revelation, the poet surpasses his readers: he knows something of the highest importance which they have to learn from him. In spite of the charity that he exercises toward his fellow men, by imparting his knowledge, and of the fact that, as a human being, he is their equal before God, Divine Grace, by electing him for this special revelation, has raised him above all other mortals. The reader is not his equal. He may well repudiate Dante's message, accuse him as a liar, a false prophet, an emissary of Hell, yet he cannot argue with him on a level of equality, he must "take it or leave it." These last sentences, of course, are exaggerated; the contemporary reader already knew that all this: mission, journey, and actual revelation in Purgatory and Heaven, was poetical fiction. But a fiction so fused with reality that one easily forgets where its realm begins; and Dante's narrative is so dense, so invariably consistent in its linking of true events that some of its realistic suggestion survives, at least temporarily, in many minds. At any rate, his relation to the reader, as expressed in the addresses, is inspired by this "poetic fiction": Dante addresses the reader as if everything that he has to report were not only factual truth, but truth containing Divine Revelation. The reader, as envisioned by Dante (and in point of fact, Dante creates his reader), is a disciple. He is not expected to discuss or to judge, but to follow; using his own forces, but the way Dante orders him to do.

I know of, at least, one classical apostrophe, linked with an address to the hearer, which seems comparable to Dante's loftiest addresses as regards its sublimity and its urgency. It is due to a man who is himself comparable to Dante—both had the same psychagogical power, the same partiality, the same vindictiveness and cruelty toward their enemies; also, both experienced an utter failure of all their political aspirations. I am thinking of Demosthenes. In 330 B.C., when Philip of Macedon was dead and his son Alexander far advanced in the conquest of Persia, Demosthenes had to defend his policy of resisting Philip's power in the past. At the time when he made his famous speech on the Crown, everyone, including himself, knew that the policy of resistance had failed. The battle of Chaironeia (338) had decided against Greek independence and against the course of Demosthenes. In a certain passage of the speech (199 ff.), he raised the question whether a policy worthy of the Athenian tradition of defending Greek independence should be condemned because fate had denied it victory. His answer was, no.

Even had we been able, he says, to foresee what was to happen, we should have acted as we did. You followed my advice at that time. That is your glory as it is mine. If you now condemn this policy, as my opponent [Aeschines] requires you to do, that would rob you of the enduring praises of posterity; you would appear not as men who suffer the blows of insensible fate, but as men who have done wrongly.[23] But it cannot be, no, men of Athens, it cannot be that you have acted wrong, in encountering danger bravely, for the liberty and the safety of all Greece. No! by those generous souls of ancient times who were exposed at Marathon, by those who stood arrayed at Plataeae, by those who encountered the Persian fleet at Salamis, who fought at Artemisium; by all the brave men whose remains lie deposited in the public monuments. All of whom received the same honorable interment from their country, Aeschines: not those only who prevailed, not those alone who were victorious. And with reason. What was the part of gallant men they all performed; their success was such as the deity dispensed to each.

This apostrophe of §208: μὰ τοὺς Μαραθῶνι προκινδυνεύσαντας was the most famous passage of oratory in Graeco-Roman history. In modern times, as long as Greek was an essential part of higher education, many generations of students read and admired it. Read after more than twenty-two centuries, in a private study (not, as it once was, delivered in a stormy political assembly by an incomparable master of rhetoric), it still has the power to make the reader's heart beat faster. It represents the most magnanimous, and also the most violent, attempt to win the support of the audience which classical literature has bequeathed to us. Still, there can be no doubt that Demosthenes is arguing a cause, and that he awaits the decision of his hearers. He is not supported by the infallible judgment of the Divinity. On the contrary, this lack of an unerring ally becomes his strongest argument. He argues against the Divinity. For his divinity, Fate, decides only what happens; it cannot decide what is right or wrong. This decision belongs to the men of Athens, to their conscience, guided by the traditions of their city. Demosthenes, a man of Athens, appeals to the judgment of his equals, the citizens of a community proud of having been, since the days of Marathon, the champion and protector of Greek independence. He does not know the future; the object of his interpretation is the past; and his opponent, Aeschines, has the same right as he to submit another interpretation of that past to the decision of their fellow citizens.

Dante's position is quite different. The Christian God is not only the ruler who governs the universe, he is also the sole source and the sole arbiter of justice. Therefore, whoever advocates a cause on earth, has to present it as the will of God. Now, God has disclosed his will; his revelation, linked through the Incarnation to human history, involves a providential plan of this history. But the revelation—the Holy Scriptures as well as earthly events taken as expressions of Divine Providence—may be interpreted in many different ways, especially if practical issues are at stake. The ambiguity of God's revelation creates an uncertainty even greater than that facing Demosthenes and his contemporaries. Their criterion (i.e., their conscience as citizens of a "polis") has lost its decisive authority; and the new criterion, God's will, is inscrutable. Demosthenes' argument, that one must not judge by the event, has not lost its strength. The argument stands, only its basis has changed. God does not reveal his decision on a particular earthly issue by bestowing victory upon the righteous. The victory of the righteous will be manifest only at the last judgment. On earth, evil will always play its part, and will very often prevail, since it has an essential function in the drama of human redemption.

The struggle over political issues (I use the word "political" in its widest sense) had thus become a struggle over the interpretation of the will of God; Dante was not the first to present his interpretation as an authentic one. The appeal to divine authority was the natural and normal way to express strong political convictions in medieval civilization, as it had been at the time of Jewish prophecy. Indeed, very few of Dante's medieval predecessors had gone so far as to claim that a special revelation had been granted them; and never before had this claim been asserted with such an encylopedic unity of vision and with such a power of poetic expression. Politically, it was a failure. Dante's idea, the re-establishment of the Roman Empire as the providential form of united human and Christian society on earth, was a lost cause long before the *Commedia* became known. The life which the great poem won "tra coloro che questo tempo chiameranno antico" (*Par.* XVII, 119–120) is not due to its political doctrine, but to its poetic power. Yet Dante's poetic power would not have reached its highest perfection, had it not been inspired by a visionary truth transcending the immediate and actual meaning. The Christian revival of the Imperium Romanum is the first conception of political unity on earth, and the Christian interpretation of human life as fall and redemption is at the root of all dialectical understanding of history. Dante, in his vision, combined both. He reached conceptions far beyond the horizon of Demosthenes' Athenian democracy. Thus it may well be legitimate that he spoke to his readers, as he still speaks to us, with the authority and the urgency of a prophet.

Notes

1 *Inf.* VIII, 94–96; IX, 61–63; XVI, 137–142; XX, 19–24; XXII, 118; XXV, 46–48; XXXIV, 22–27; *Purg.* VIII, 19–22; IX, 70–72; X, 106–111; XVII, 1–19; XIX, 98–103; XXXI, 124–126; XXXIII, 136–139; *Par.* II, 1–18; V, 109–114; X, 7–27; XXII, 106–111. Gmelin adds *Par.* IX, 10–12, and XIII, 1–12.

2 *Deutsches Dante-Jahrbuch*, XXIX–XXX (Weimar, 1951), 130–140.

3 E.g. I, 7, 32; I, 11, 35; IV, 1, 2; IV, 10, 131; V, 1, 66.

4 Examples: I, 1; I, 113; II, 1; IV, 55, 27; IX, pr., 5; X, 2; XI, 16; XI, 108.

5 E.g. X, 2.

6 *Metam.* I, 1, 16; X, 2, 12; XI, 23, 19.

7 Lib. II, Prol.; IV, 7, 21. Horace's *fauete linguis* will be mentioned later. The editorial office of the ThLL (W. Ehlers) kindly sent me, at my request, a list of passages where *lector* is used as a vocative. Apart from the passages mentioned above, it includes Avienus (*Orb. terr.* 257 ff.), Ausonius (118, 15 [p. 421] and 159, 15 [p. 29], ed. Peiper), Rutilius Namatianus (1, 1), several inscriptions and *carmina epigraphica*, and Christian authors, some of whom I quote in n. 11.

8 CIL I, 1007 and VI, 15346; also in many anthologies, e.g., W. M. Lindsay, *Handbook of Latin Inscriptions*, p. 79, or Diehl, *Altlateinische Inschriften* (2d ed.), No. 494.

9 Let me quote a few texts. Nigel Wireker, at the beginning of a collection of his poems (quoted by Raby, II, 99, cf. J. H. Mozley in *Spec.*, VII, 398 ff.):

> In quascunque manus peruenerit iste libellus
> dicat, in eterna requiescat pace Nigellus.
> si quid in hoc modico quod te iuuet esse libello
> contigerit, dicas: sit lux eterna Nigello.
> huius quisquis eris conspector forte libelli,
> dic ita: Christe Ihesu, miseri miserere Nigelli.
> factoris memor esto tui: sic parue libelle
> sepius et dicas: uiuas sine fine Nigelle.

Gottfried of Viterbo, *Pantheon* (Raby, II, 165, cf. MGH, *Scriptores*, XXII, 135):

> O uos qui me legitis, uiri literati,
> super hoc uolumine iudices uocati,
> si non satis fuerint uersus elimati,
> indulgeri conpetit mee paruitati.

Note a rather amusing example at the end of a poem (early 13th cent.) against sacerdotal celibacy (Raby, II, 225, cf. T. Wright, *Poems Attributed to Walter Mapes*, pp. 171–173):

> ecce iam pro clericis multum allegaui,
> necnon pro presbyteris multa comprobaui;
> paternoster nunc pro me, quoniam peccaui,
> dicat quisque presbyter cum sua suaui.

9a The oldest Italian example I know is the beginning of the *Ritmo Cassinese*: "Eo, siniuri, s'eo fabello, lo bostro audire compello. . . ." (quoted after E. Monaci, *Crestomazia italiana dei primi secoli*, p. 17).— For Spain, see R. Menéndez Pidal, *La España del Cid* (2d ed., Buenos Aires, 1943), pp. 422 f. My colleague Stephen Reckert has kindly drawn my attention to the great number of analogous addresses in the poems of Berceo.—See also W. Hövelmann, *Die Eingangsformel in germanischer Dichtung* (Diss. Bonn, 1936).

10 In the same way, the Arabic story of the journey of Mahomet to the other world (*al Miʾ rāǧ*) is addressed to the reader. Cf. *La Escala de Mahoma*, ed. J. Muñoz Sendino (Madrid, 1949), pp. 265 ff. See also M. Asín Palacios, *La escatología musulmana en la Divina Comedia* (2d ed.;

Madrid-Granada, 1943), p. 37. I am indebted for this information to Da. María Rosa Lida de Malkiel.

11 For Augustine, cf. his "vide si potes" (*De Trinitate*, VIII, 3; commented upon by me in "*Sermo humilis*," RF LXIV [1952], 329–331). Other patristic addresses to the reader:

Jerome, *In Matth.* 10, 29 (Migne, XXVI, 66); "Prudens lector, caue semper superstitiosam intelligentiam, ut non tuo sensui attemperes Scripturas, sed Scripturis iungas sensum tuum . . ."; Prudentius, *Hamartigenia* 624, with a movement of interruption: "Sanctum lector percense uolumen. . . ." Verecundus, *In Cant. Ionae* 8, 14 (Pitra, *Spicilegium Solesmense*, IV): "Excita, lector, auditum; rimare secreta prudentissimi regis; et ultro reperies quod debes admirari. . . ."

12 Quintilian, *Inst. orat.* IV, 1, 63; IX, 2, 38, and 3, 24; cf. also the figura called *communicatio*, ibid. IX, 2, 20–22 and the author Περὶ ὕψους, XXVI, on the figure called τῶν προσώπων ἀντιμετάθεσις.

13 Demosthenes: μὰ τοὺς Μαραθῶνι προκινδυνεύσαντας . . . Cicero: "Quousque tandem, Catilina," or "O leges Porciae legesque Semproniae" (*Verr*. V, LXIII, 163) or Horace: "O quae fontibus integris gaudes. . . ." (*Carm*. I, 26).

14 *Poetria nova*, written in the first decades of the 13th century, vv. 264–460; Faral, *Les Arts poétiques*, pp. 205 ff.

15 One may here remember Lucretius who says *tu* rather frequently, if not to the general reader, at least to C. Memmius.

16 Dante liked the image *acuere oculos*; cf. "aguzzavan le ciglia" (*Inf.* XV, 20). In spite of the meaning of *acies* (*oculorum*) there are no examples of Dante's image in the ThLL.

17 *Inf.* VIII, 94; XX, 20; XXXIV, 26; *Purg.* X, 110; XXXI, 124; *Par*. V, 109.

18 The movement *Leva* may well be inspired by biblical and liturgical passages, just as *ciba* in the following verses.

19 See e.g. the letter of Anselm of Lucca to Bishop Hermann of Metz, written probably in 1085, in *Briefsammlungen der Zeit Heinrichs IV*, ed. C. Erdmann and N. Fickermann, MGH, *Die Briefe der deutschen Kaiserzeit*, V (Weimar, 1950), pp. 50 f. Cf. C. Erdmann, *Die Entstehung des Kreuzzugsgedankens* (Stuttgart, 1935), p. 224, n. 56.

20 Augustine, *Sermo* 362, 29; Petrus Damiani, *Hymnus de gloria Paradisi*, Migne, CXLV, 862 and in many anthologies; Richard of St. Victor, *De gradibus charitatis*, ch. ii, Migne, CXCVI, 1198–1200 (on our subject col. 1200).

21 See Thomas Aquinas, *Commentum in Johannem*, ch. vi. lectio 4.— For the meaning of *pan degli angeli* see B. Nardi in *St. Dant.*, XXV (1940), 131–136.

22 I owe this observation, and some other useful suggestions, to my colleague Thomas G. Bergin.

23 Up to here, I have given a summary, rather than a translation, of Demosthenes' text. In the next sentences (208), I follow T. Leland's translation (*The Orations of Demosthenes*, II [London, 1802], pp. 349 f.), with slight changes.

Ernest Hatch Wilkins

5 · Reminiscence and Anticipation
in the Divine Comedy

IT IS to be expected that in the course of a fictional narrative an author should occasionally refer backward to experiences set forth in previous passages, and that he should occasionally refer forward to experiences that are to be set forth in later passages. Dante's use of this natural technique of reminiscence and anticipation is, however, so extraordinary that some discussion of it may be of interest.

I

By Dante's "reminiscences," I mean references made by him in the course of his account of a given region to experiences—or persons, or objects, or circumstances—pertaining to some region or regions that he has previously described. There are in the *Divine Comedy* a hundred or more such reminiscences, remarkable not only in their number and in their great variety but in the wideness of their range: not only does Dante refer, in the course of a given *cantica*, to regions described in previous portions of that *cantica*, but he refers similarly, also, in the course of the second and third *cantiche* to regions described in a previous *cantica*. There are in the *Purgatorio* a score of references to the Hell, and in the *Paradiso* about a score of references to the Hell or to the Mount of Purgatory.

Reprinted by permission from *The Seventy-Fourth Annual Report of the Dante Society of America*, published by the Dante Society of America in 1956.

In the first canto of the *Purgatorio*, for instance, Vergil says to Cato:

> Of myself I came not. A lady came down from Heaven through whose prayers I succored this man with my company . . .

a reference, of course, to the descent of Beatrice into Limbus. And in the same canto Minos, who has been referred to over and over again in the *Inferno*, is mentioned, for the last time, by Cato.

In *Purgatorio* XXVII Vergil says to Dante:

> Remember thee, remember thee, . . . and if on Geryon I guided thee safely, what shall I do now nearer to God?

a reference, of course, to the descent from the seventh circle to the eighth.

The very last words uttered by Beatrice, in *Paradiso* XXX, are these, spoken with regard to Clement VII:

> But short space thereafter shall he be endured of God in the sacred office; for he shall be thrust down where Simon Magus is for his desert, and lower down shall force him of Anagna . . .

a reference, of course, to the *bolgia* of the simonists.

The last reminiscence of all is St. Bernard's reference, at the end of the next-to-last canto of the poem, to events narrated in its first two cantos:

> And o'er against the greatest of housefathers sitteth Lucy who moved thy Lady when thou wert stooping down thy brows to thy destruction.

Many of the reminiscences that range just within a single *cantica* are similarly impressive.

Particularly noteworthy are those reminiscences that are of one or the other of two special types. Those of the first type might be called "supplementary" or "additive" reminiscences.

The first twelve lines of the poem recount Dante's experiences in the *selva oscura*. Despite the deep impression of horror which they leave, the only specific elements of description are those afforded by the adjective *oscura* and by the line

what a wild, and rough, and stubborn wood this was,

and the only specific narrative element is that afforded by the
statement that Dante was *pieno di sonno* when he lost his way.
Immediately afterward, however, we are told that the sun was
rising as Dante made his way out of the forest, and we know,
therefore, that his wandering in the forest took place at night.
That fact is indeed brought out specifically in the lines

> Then the fear was somewhat calmed, which had con-
> tinued in the lake of my heart the night that I passed so
> piteously.

That is all, as far as the original narrative is concerned. But
at the end of Canto XX, as Vergil and Dante prepare to leave
the bridge over the fourth *bolgia*, Vergil says:

> and already yesternight the Moon was round; well must
> thou remember: for she did not hurt thee any time in the
> deep wood.

The full moon was shining, then, as Dante struggled through
the dark forest. And when, after reading Canto XX, one rereads the first canto, this additional element is present to one's
mind. That it remained present to Dante's mind is evidenced by
the fact that it is mentioned again in Dante's words to Forese in
Purgatorio XXIII:

> From that life he who goeth before me did turn me, the
> other day, when full was shown to you the sister of him
> (And I pointed to the sun).

As Dante, escaped from the forest, starts up the *colle*, his
progress is contested by a leopard:

> And behold, almost at the commencement of the steep,
> a Leopard, light and very nimble, which was covered with
> spotted hair.
> And it went not from before my face; nay, so impeded
> my way, that I had often turned to go back.

He finds some occasion for hope (lines 41–43):

> first moved those fair things: so that the hour of time and
> the sweet season caused me to have good hope of that animal
> with the gay skin. . . .

That is all, as far as the original narrative is concerned.
But at the end of Canto XVI, when Dante and Vergil are

standing on the edge of the precipice that falls from the seventh
circle to the eighth, there comes an additive reminiscence:

> I had a cord girt round me; and with it I thought some
> time to catch the Leopard of the painted skin.

Consequently, when, after reading Canto XVI, one rereads the
account of Dante's struggle with the leopard in the first canto,
this additional fact is present to one's mind.

The Limbus was evidently a favorite region in Dante's imagination. The original account of it, in *Inferno* IV, opens thus:

> Here there was no plaint, that could be heard, except of
> sighs, which caused the eternal air to tremble;
> and this arose from the sadness, without torment, of the
> crowds that were many and great, both of children, and of
> women and men.

In the following lines Vergil tells of the conditions that cause
confinement there, and of eternal desire without hope. After
Vergil has mentioned the virtuous Hebrews rescued at the time
of the Descent of Christ into Limbus—of whom seven are
identified by name, and two otherwise—the travelers meet
Homer, Horace, Ovid, and Lucan, and with them enter the
nobile castello, wherein thirty-five spirits are identified. All in
all, not counting the rescued Hebrews, but counting Vergil,
whose own place this is, forty spirits are identified in this canto
as dwelling in the Limbus—more than are identified in any
other region visited in the course of the journey.

Among those mentioned, by name only, is Marcia. In the
first canto of the *Purgatorio*, Vergil seeks to win Cato's favor
by reference to her, and in so doing gives her a more developed
poetic existence:

> but I am of the circle where are the chaste eyes of thy
> Marcia, who visibly yet doth pray thee, O holy breast, that
> thou hold her for thine own. . . .

But despite Vergil's offer to carry back a grateful message, and
despite Cato's expressed love for the living Marcia, his answer
adds something to the hardness of the lot of those in Limbus:

> Now that she dwells beyond the evil stream, no more may
> she move me, by that law which was made when I thence came
> forth.

The conversation between Vergil and Statius in *Purgatorio* XXII adds several new names to the already long list of those specified as dwellers in the Limbus. Lines 13–15 tell of the coming of Juvenal:

> wherefore from that hour when Juvenal, who made thy affection manifest to me, descended among us in the limbo of Hell

And lines 97–114, beginning

> tell me, where is our ancient Terence, Caecilius, Plautus, and Varro if thou knowest;

and ending

> There is seen she who showed Langia; there is Tiresias' daughter, and Thetis, and Deidamia with her sisters.

constitute a remarkable return to and development of the account of the Limbus—an enclave, as it were, within the Purgatory. Seventeen new names, in all, are in this canto added to the list.

A final reference to the Limbus, in the next-to-last canto of the *Paradiso*, adds the name of John the Baptist to the list of the Hebrews specified as dwelling in the Limbus for a time:

> so, over against her, doth the seat of that great John who ever holy endured the desert and the martyr death and thereafter Hell for two years' space. . . .

When, after reading the whole poem, one rereads the original account of the Limbus, that rereading is enriched by knowledge of the several additional elements first set forth in the later cantos.

In *Inferno* XXIX we are told that while Vergil and Dante are traversing the ridge that lies between the ninth *bolgia* and the tenth, Dante bethinks himself of a spirit whom he might have expected to see in the ninth *bolgia* and had not seen. But Vergil had seen him:

> let him
> stay there: for I saw him, at the foot of the little bridge, point to thee, and vehemently threaten with his finger; and heard them call him Geri del Bello.

When one revisits the dread scene, not even the terrible sight of Bertran de Born will keep one from watching for Dante's kinsman.

The account of the Terrace of Pride in *Purgatorio* X–XII tells of the circling of spirits bowed down like caryatids under their heavy burdens, and identifies, as found there, Omberto degli Aldobrandeschi, Oderisi da Gubbio, and Provenzano Salvani. In *Paradiso* XV Cacciaguida speaks of still another person as circling, long delayed, on that same terrace:

> He from whom thy kindred hath its name, and who a hundred years and more hath circled round the Mount on the first terrace,
> was son to me, and thy grandfather's father. . . .

When, after reading this passage, one rereads Cantos X–XII of the *Purgatorio*, the bowed spirit of this other kinsman of Dante is present to one's mind.

The reminiscences of the second special type are those that occur in reviews that cover several regions.

In *Inferno* XI, while Vergil is seeking to make clear to Dante the organization of the Hell, Dante refers thus to the spirits seen in circles already visited:

> Those of the fat marsh; those whom the wind leads, and whom the rain beats; and those who meet with tongues so sharp. . . .

Each of the four phrases, in its intense brevity, summons up, and makes more vivid still in memory, the sights and sounds of a whole infernal region.

A curious clause, which if given its due measure of thought, forces one to renew, in his mind, the sufferings of the first five of the refining terraces, occurs in *Purgatorio* XXI, when Statius, explaining the earthquake, says:

> It quakes here when some soul feeleth herself cleansed, so that she may rise up, or set forth, to mount on high. . . .

For the word *surga* implies the action of the caryatids of the first terrace, the seated blind spirits of the second, and the prostrate spirits of the fifth; while the spirits purged of anger and of sloth have only to move forward.

Most impressive of all are the reviews in the *Paradiso*, especially three passages that occur in Canto XVII in the course of Dante's conversation with Cacciaguida, and his two downward glances from the Twins.

Dante, speaking to Cacciaguida, reviews the journey thus:

> whilst I was companioned by Vergil along the mount which cureth souls, and down-going through the world defunct,

and again thus:

> Down in the world endlessly bitter, and along the mount from whose fair summit my Lady's eyes uplifted me,
> and after, through the heaven from light to light,

and Cacciaguida's last reply contains this tercet:

> Therefore have been displayed to thee, in these wheels, upon the mount, and in the dolorous vale, only souls known to fame. . . .

The first of the two surveys of the planetary heavens and the tiny earth begins, in Canto XXII, with the lines:

> With my sight I turned back through all and every of the seven spheres, and saw this globe such that I smiled at its sorry semblance;

continues with mention of the seven great heavenly bodies; and ends thus:

> The threshing-floor which maketh us wax so fierce, as I rolled with the eternal Twins, was all revealed to me from ridge to river-mouth. . . .

II

By Dante's "anticipations," I mean references made by him in the course of his account of a given region to experiences— or persons, or objects, or circumstances—pertaining to some region or regions that he has not yet described. There are some fifty such anticipations in the *Comedy*. Several of them range forward from the *Inferno* to the Mount of Purgatory or the Paradise, or from the *Purgatorio* to the Paradise.

In the second canto of the *Inferno*, for instance, there is depicted a scene in the Empyrean in which Mary, Lucia, Beatrice, and Rachel are beheld as they will be beheld in the celestial

Rose; and in the third canto Charon, protesting Dante's presence on the bank of the Acheron, suggests another ferrying, between other ports, of which no uninitiated reader will have further knowledge until he reaches the second canto of the *Purgatorio*.

In *Inferno* XIV, at the close of Vergil's discussion of the rivers of Hell, Dante asks where Lethe is to be found; and Vergil replies:

> Lethe thou shalt see, but out of this abyss, there where the spirits go to wash themselves, when their guilt is taken off by penitence.

In *Purgatorio* XXIV Forese Donati, answering Dante's question as to Piccarda, replies:

> My sister, who, whether she were more fair or more good I know not, now triumphs, rejoicing in her crown on high Olympus.

Among the anticipations, as among the reminiscences, there are some that are of one or the other of two particularly noteworthy types. Those of the first type, which correspond, in a sense, to the additive reminiscences, might be called "unfulfilled" anticipations.

In *Inferno* V Francesca says, of Gianciotto:

> Caïna waits for him who quenched our life.

But in Dante's account of the Caïna there is no reference to the coming of Gianciotto.

In *Inferno* VI Dante asks Ciacco the whereabouts of five of their fellow citizens:

> Farinata and Tegghiaio, who were so worthy; Jacopo Rusticucci, Arrigo and Mosca, . . .
> tell me where they are,

and Ciacco replies:

> They are amongst the blackest spirits; a different crime weighs them downwards to the bottom; shouldst thou descend so far, thou mayest see them.

Four of the five are indeed seen below; but Dante never finds Arrigo.

When the ascent of the Purgatorial mountain grows hard, Vergil encourages the weary Dante, in *Purgatorio* VI, by speaking to him of Beatrice, saying:

> thou shalt see her above, on the summit of this mount smiling and blessed.

But when Beatrice first appears there is no laughter and no felicity: instead, she smites Dante with a swordlike reproof; fulfillment of Vergil's assurance comes only through and after an experience of intense dismay.

In *Purgatorio* XVI Marco Lombardo asks that Dante, when in Heaven, pray for him, and Dante replies:

> By my faith I bind me to thee to do that which thou askest of me. . . .

But we never hear that prayer, nor the prayers desired by Guinizelli and by Arnaut Daniel.

In the third canto of the *Paradiso* Piccarda says, speaking of St. Clare:

> Perfected life and high desert enheaveneth a lady more aloft . . . by whose rule down in your world there are who clothe and veil themselves. . . .

But St. Clare is not made manifest to Dante.

As there are reminiscences that occur within reviewing surveys, so there are anticipations that occur in passages that are virtually tables of contents, such as those in *Inferno* I, *Inferno* XI, and *Purgatorio* XVII, or in the many passages, in all three *cantiche*, that bear the poem forward to its three great climaxes.

The experiences of the Empyrean, first suggested in the second tercet of the *Paradiso*,

> In that heaven which most receiveth of his light, have I been; and have seen things which whoso descendeth from up there hath not knowledge nor power to re-tell,

are approached with a gradually increasing clarity in several later passages. The infinitesimal Point that is the one perfect symbol of the Infinite is first mentioned in Canto XVII; and long before Dante attains his supreme vision of that Point, he tells us thus, in Canto XXVIII, of his awareness of it:

a point I saw which rayed forth light so keen, needs must
the vision that it flameth on be closed because of its strong
poignancy;
and whatever star from here appeareth smallest, were seen
a moon neighboured with it, as star with star is neighboured.

III

Closely related to the techniques of reminiscence and anticipation is the technique shown in three pairs of pendant
passages, two of the three pairs linking the *Inferno* and the
Purgatorio, the other the *Purgatorio* and the *Paradiso*.

The most striking of these pairs consists of the passage in
Inferno XXVII which tells of the eternal fate of Guido da
Montefeltro and the passage in *Purgatorio* V which tells of the
contrasting fate of his son, Buonconte. At the death of Guido,
the choice for him as between Heaven and Hell is so narrow
that both an angel and a demon come to receive his soul: the
demon wins. At the death of Buonconte, the choice is likewise so narrow that both an angel and a demon come to receive
his soul: in this case the angel wins.

A similar balance exists between the account of the passage
of Acheron in the third canto of the *Inferno* and the account
of the passage from Tiber to Purgatory in the second canto of
the *Purgatorio*. The contrast in this case extends to many specific elements of the two pictures: Charon versus the Angelic
Pilot; the *livida palude* and the *onda bruna* of the Acheron
versus the dawn-lit waters of the Purgatorial island; the oar so
terribly plied among the damned versus the angelic wings that
speed the boat of the redeemed; the blasphemies of the infernal
passengers versus the hymn that the newcomers to Purgatory

sang they all together with one voice,

the *nave* of Charon versus that which is foretold as a *più lieve
legno* and is fulfilled as *un vasello snelletto e leggiero*.

The twenty-third canto of the *Purgatorio* tells of Dante's
meeting with Forese Donati. Dante is unable to recognize
Forese by sight, because Forese's face is so horribly disfigured,
but when Forese speaks Dante does recognize him by his voice:

> Never had I recognized him by the face, but in his voice,
> was revealed to me, that which was blotted out in his counte-
> nance.

In the following canto, as has already been noted, Dante asks
Forese where his sister Piccarda is, and Forese replies that she
is in Heaven. There Dante, as we learn in *Paradiso* III, finds
her, in the Heaven of the Moon. And here again Dante is unable to recognize by sight, but does recognize by voice. But
his inability to recognize by sight is due, in this instance, not
to disfigurement, but to transmuting splendor:

> In your wondrous aspects a divine somewhat regloweth
> that doth transmute you from conceits of former times.
> Wherefore I lagged in calling thee to mind; now what
> thou tellest me giveth such help that more articulately I re-
> trace thee.

IV

There are other techniques that are associated, though less
closely, with those of reminiscence and anticipation, such as
the technique whereby Dante links his accounts of adjacent
regions, and the technique whereby he conveys a sense of grad-
ual approach; but these lie beyond rather than within the scope
of this essay.

There remain to be considered, in brief conclusion, the two
outstanding poetic values of the techniques we have been considering, namely, the more perfect unification of the poem and
the enhancement of its reality.

The cumulative linking effect that results from the many
case of reminiscence and anticipation is extraordinarily powerful. There are, on the average, about two cases of reminiscence
or anticipation in each of the hundred cantos. The linkings, as
we have seen, affect not merely adjacent regions, but widely
separated regions, not merely cantos in the same *cantica*, but
separate *cantiche*—even the very beginning of the poem and
the very end.

It is quite obvious that Dante held the whole poem in his
mind—so insistently, indeed, that its unity is forced convinc-
ingly upon the reader. The poem, for all its diversity, is one
poem: its unity is elaborate, unmistakable, organic, and therefore vital.

That which is vital is real: the very organic unity of the poem thus contributes directly to one's sense of its reality. And that sense of reality is directly built up by the repeated instances of reminiscence and anticipation. One does not keep remembering that which is not real. The remembered figure or incident becomes increasingly real with each new reference to it as to a thing already known. And that which comes as the fulfillment of anticipation comes with a surge of satisfaction: the reality has been reached at last.

Within the series of passages that have been reviewed, the group that contributes most strikingly to the sense of reality is, it seems to me, the group of additive reminiscences—those in which something new is added to the original account, such as the one that brings moonlight into the darkness of the forest. Such passages assert that the original account of the experience in question, though it seemed complete, was in truth incomplete: in other words, that there was more to the experience than was related, that more happened than the author has time to tell. This gives to the passages concerned, and in some measure to the poem as a whole, a depth, a fourth dimension of the untold, as it were, which certainly enhances the reader's sense of a profound reality.

Many of the instances of reminiscence and anticipation also give the poem extended life in a different way, in that they, as well as other related passages, refer to experiences in the other world which had taken place prior to the time of Dante's visit, or were to take place at a later time. One may cite as instances Statius' reference to the coming of Juvenal to Limbus, or Francesca's prophecy of the coming of Gianciotto to Caina, or those terrible last words of Beatrice in which she prophesies that Clement VII

> shall be thrust down where Simon Magus is for his desert,
> and lower down shall force him of Anagna.

The regions visited thus gain depth and extension in time. They have existed and they will exist *ab aeterno* and *in aeternum*. And that which so exists is profoundly real.

Helmut Hatzfeld

6 · The Art of Dante's Purgatorio

> *Il mito non è favola, ma . . .*
> *"storia vera."*
> RAFFAELE PETTAZZONI
> Not merely a story told,
> but a reality lived.
> B. MALINOWSKI

1. INTRODUCTION

The considerable amount of critical literature on Dante's *Divine Comedy* contains very few items which concern esthetical, structural, and stylistic problems. The *Purgatorio* is the most neglected and allegedly the most debatable part of the three Canticles of the *Commedia*. Consequently, what we need most of all in Dante criticism is an artistic, accurate analysis and appreciation of the *Purgatorio*. Certain random remarks on Dante's poetics in recent commented editions, particularly that of Momigliano or in refined critics like Olivero, T. S. Eliot, and Singleton, together with new insights into the problems of poetic myth, symbolism, archetypes, psychology of religion and of the human depths, mysticism, and liturgy, now enable us to make at least a sketch of the art of Dante's Purgatory with some hope of success. This attempt may receive a certain significance from the conviction of the modern literary critic that the true poetic symbol or image conveys a kind of wisdom

Reprinted from *Studies in Philology* (XLIX, 1, 1952) by permission of the University of North Carolina Press. Copyright 1952 by the University of North Carolina Press.

which is irresistible [1] to the reader and transcends in his catharsis the subjective discovery of the artist, because it suggests secret affinities which must be rooted in the very nature of reality.[2]

Since many points, which I shall mention, have been told and retold by others, though under quite different aspects, I reluctantly suppress a list of general bibliographical items at the request of the editor. What I am adding beyond the new general synthesis is:

1. the exclusive stress on esthetical problems,
2. the identification of Dante's general style with magic realism,
3. the explanation of Dante's participation in the mystical purgation of the souls as a miraculous and not as a mystical phenomenon,
4. the *artistic* identification of the *Purgatorio* with the Suffering Church,
5. the interpretation of the purification of the souls as an analogy to the later so called passive dark night of the soul coinciding here with illuminative processes, which are in turn visionary and auditory.

2. THE FOUNDATION OF THE POETICAL MYTH

Dante's *Purgatorio* is first of all the artistic product [3] of a myth-maker who, with selective skill, weaves together Christian, Pagan, Mohametan, and folkloric traditions, to erect his own magic seven story mountain: When Lucifer with his army of revolting angels (*Par.* XXIX, 49–57) was hurled from Heaven like a thunderbolt (XII, 25–27) to the very center of the Earth, masses of stone and clay, as though they had a presentiment, withdrew in horror from Satan. What Lucifer's body hollowed out appeared on the surface of the Southern hemisphere (*Inf.* XXIV, 121–126), opposite Jerusalem in the shape of a cone, on top of which the Earthly Paradise was placed, since this point was closest to Heaven. The rest of the hemisphere was covered with water. Thus it came to pass that an isolated mountain, high and steep (IV, 81), far removed from the lands later inhabited by the fallen men, was provided for souls to be purged and brought to salvation after the divinely foreseen Redemption.

But how should the souls get there in visible shape making possible their expiatory punishment by the pain of the senses (III, 31 ff.)? Dante, the myth-maker, having entered with his first step the poetic sphere of magic realism has no difficulty in making the second. The not as yet perfect but chosen (III, 73) Christian souls are at the moment of death miraculously (XXV, 86) "jet-propelled" by an inner urge (XXV, 85) to the mouth of the Tiber (XXV, 85 ff.). Thus they are poetically undergoing their particular judgment. As opposed to the thick, black air of Acheron out of which the bodies of the damned are formed, the thin, clear, holy Tiber air of Ostia (XXV, 89), near the Eternal City, is offered to these souls for creating their new aerial bodies (XXV, 88 ff.). This is again a magic process, comparable to that by which the sun forms a rainbow (XXV, 91 ff.).

As soon as a sufficiently large group has gathered, an angel will arrive with a very light and swift boat to take these fine "soul-bodies" preshaped for the halleluia of the resurrection [4] (XXX, 15), to the shores of the purgatorial island (II, 13–57). In spiritual profundity this magic isle is as different from Pindar's island of the Blessed and Homer's Ogygia and all the Atlantic types of mythical Western islands, as it is different in poetical beauty from the Earthly paradise islands of Peter Lombard and St. Thomas,[5] not to speak of the prosaic purgatory of St. Patrick on Station Island in Ireland.

Dante's poetic genius furthermore has understood that to climb a mountain step by step over rocks, narrow paths, and crooked terraces was the ideal symbolic setting for a painful purgation. His sense of magic landscape makes these terraces appear as though hewn into steep declivities in fantastic altitudes. Dante's poetic instinct also saw clearly that an island in distant waters (VIII, 57) could best give the vague sensation of limitless space and of a place in which the finite world would fuse with the metaphysical infinite. At this point a new idea, the third one to be poetized, surges in Dante's mind, namely the fact that in the spiritual life on Earth the great purgatorial sufferings start only after a time of a more consoling expectation. To work in this concept he creates an Ante-Purgatorio, consisting of a beach, a colorful meadow (VII,

73–84), and a blooming valley at the foot of this very steep mountain. It is there that certain souls, now called shades (VIII, 45), gentle forms (IX, 58), but also vanities (XXI, 135) are destined to delay their purgatorial sufferings, because they have not developed any spirituality in their earthly life. These souls are worldlings who died in excommunication with only a last sigh of contrition, or elegant gentlemen and ladies who hoped for a long life, but were killed in their youth, and princes who, having yielded to trifles, neglected their duties, or conversely, lost themselves entirely in the affairs of State. Again Dante poeticizes everything, even canon law. He knew that the threat of excommunication gave to the person warned thirty days for a possible resipiscence before the excommunication itself took place. Consequently, as in a fairy tale, though with an unusual reverence for the power of the Keys (IV, 135), Dante makes the excommunicated stay in his Ante-Purgatorio thirty times the period which elapsed between the beginning of their exclusion from the Church and their death.

3. THE POETIZATION OF THEOLOGY

Of course, if we are well aware of Dante's keen psychology of these aerial creatures, the respite in this Ante-Purgatorio is only an external boon. These souls are unhappy because their eagerly awaited, though feared, purgation is delayed. They feel like accused persons who have been released on bond and have a certain freedom of movement (VII, 41) but who are none the less worried in view of the threat of the penitentiary. These and all the other souls finally will go through all the seven terraces of Purgatory, to atone for and become entirely purged of pride, envy, anger, sloth, avarice, gluttony and lust, with a different length of time, of course, on the different terraces, according to the individual case. Again, Dante's poetic instinct is at work when he chooses among the many systems of the seven capital sins that of Hughes of St. Victor and Saint Bonaventure. Only with this system at hand could he drastically reduce his distribution of the penitents to the principle of the whole *Commedia*, namely to that Love which moves the sun and all the stars. Actually, on the middle circle of sloth the shades are atoning for their lack of vigor in explicit love of God, higher up for too much inordinate vigor in love for persons or things, lower down for too little implicit love of God by definite forms of erroneous love of self. These latter forms are almost identical with forms of hatred of one's neighbor.

Dante's next problem was the poetization of the "spirits to be ripened by weeping" (XIX, 91) with their single corrective pains in harmony with the concept of the magic mountain. How was Dante to symbolize what the theologian would call their tribute or debt to be paid (X, 108; XI, 188; XIII, 126), the money to be restored by them (XI, 125)? Dante rejected at the outset the prosaic solution of the Middle Ages that the souls are tortured by devils or angels. Dante's penitential souls carry with and in themselves a divinely supported, organic system of painful correction just as they carried their particular judgment in themselves. That means in terms of Dante's poetic symbolism that the proud must moan under the heavy stones they carry, in order to learn humility, that the envious must weep bitter tears from their closed eyes with which they used to squint at their neighbors. Now their lids are painfully sewn like those of a sparrow-hawk. The angry are steeped in a stifling smoke which hurts their eyes as their irascibility hurt their hearts. The slothful have to run relentlessly around the mountain, day and night, to the point of exhaustion, in order to overcome spiritual inefficiency, e.g., scorn of meditation, lack of vigilance, negligence, and procrastination. The avaricious cannot rise from the soil symbolic of their clinging to earthly goods. They appear as if they were irremissibly prostrated before the Golden Calf. The bitterness of their pain consists in not being able to turn their faces to Heaven. The gluttonous are literally tantalized by being placed around the finest trees laden with juicy fruits. Their aroma enhanced by a constant shower from the rocks (XXIII, 68–69) makes them all the more attractive, so that the souls behave like children who stretch out their hands for things they cannot get (XXIV, 108 ff.). Emaciated, with shining teeth (XXIV, 28) and fleshless skeletons, these dead persons seem to have died a second time. Here, Dante's magic realism reaches a climax. The souls, aerial bodies, seem, but only seem, forgotten and we are under the spell of living skeletons. With their eyeballs deeply hidden in their orbits

(XXIII, 40) forming two eerie O's and the fleshless nose between them appearing like an M, these souls seem to say: We are the picture of miserable man OMO (*homo*) (XXIII, 31–33).

We see that with the progress of the action on the higher terraces the artistic rendering of the supplices is also growing. Therefore when Dante climbs through the last narrow gate and stair to the seventh circle, there he finds for the first time the real fire of purgatory as the adequate cleansing punishment for the lustful who were devoured by the fire of erotic passion. This fire is for Dante's art and logic a poetic magician's synthesis of the material fire of the Latin Fathers and of the fire wall surrounding Earthly Paradise of the Orientals.[6] Stressing the Oriental concept Dante's artistic skill uses this new synthetic symbol at the same time for his particular politico-spiritual doctrine, that the natural virtues when duly developed lead to an earthly beatitude which is the "conditio sine qua non" for the spiritual soaring to the beatific vision: The Earthly Paradise.

4. THE POETIZATION OF ASCETICISM AND MYSTICISM

But Dante does much more with the penitent souls. Although he constantly stresses the fact that atoning pain is never disgusting, revolting, or horrifying (XXXIII, 72), there is, he also brings out, the souls' privation of God, their desire for Him, their temporary loss and inhibition of the beatific instinct.[7] And to make this desire for God almost unbearable, and the insight into their own unworthiness intolerable, these souls undergo for their purification and perfection the same treatment which the mystics do on Earth. Visions and voices both exalt and depress them at the same time. All this occurs simultaneously in well-devised and artistic compounds. For instance, on the terrace of the proud, sculptures on the wall representing examples of humility attract these souls so much that they try with difficulty to lift up their eyes to these consoling corporal visions, curbed as they are under the weight of the stones they carry. But when they keep their eyes down upon the ground, they see only engraved pictures of pride, taken from the Bible and classic antiquity which show them their own disgrace and they cannot help trampling on them in shame-faced repentance. But a more unearthly "mysterious" impression—to stress our critical magic principle—comes from the fact that it appears as if these living caryatides (X, 130) seem to move in a museum of bas-reliefs, onlookers and at the same time part of this sculpture gallery of God's direct products of art (X, 99). Dante's scrupulousness in reproducing St. Thomas' ten subdivisions of pride [8] thus works out very well artistically; with fewer sculptures there would not be the convincing impression of a museum, or of an art exhibit, a concept which Dante's artistic imagination anticipates, just as it does in other cantos, aviation or moving pictures, as we shall see later.

On the terrace of the envious, things shape up quite differently. The walls and the pavement with their bareness in contrast to the preceding circle offer no pictures because sewn eyes cannot see. The livid souls there, in their pale gray cloaks (XIII, 47), not only particularly pathetic because as spirits they wear clothes, but also because they behave in all their gestures like truly blind people, supporting one another, lifting their chins when they seem to hear something, undergo another type of mystical inner purgation. These envious souls strike Dante by their constant listening to mystical voices alternately relating instances of charity and envy. The psychological effect with the aid of this auditive means seems still more forceful than was the case in the preceding circle with the means of visualization. While the good examples are like a hearty rain, the examples of punished envy appear like claps of thunder.

Dante's magic realism is most varied and resourceful in demonstrating this inner passive purgation in the circle of the avaricious. The penitent souls themselves record the examples by an inner ecstatic urge, the same which makes the mystics cry out their pain and love. On the terrace of the lustful, vision, voices, and ecstatic cries are even supplemented by touch. The souls, marching in opposite directions, embrace one another upon meeting, but so brief is their kiss that it is almost a *pax tecum*. This, says Dante, looks mysteriously like ants meeting and stopping to ask one another the right direction (XXVI, 34–36). For these souls it is the method by which they learn how to give a chaste kiss of charity and embrace the others out

of love of God, by the kiss to the leper. This experience makes
them so disgusted with their old kind of life that they shout
into the air the most horrible examples of sins of the flesh,
some: "Sodom," others: "Pasiphae," each group outdoing the
other, and then they are themselves ashamed of their outcries
(XXVI, 81).

5. THE POETIZATION OF DANTE'S PARTICIPATION
IN THE PURGATION OF THE SOULS

Dante, who cannot help crossing their fire in order to reach
the Earthly Paradise, experiences their purifying pain to the
point that he states that a bath in burning glass would be refreshing compared to this unimaginable heat. So much is
needed to turn love into charity. But, lo! Dante's garments are
not singed, because this is a cleansing, not a consuming fire
(XXVII, 29–30). This example proves that Dante as the living
man among the dead is given the particular grace of partic-
ipating miraculously, not mystically, in some of the different
mystical trials and illuminations of the souls. Therefore, this experience is not his own purgation. It is a type of instruction in
purgation and a lesson in charity, an initiation, a most drastic
retreat, a series of spiritual exercises which prepare him for his
general confession on the top of the mountain in the presence
of Beatrice. Stranger still than Dante's fire ordeal is his participation in the imaginary visions of the angry (XV) who like
the blind envious cannot have corporeal visions because of the
dark smoke. On their terrace it seems to Dante as though a
screen (XVII, 21) were prepared inside his head on which to
project, nay to flash (XVII, 25), in a quick sequence what we
would call a series of changing moving pictures, seven hundred
years before they were invented, as we mentioned before. Thus
he sees in an ecstatic vision (XV, 85–86), Mary meekly entering the temple in search of her lost Child (XV, 89 ff.); he sees
Aman, looking wild, on the gallows (XVII, 26); he sees the
stoning of St. Stephen (XV, 106 ff.), who is at the same time
pardoning his murderers. These ecstatic pictures are given in
dynamic form, in foreshortenings and on double planes, and
always a new picture breaks the preceding one like a soap bubble
(XVII, 32). Dante, perturbed more than ever before and like

a person just awaking from sleep, rubs his eyes and Vergil sees him stumbling along wholly benumbed (XV, 118–123).

6. SOME POETICAL TRIMMINGS OF MAGIC REALISM

Dante, wandering from terrace to terrace, makes still other truly amazing discoveries. He finds that the very door to Heaven is at the entrance of Purgatory. This seems bewitching, but is actually very logical in this magic architecture, because any soul passing through this door is well confirmed in grace. Dante experiences that at the beginning of the climbing he needs an almost superhuman effort, because the stairs leading from one circle to the other through the narrow gates (XII, 108) are very steep. On the higher terraces, however, the gates widen, and movement becomes easier. Another surprise: after having witnessed the explosions of hatred in Hell, Dante is now astonished to hear himself called "Brother" by every soul. Thus he understands the growth in grace and charity. But lending a helping hand upward over difficult crevasses is even beyond the strength of such a spiritual guide as Vergil. Therefore, Heaven must interfere more directly. Dante, having fallen asleep (IX, 13 ff.) in the valley of the Princes, dreams that a mighty eagle has caught him like another Ganymede and carried him to the sphere of fire (IX, 17–30); and at his actual awakening Vergil can explain to him that Santa Lucia in cooperation with Beatrice had come down from Heaven and, light-footed and nimble, had carried him a good part of the way up to the great gate of purgatory. Dante undergoes other shocks, as when he sees sun (IV, 56–57) and moon (XVIII, 79–81) not on the expected but on the opposite side.

The magic mountain also has curious laws for earthly visitors. There are only right turns (XXII, 123), as any move to the left, the usual one in the Inferno, would mean danger. At nightfall the movements of the wanderers are hampered (XVII, 67–69; XXVII, 70–75). On the terrace of the slothful this law is aggravated, so that even Vergil seems paralyzed, and Dante feels like a stranded ship (XVII, 78). He fully realized what Jesus (John XII, 35) means when he urges us to walk as long as there is daylight. Dante sleeps and dreams three times (IX, 13 ff.; XIX, 1 ff.; XVII, 94 ff.) on his three-day journey and in each dream, conceived of as a magic superstratum in a magic world, equally introduced by the solemn expression "In the hour when," there appear to him his protective helpers. After Santa Lucia who carried him off (IX, 59–60; 19–33), it is Beatrice herself [9] who drives away the slothful and voluptuous siren at whom Dante still dared to smile in a dream, since he could not resist her smooth, sensuous, and melodious insinuations. Following Beatrice it is the young and beautiful Lea (XXVII, 97), who shows him in the third dream the beauty of active life, gracefully depicted by her gathering of the choicest flowers for a beautiful nosegay. Thus Dante may vie with St. Francis de Sales for the invention of the concept of a spiritual bouquet. Lea tells him of her more beautiful contemplative sister Rachel, who never leaves the mirror in which she sees God. This last dream is a gentle preparation for the apparition of Beatrice.

Dante also realizes the seriousness of the purgatorial pains in a concrete lyrical fashion. Even the souls which suffer least seem to say: "I can no more" (X, 139), and sometimes the pain changes their moaning prayers into an inarticulate: "hui" (XVI, 64). Nor is theirs an immediate purgation. The Roman poet Statius is released from purgatory just at the moment, when Dante passes the terrace of the avaricious, after a stay of 1200 years, of which he spent 500 with the spendthrifts. None the less, Dante also discovers that the holiness (XXVII, 11) of the so-called poor souls outshines their helplessness. Therefore they are always first encouraged by the positive example of virtues before they envisage the opposite disgraceful, remorse-provoking deterrent vices. But to make things lyrically still more beautiful, the first example given in each case is taken from the model life of the Blessed Virgin (XVIII, 113; XX, 22–23, etc.), the Immaculate, whom Saint Bonaventure, in this case the pattern for Dante, had praised as "septem vitiis capitalibus immunissima." [10] Mary is present still in another way. Her name on his lips, says Buonconte, killed in battle, saved him at the last moment (V, 102); the angels (VIII, 37) sent to the purgatorio came from her arms and motherly embrace and defeated the Serpent in her name; and now when the purgatorial "Prisoners of Hope" unconsciously pregnant with virtue already suffer like mothers giving birth to a child, they mitigate their pain by the ejaculatory cry: "O sweet Mary" (XX, 20). Even on the sculptures she seems to live and talk (X, 95) and Dante would swear when looking at the picture of the Annunciation that he could hear her say: "Behold the handmaid of the Lord" (X, 43). Thus also the lyrical Mary theme appears incorporated in the magic realism of the Mountain.

7. THE POETIZATION OF LITURGY

One of the greatest discoveries made by Dante, the wanderer, during his four days in purgatory is that he does not find here a disorderly mass of souls, as was the case in the Inferno, but a well-ordered, silent and devout crowd (XXIII, 21), a part of the "turba magna" (ib.) once to adore the Lamb, in other words: he meets the Suffering Church. Consequently the souls as a group add to the mystical individual suffering and contemplation, the collective liturgy of hymns and prayers, and sacramental attitudes. For the most part they form processions as pilgrims to which the pilgrim Dante feels attracted (XXIII, 15). They also gather for devotions fit for their particular purposes. As Dante arrives in the different terraces at different hours of the day, he witnesses many of these canonical hours, according to the "religion of the Mountain." The awe and recollection of the worshipers is only endangered by the frightening strangeness of the shadow of Dante's body, a recurrent motif. Dante's shadow seems as unreal to them as the voices and the gestures of the spirits seem outlandish to the earthly ears and eyes of Dante.

On the terrace of the angry, Dante overhears a wondrous *Agnus Dei* by which the souls implore the Lamb for mercy and peace (XV, 16–19) and all the voices unite in a choir of the sweetest harmony (XVI, 20–21). The proud souls of the first terrace say the *Our Father*, changing the text to correspond with their own situation. Thus they are praying for their daily *manna* in their purgatorial desert as the Jews did in theirs, and this manna is the suffrage of the faithful for which all the souls on all terraces will implore Dante (VIII, 71; XI, 32; XIII, 147). Dante is impressed by the reciprocation of these souls who offer on their part the petition "And lead us not into temptation," for the living because there are no temptations in purgatory. The hymn "Te lucis ante terminum" in the Ante-Purgatory is not only sung but the whole Compline is staged by human and heavenly actors. The "leo rugiens" (*lectio brevis* from I Petr. 5, 8), the "pestis quae vagatur in tenebris" (Ps. 90), and the "noctium phantasmata" (Hymnus) are not mentioned, but to the horror of the souls who never can be tempted any more, a frightful spectacle occurs every evening: The temptations to which these souls consented and succumbed on earth reappear here much more frightful than any "negotium perambulans per noctem," in the shape of the Serpent (VIII, 131), perhaps the same, says Dante significantly, which once gave Eve the bitter apple (VIII, 99). But every evening also two heavenly messengers "Angeli sancti . . . qui omnes insidias inimici . . . longe repellunt" (Oratio) appear with drawn flaming swords to drive the serpent away (VIII, 25–42; 94–108) and thus protect the still "exiled children of Eve" as the souls call themselves in the "Salve Regina" which they intone (VII, 76 ff.).

When Dante approaches the main door of purgatory, it not only opens automatically as in the Vision of Tundale [11] but it starts also wondrous organ music and all the souls sing the *Te Deum* solemnly and beautifully (VIII, 145). At the quasi-resurrection of Statius from purgatory to Heaven the whole mountain trembles as the Earth did at the death of Christ, and Statius appears to Dante and Vergil as suddenly and mysteriously as Christ the Risen once appeared to the disciples on the way to Emmaus (XXI, 7–13). At the same time a *Gloria* is heard, sung by the rejoicing souls, forgetting their own sorrow, Dante listening to the heavenly tunes feels something of the bliss of the shepherds on the memorable Christmas night (XX, 140).

Of course, it is fitting that Dante meets more often slowly moving penitential processions of praying shades (XI, 20), mostly weeping and singing at the same time. They entune the *Miserere* (V, 22) or cry for help with the Litany of all the Saints (XIII, 50; XVI, 19). The processional hymns of the angry are heard, although the singers cannot be seen in the stifling smoke of their dark night (XVI, 1 ff.). The gluttonous who have opened their mouths for good food rather than for the praise of the Lord suddenly understand altogether why their Divine Office stresses so much Psalm 50, 17: *Domine, Labia mea aperies* (XXIII, 11). The hymn of Saturday at Matins, *Summae Deus Clementiae,* containing the strongest prayer for the preservation of chastity, is sung even twice at each occasion by the lustful (XXV, 121). They have no other hymn but this (XXV, 131). These are some examples of Dante's inexhaustible variations of the liturgical theme embedded in the magic-realistic action.

For helping to perform all the liturgical ceremonies there are no priests. Priests are not needed where there is no sacrifice. But those who take care of the penitential rites are angels with priestly functions, beautiful angels, clad in the splendor of white rays (XVII, 52–57), their faces shining like the trembling morning star (XII, 89–90). They have delegated powers in a mystical penitentiary where it would be not compatible with the dignity of the Master to appear Himself. These angels with their blessings by the sign of the cross (II, 49) convey the sacramental atmosphere to the Mountain. They stand watch on the highest point of each circle to keep any soul from leaving the terrace assigned to it before its time is up. This function is merely formal, however, because no soul would do so; on the contrary, all of them are so eager to please the Lord, that despite their pain, they keep straight to their particular mode of purgation and try to accelerate the process so earnestly that they scarcely take time out to talk to Dante, which Oderisi, Pope Hadrian, Guido del Duca, Marco Lombardo bluntly tell him.[12] Conversely, the souls in the Inferno only thought of tricks to escape the devils. Therefore the much more important function of these reigning angels with their loving voices is to welcome the souls, first to the main purgatory with the symbol of the keys (IX, 76–132) and then to each one of the higher circles after their penance on the lower one is fulfilled. They open their arms wide to the redeemed sinners like Christ on the cross (XII, 91). They greet them with the *beatitude* most appropriate to their situation (XII, 109 ff.; XV, 37 ff.; XVII, 67 ff.; XIX, 49 ff.; XXII, 4 ff.; XXVII, 7 ff.), hinting in a melodious, poetical manner to the fact that purgation has brought about the heightening of the virtuous capacities of the souls to the full gifts of the Holy Spirit, which, when accumulated, will give them the power to soar automatically to Heaven from the plateau of Earthly Paradise. Thus the inner process of sanctification hinging on a major automaton is stressed as were the others.

The angels have more priestly functions: They bless, aid, and direct Dante in his symbolic penitential initiation into the mysteries of the Mountain (XXX, 82–99). The first angel draws the seven Peccata signs on Dante's forehead (IX, 112) like a penitential cross of ashes and each of the following angels removes one of these P's, revealing to him the true meaning of a heavy conscience and a conscience at ease. Their work is crowned after Dante's most perfect contrition and confession on the plateau when Matelda washes the remembrance of any guilt from him (XXXII, 1–3) and makes him drink the memory of good works instead.

8. THE POETIZATION OF VERGIL'S GUIDANCE

Dante's spiritual guide, ever present and blindly obeyed (XVI, 6), is not an angel, but Vergil; Vergil who, though not a Christian, could not help becoming for many a guide by his literary work, and a directing-sign to Christ. Much to Vergil's own sorrow, he is so informed by Statius, the Crypto-Christian, who had read the poet's fourth eclogue with its curious prediction of the birth of a savior from a virgin and of a new golden age. This is the topic to be discussed by the two spirits, Vergil and Statius, on the way from the terrace of the avaricious to that of the gluttonous. Vergil cannot help envying Statius, who is on his way to Heavenly peace (XXI, 17), while he himself will return to the sad limbo, the "eternal exile" (XXI, 18), as he says bitterly. If some critics wonder why Vergil, the pagan, has such high powers as Dante's guide, one may conclude from the text that he, who particularly led Statius and others to Heaven, is also capable of guiding Dante at least to Beatrice and to "crown and miter" him (XXVII, 142).

Vergil is the most affectionate (XVII, 82), true (XVIII, 7), dear (XV, 25; XVIII, 13), and sweet leader (XII, 3) as well as wise adviser (XIII, 75), as Dante, Vergil's spiritual son (XVII, 92) and dear child (XXIII, 4), calls him. He awakens

him when he has weird dreams (XIX, 34–35); he offers encouraging words (XIX, 25); and against temptation he gives
him a simple, natural remedy: an upward glance toward the
stars (XIX, 62–63). The most charming scene is that of Dante
the child (XXVII, 20–45) who, refusing to cross the zone of
fire, keeps so near the outer edge that he is in danger of toppling
thousands of yards into that mythical ocean (XXV, 117),
which no human eye has ever seen. Vergil must lure him into
the flames by stratagem, the casual remark, that he already sees
faintly on the other side of the fire the long-sought eyes of
Beatrice (XXVII, 54). Upon other occasions he assumes strictly
sacerdotal attitudes, such as teaching (XII, 84) and imparting
blessings (XXVII, 142).

The situation of a pagan, such as Vergil, guiding a Christian, Dante, leads poetically to the development of the motif
of the blind leader. Vergil who must show the way to Dante
does not know the way himself. Although he finds the wide
road, he does not discern the narrow gates. Therefore he must
ask continually, first Cato, later the angels and the souls, what
path to take in this strange "cloister of charity" (XV, 57).

9. THE POETIZATION OF DANTE'S MEETING
WITH HIS DEAD FRIENDS

The meeting of Dante with his dead friends is a breathtak-
ing, lyrical motif. In their dialogues Dante reveals himself as a
pitiful soul (XIII, 53–54) of thoughtful manner (XIII, 85),
while his erstwhile companions have become so gentle, brotherly
and self-effacing, that they already speak another language.
Upon seeing Dante, they do not exclaim like Dante's friends in
Hell: "What a surprise!" but "What a grace!" (XXIII, 42).
The souls, in a discreet (XXIII, 43–45) and noble manner,
delicately share certain of Dante's earthly interests, whereas
Dante learns unconsciously and gradually to view things from
the standpoint of true eternity. Here are some concrete artistic
consequences of this situation. When Pia dei Tolomei wants to
relate to Dante her brutal assassination at the hands of her
husband, she only evokes in a melancholy way the time when
he lovingly gave her the dear wedding ring and then adds with
a sigh: Well, "Siena brought me to life; Maremma to death"

(V, 133–136), and she urges Dante to say some prayers for her only after having had a good rest from the hardships of his trip. The painter Oderisi (XI, 82) and the poet Guido Guinicelli (XXVI, 114), both once eager for glory, now gently reject Dante's praise of their artistic achievements. Upon meeting with Pope Hadrian V, Dante falls to his knees, whereupon the pope says: "Brother, get up (XIX, 133 ff.), here I am a servant like you" (XIX, 134). The *neque nubent* (of Math. XXII, 30) in the other world has its analogical extension also for the relationship between the faithful and the pope, "The only value left to me is a niece on earth." With this imperceptible suggestion that Dante should try to procure the niece's suffrages in a kind of spiritual topsy-turvy nepotism, this unearthly dialogue abruptly ends the canto and leaves Dante perplexed.

Dante does not forget that these spiritual souls must also fit into the atmosphere of his Purgatorio. Therefore his friend Forese Donati, appearing as a meager skeleton (XXIV, 16 ff.), is recognized only by his voice. The beautiful Manfred, fatally wounded in battle, even in Purgatory retains his youthful blond hair and the scar on his forehead (III, 107–108). The Mantuan troubadour Sordello, to the great surprise of Dante, is able to embrace Vergil (VI, 75), whereas Statius is discouraged by Vergil in his attempt to do so (XXI, 132); and Dante never will know the exact code of the sentimental life of shadows. Similarly Dante is astonished by the abrupt manner of departure of the shades who rush back to their purgation, as does Marco Lombardo (XVI, 142–145) or Forese Donati (XXIV, 75 ff.). One of the most mysterious persons of all is Cato, the Pagan enthusiast of liberty, who, with his parted white beard, and surrounded by a halo of four stars, appears like a patriarch liberated from limbo. Dante has made him a half-saint and superintendent of the seven kingdoms (I, 82), a solemn creature, certain of a glorious resurrection on doomsday, despite his paradoxical suicide.[13]

The greatest shock is the appearance of Beatrice, who is far from being the lovely girl from Florence when she descends from Heaven. She is similar to the bride of the Canticle, or to the morning sun clouded in the East (XXX, 20–27); she is like an admiral in battle array (XXX, 58), or an adored mother who

even when scolding would appear superb and beautiful to her
son (XXX, 79). Dante's bewilderment reaches its peak when
with the mysterious griffin she disappears heavenward. These
are moments when logical allegorization would destroy all the
poetry, while the literal sense finds the modern critic and artist
entirely at ease.

10. LYRICAL ELEMENTS IN THE CREATION
OF A MAGIC LANDSCAPE

Until now we have considered, so to speak, only the necessary poetically transformed elements of the subject matter of
Dante's *Purgatorio*. But what makes the poem more lyrical and
underscores the magic realism decisively is the exploitation of
astronomical and atmospheric conditions for a gamut of landscapes, seascapes, and skyscapes, whose beauty creates a melancholy mood of sadness and nostalgia in the reader. These scenes
with their half-descriptive foreground and half-lyrical background create with comparative means a counterpoint to the
leading melody of the main action and the dialogues.

When Dante comes out of the infernal mines of the Earth,
the dawn of a dreamlike Eastern morning greets him. There are
shining on a greenish-blue sky (I, 13–27) four unknown stars,
grouped around the smiling, serene, and pure Venus (I, 19). The
still, dark sea is moved by a slight breeze (I, 117), and with the
growth of light it seems to tremble, covered as it is with tiny
rippling waves. Not far from the beach appears a very unusual
scene; there are meadows with flowers of all imaginable colors,
and a beautiful, little, wondrous valley which, at nightfall under
the setting sun of a foreign sky, evokes nostalgia. It is the kind
of melancholy known to the sailor who finds himself at sea
the first night after having kissed his beloved ones good-bye,
or it is the type of sadness which overcomes the pilgrim who,
deep in thought, approaches an unknown village at the hour
when the Angelus starts to mourn the parting day (VIII, 1–6).

Later, Dante's and Vergil's silhouettes appear on the third
terrace enveloped in the smoke of the angry souls; one is following the other, and Dante is rubbing his sore eyes (XV, 139–
140) when the weak rays of the setting sun pierce the smoke
clouds as suddenly as though they were alpine mist on a rainy

day (XVII, 1–20). It is a totally different picture when in the late morning sun the glittering Holy Mountain appears like a blast. Dante has overslept because of the spell of the terrace of the slothful, and it is as though the sun were smiling ironically and blaming Dante for his nasty dreams (XIX, 37–38), which occurred under a condoning moon, which had had the uncanny form of an overturned bucket (XVIII, 76–81). An eerie impression comes also from Dante's walking between the setting sun and the fire of the lustful, keeping to the outer edge; but Dante's shadow, nevertheless, makes the flame darker, and it seems, more glowing (XXVI, 4–8), a most astonishing observation and artistic setting some hundred years before the impressionists discovered color reflexes in shades. The starry sky over the last stair on which Dante is resting during the final night is reminiscent of those clear nights, during which the flocks stay in the open, protected by their shepherd leaning on his staff. In like manner is Dante protected by Vergil until Dawn jubilantly chases the stars and the darkness away in all directions (XXVII, 112).

The most magic landscape, of course, is the dark green shadowy pine wood of Earthly Paradise. Streamlets, fresh and transparent, although appearing almost brown like the trunks of the trees, murmur in union with the birds singing on the ever peacefully moving branches (XXVIII, 1–33). Since a fiery but none the less mild sunlight casts a sea of light through the thicket (XXIX, 34–35), and rosy blossoms come from leafless branches (XXX, 22–24), and virtuous nymphs (XXIX, 4–5) dance in this woodland, Dante understands that Ovid, in speaking of the Golden Age, had in mind this Garden of Eden.

Dante as a poet knows that he does not have to compete with the painter in description and he draws mood and climate, as we have said before, rather from lyrical suggestions. Therefore there is still another layer of remembered earthly landscapes which become magic in the light of the remembrance of souls who lived or died therein. Thus is portrayed the battlefield of Campaldino (V, 92 ff.) with the wounded Buonconte, who, fleeing with his throat pierced, tinges the field with dripping red blood (V, 99 ff.); then he collapses and is dragged into the river on that stormy day (V, 119 ff.). Or to choose a brighter picture: There looms in the mind of Dante, who is on his way to Earthly Paradise, a Proust-like landscape-comparison of a balmy May air, full of the perfume of blossoms announcing an as yet unseen orchard full of blooming trees (XXIV, 145–154).

11. THE ART OF USING COMPARISONS

There is even a third layer of pictorial-lyrical evocations, those existing only in comparisons. Dante's casual remarks, actually, are full of imagery. Beatrice's name is in his mind like a refreshing spring (XXVII, 41–42), which will help him courageously even through the fire. It makes him feel like Pyramus, who on the verge of death opens his eyes again upon hearing the name of Thisbe (XXVII, 37–42). The souls with Dante among them as one able to procure prayers for their earlier release, feel as if they were being visited by a messenger of peace bearing the olive branch (II, 70–75). Dante on his part, surrounded by a pressing crowd of souls pleading for *Our Fathers* (XXVI, 130), feels like the winner in a dice game called *Zara* who tries to brush aside people who want to share in the winnings (VI, 1–12). Or he looks at the magic trees on the terrace of the gluttonous with such a concentrated attention that he could be taken for a birdhunter (XXIII, 1 ff.). Similes make the magic atmosphere appear quite natural. When Dante feels the Angel's wing touch his forehead for the first time, he lifts his hand up to his head like someone warned by the gestures of passers-by that he has something on his face which he cannot himself see, and Dante discovers that one of the seven P's on his forehead has vanished (XII, 127–135); Vergil cannot help smiling, having noticed Dante's surprise. When Dante comes back to himself from the vision of examples of anger, his ecstasy fades away and like a person awakening from a heavy dream, asks: "Where am I?" Finally, a voice heard all of a sudden, brings him to full consciousness (XVII, 40–48). Under the taunt of Beatrice, Dante bursts forth into tears as a crossbow bursts from extreme tension, so that the bolt flies through the air in lessened speed (XXXI, 16–20). On a more symbolic scale, the concept of the Suffering Church, as a flock: *pecorelle* (III, 79), *capre* (XXVII, 77), *mandra* (III, 86), is repeatedly suggested by the similes of the sheep either fearful or disturbed, trembling and timidly following the leader, with eyes and mouth turned down to earth (III, 79–93), or of sheep well under the protection of the shepherd (XXVII, 76–84).

Psychological similes of a resounding vibration come up even in the conversations, as when Statius, the saved, explains to Vergil, the non-saved, the latter's tragic mission: "You carried the lantern in the night, giving light to others, and remaining yourself in the dark" (XXII, 67–69), or when Dante compares his timidity in restraining his eagerness to ask questions to the behavior of the little storks who want to lift their wings, not daring however to leave their nest (XXV, 10–14). In other words Dante compares his preconceived but not uttered questions Mallarmé-like to flights desired but not made.

A simile sometimes transfers the central theme of the Purgatory into an analogy, taken, e.g., from the realm of insects, an analogy which will be dear to Santa Teresa one day later in history: We are worms destined to form the heavenly butterfly; we are insects in their deformity, helplessly exposed to the transforming power of divine justice and grace (X, 124–129). Guido Guinicelli, in order to demonstrate that the purgatorial pain is at the same time a solace, leaps back into the fire like a fish plunges into the water seeking its life element (XXVI, 135). Nothing could make clearer the implications that the poor souls are holy souls.

12. THE TECHNIQUE OF AWARENESS AND SURPRISE; CONTRASTS OF SILENCE AND SOUNDS

To underscore Dante's bewilderment on this unusual mountain, there is furthermore a technique of awareness. Confronted with new and strange things, Dante often gets an enigmatic impression which announces something tremendous and unheard of and which grows still more in importance when elucidated. Long after having talked, sung, and initiated Dante, the enigmatic Primavera and forerunner of Beatrice reveals her name: Matelda (XXXIII, 119). The voices, heard by Dante, often are veiled. He is not able to ascertain whence they come, whether from the souls or the angels, from invisible spirits (XIII, 25), from a tree, from a rock, or from Heaven. There-

fore Dante, in his poetically exact reporting, remarks: It was
not clear whence the words came, but actually they were spoken
(XI, 46–49). Little wonder that Dante is frightened by such a
mysterious (XXIV, 133 ff.) hierophany. When Dante beholds
in an imaginary vision Mary's meekness in admonishing Jesus
in the Temple, he first sees an unknown lady and several persons in a church until he is able to identify the scene (acc. to
Lucas II, 46–48). When the first angel arrives with the ghostly
speedboat, Dante has not even time to coordinate his impressions: a wondrous light, something white, white wings, before
Vergil cries: kneel down, God's messenger (II, 13–29). Suspense and incertitude are conveyed in a similarly impressionistic
way when the abbot of San Zeno on the terrace of the slothful
breathlessly tells his story without interrupting his course; and
at a certain moment when the abbot moving away is heard from
a distance only, Dante is unable to say whether he is still talking
or has become silent (XVIII, 127). When the proud with
their stones on their shoulders appear in the distance, Dante is
frightened by the moving stones, or rather by something that
moves and does not seem to live, it is to him just an "I don't
know what" (X, 112–114). Thus Dante's magic invention of
moving stones anticipated Shakespeare's marching wood of
Dunsinane in *Macbeth*. But the greatest suspense of all is, as
Professor Singleton discovered, the moment when the procession of the Church entunes the *Benedictus* as though Christ
Himself were to appear—but who actually appears is Beatrice
(XXX, 19–32).

Despite the many happenings in the Purgatorio, the wanderers go long stretches in solitude and silence high above the
deep ditch of this unique quasi-Carthusian monastery-fortress
of God's honored prisoners. Solitude and silence are actually a
dominant note in the lyricism spread over the mountain-city,
which links Earth to Heaven.[14] This mood is stressed from
the outset by the appearance of only one old man, Cato, on the
wide, vague and lonely beach (I, 31); it is emphasized by the
wanderer's feeling entirely lost on the pathless plain (I, 118–
120), and again by the already mentioned recurring silhouette
of Vergil and Dante, one behind the other, on almost all the
terraces as though seen from a ship in the magic ocean (IV,

136; XV, 40). It is stressed by the gigantic shadow of the Mountain covering a hilly, lifeless landscape (VI, 51); it is brought out by Sordello's isolated appearance in a complete solitude (VI, 59) like a lion in a desert (VI, 66) made more lonesome still by Dante's motifs and metaphors in his political remarks on the forsaken weeping widow, Rome, and the sick, neglected woman, Florence (VI, 112–113; 149–151). Even the path covered with those interesting bas-reliefs is said to be more deserted than the desert (X, 21); the terrace of the silent blind is, in the livid greenish-gray, terrifyingly lifeless (XIII, 7), particularly since not the slightest sound is heard (XIV, 142). We are definitely in the land from which no traveler returns. Dante, so talkative in Hell and Paradise, is here merely pondering over spiritual problems, a mute *pensieroso* who soon will see as a spirit the very places he now sees in the flesh. Thus he feels still more lonely, even in the presence of his paternal friend (XX, 151). Vergil's exclusive discussion with Statius makes him almost jealous and more forsaken than ever, *soletto* (XXII, 127). Dante's solitude assumes heart-rending proportions when the austere Beatrice has summoned the angels to ostracize him as a sinner among the saints (XXX, 103 ff.). Thus Dante experiences the inner loneliness of the lonely souls he has visited.

In this silence of the Purgatorio, paradoxically, there is much music, not only liturgical hymns befitting a church. The souls seem attracted by the soothing element of music as a healing medicine for their wounds. Therefore the angels sing the beatitudes to them. Casella is not hindered, except by the austere Cato (II, 120), from singing one of Dante's songs with a celestial sweetness (II, 113). We may recall also that the murmuring trees in the Earthly Paradise are tuned in as counterpoint to the singing birds, that the door to Purgatory is a resounding organ, that all the processions are singing, though in tears, and the procession of the triumphant Church fills the luminous air with the sweetest melody (XXIX, 22–23). The voices of unseen spirits flitting through the air are arranged in a concerto rolling forth and fading away pianissimo (XIII, 25–35). One thinks of the expression of St. John of the Cross: Silent Music.

13. THE ARTISTRY OF THE WORD

Wondrous suggestions come often from single words. The terraces larger below, smaller above, are called by different names according to the circumstances: *giri, gironi, cinghi, piani, cerchi, gradi,*[15] the process of purgation is called *purgare* (I, 5, 66; XI, 30), *mondare* (XVI, 31; XIII, 103), *dismalare* (XIII, 3), *far lieto* (XIV, 83), *far bello* (II, 75), *assotigliare* (XXIII, 63), *rifar santo* (XXIII, 66). The spirit of charity appears incarnate in the many diminutives: *vedovella* (X, 77; XXIII, 92), *miserella* (X, 82); enjambements express shock and surprise, as when Dante deep in thought, sees suddenly his path barred by a tree (XXII, 130–131). The most uncanny impression comes from the repeated use of the very strong verb *gridar* for expressing surprise, joy, disgust and other reactions of the souls, whose ecstatic utterances cannot be grasped by a non-superlative expression. Very strong syntactical condensations and far-fetched allusions enhance the mysterious atmosphere. The appearance of a white bas-relief is cast into one verb: *biancheggiare* (X, 72). The fundamental difference of the earthly existence from the post-mortem existence is underscored by Dante's using the past tense in inquiring of the personalities behind the souls: "chi *fosti* anzi la morte" (XVI, 43). Metaphors do the work of a metaphysical irony, e.g., when the slothful souls running relentlessly are likened to the slackened oar, which is plied again steadily (XVII, 87); or when Beatrice calls Dante's face, in contempt of his spiritual immaturity, a "bearded chin" (XXXI, 76), Metonymies contribute to representative dignity, as when the angels are called "Messengers of the eternal realm" (XXXII, 78), or when the hour of death becomes "the hour of good pain which unites us to God" (XXIII, 81). For more minute details in Dante's verbal art one can refer now to the book of Luigi Malagoli.

14. CONCLUSION

In conclusion we may say that, while Dante's Inferno is a very "earthly world" and the Paradiso a spiritualization which almost neglects the human element, the art of the Purgatoric consists in the creation of a very human, magic myth, including the poetization of theology, spiritual life, human relations, liturgy, landscapes, actions, and situations. The real meaning of Dante's display of creative imagination and captivating symbolism in his Purgatorio does become still clearer when we reduce his fantastic variations to their theme which scholars found very closely preformed in the sentence of Hughes of Saint Victor: "The virtues drive out the vices . . . , the virtues finally taking over the place of the vices are called sanities or healings. The joy over the recovered health are the beatitudes." [16] Such a retranslation from poetry into prose, which is supposed to have engendered that very poetry, is not only helpful to our own inadequate understanding of the spell of Dante's symbolic, magic, and persuasive reality. There is still implied the problem of the significance of Dante's poetry. Theologians, philosophers, and historians have done very much to find out Dante's sources. The literary critic, allegedly their opponent, is nevertheless grateful to them, because their doctrinal interpretations and verifications make Dante's subtle imagery and symbolism much more transparent, solid, secure, meaningful, and existentially important. Dante's painstaking in keeping strictly to the fundamental Catholic doctrine on purgatory is discernible in every line. Despite his apparent independence in the transformation of a traditional fire into a mountain, or in inserting an Earthly Paradise between Purgatory and Heaven, transformations more radical than the poetical changes in his Inferno and Paradiso, Dante's Purgatorio remains the dogmatic purgatory with its ontological truth. However, the formal truth is seen by a temperament and is broken by Dante's poetic prism into a bundle of most adequate, grandiose, and symbolic images, radiating all the more his firm, vivid, and unshakable faith (*Par.* XXIV, 142; XXV, 52–53). Therefore, Dante's Purgatorio, although it owes its reality only to the magic wand of the poet, is in the fullest sense *littérature engagée*. Modern readers under its cathartic spell cannot help feeling already with Dante the thread sewing their envious eyes and the heavy stone destined to curb their pride (XIII, 133–138).

Notes

1 Romano Guardini, *Über das Wesen des Kunstwerks* (Stuttgart: Wunderlich, 1949), p. 16.

2 Jean Daniélon, "The Problem of Symbolism," *Thought*, XXV (1950), 423–440, p. 428.

3 See however Thomas Aquinas, *Summa Theol.*, Suppl. LXIX, a, 4–7, quoted in Ernesto Trucchi, *Esposizione della Divina Commedia. Purgatorio* (Milano: Montaldi, 1943), p. 1.

4 Romano Guardini, *Vision und Dichtung; der Charakter von Dantes Göttlicher Komödie* (Tübingen: Wunderlich, 1946), p. 11.

5 Petri Lombardi *Sent.*, dist. 17 and Thomas Aquinas, *Summa Theol.*, Iª, Iªᵉ, 102, 1, 4, Quoted by Ernesto Trucchi, *op. cit.*, p. 2.

6 Bruno Nardi, "Intorno al sito del purgatorio e al mito dantesco dell Eden," *Giornale Dantesco*, XXV (1922), 289–300, p. 289.

7 Santa Caterina di Genova, *Trattato del Purgatorio*, ch. 3, quoted by Paolo Perez, *I sette cerchi del purgatorio di Dante* (Milano: Cogliati, 1896), p. 50.

8 Giovanni Busnelli, *L'ordinamento morale del Purgatorio Dantesco* (Roma: Civilita Cattolica, 1908), p. 90.

9 Giovanni Fabri, "Il secondo sogno di Dante nel Purgatorio," *Giornale Dantesco*, XXVI (1923), 97–109, p. 101.

10 Edward Moore, Studies in Dante, Second Series: *Unity of Design in the Purgatorio* (Oxford: Clarendon, 1899), p. 258.

11 Howard Rollin Patch, *The Other World. According to Descriptions in Medieval Literature* (Harvard Univ. Press, 1950), p. 113.

12 Attilio Momigliano, *La Divina Commedia commentata. Il Purgatorio* (Firenze: Sansoni, 1946), p. 411.

13 *Ibid.*, pp. 264–267.

14 *Ibid.*, pp. 262 and 268.

15 P. Perez, *loc. cit.*, p. 89.

16 Hughes of St. Victor, Sermo XI, *De spirituali sanitate*, quoted in Perez, *loc. cit.*, p. 96.

III. Meaning

7 · Dante's Allegory

IN HIS *Convivio* Dante recognizes two kinds of allegory: an "allegory of poets" and an "allegory of theologians." And in the interpretation of his own poems in that work he declares that he intends to follow the allegory of poets, for the reason that the poems were composed after that manner of allegory.

One must recall that there is an unfortunate lacuna in the text of the *Convivio* at just this most interesting point, with the result that those words which defined the literal sense as distinguished from the allegorical are missing. But no one who knows the general argument of the whole work will, I think, make serious objection to the way the editors of the accepted critical text have filled the lacuna.

The passage in question, then, patched by them, reads as follows:

> *Dico che, sì come nel primo capitolo è narrato, questa sposizione conviene essere litterale e allegorica. E a ciò dare a intendere, si vuol sapere che le scritture si possono intendere e deonsi esponere massimamente per quattro sensi. L'uno si chiama litterale [e questo è quello che non si stende più oltre la lettera de le parole fittizie, sì come sono le favole de li poeti. L'altro si chiama allegorico] e questo è quello che si nasconde sotto'l manto di queste favole, ed è una veritade ascosa sotto bella menzogna: sì come quando dice Ovidio che Orfeo facea con la cetera mansuete le fiere, e li arbori e le pietre a sè muovere; che vuol dire che lo savio uomo con lo strumento de*

Reprinted from *Dante Studies I: Commedia* by Charles S. Singleton (Harvard University Press, 1954). Copyright 1954 by the President and Fellows of Harvard College.

*la sua voce fa[r]ia mansuescere e umiliare li crudeli cuori, e
fa[r]ia muovere a la sua volontade coloro che non hanno vita
di scienza e d'arte: e coloro che non hanno vita ragionevole
alcuna sono quasi come pietre. E perchè questo nascondimento
fosse trovato per li savi, nel penultimo trattato si mosterrà.
Veramente li teologi questo senso prendono altrimenti che li
poeti; ma però che mia intenzione è qui lo modo de li poeti
seguitare, prendo lo senso allegorico secondo che per li poeti è
usato.*[1]

Dante goes on here to distinguish the customary third and
fourth senses, the moral and the anagogical. However, in illustration of these no example from "the poets" is given. For both
senses, the example in illustration is taken from Holy Scripture.
It is, however, evident from the closing words of the chapter
that in the exposition of the poems of the *Convivio*, the third
and fourth senses will have only an incidental interest and that
the poet is to concern himself mainly with the first two.[2]

It was no doubt inevitable that the conception of allegory
which Dante here calls the allegory of poets should come to be
identified with the allegory of the *Divine Comedy*. This, after
all, is a formulation of the matter of allegory by Dante himself.
It distinguishes an allegory of poets from an allegory of theologians. Now, poets create and theologians only interpret. And,
if we must choose between Dante as theologian and Dante as
poet, then, I suppose, we take the poet.[3] For the *Divine Comedy*, all are agreed, is the work of a poet, is a poem. Why, then,
would its allegory not be allegory as the poets understood it—
that is, as Dante, in the *Convivio*, says the poets understood it?
Surely the allegory of the *Comedy* is the allegory of poets in
which the first and literal sense is a fiction and the second or
allegorical sense is the true one.[4]

Indeed, with some Dante scholars, so strong has the persuasion been that such a view of the allegory of the *Divine
Comedy* is the correct one, that it has brought them to question the authorship of the famous letter to Can Grande.[5] This,
in all consistency, was bound to occur. For the Letter, in pointing out the allegory of the *Commedia*, speaks in its turn of the
usual four senses. But the example of allegory which it gives is
not taken from Ovid nor indeed from the work of any poet.
Let us consider this famous and familiar passage:

Ad evidentiam itaque dicendorum sciendum est quod
istius operis non est simplex sensus, ymo dici potest polisemos,
hoc est plurium sensuum; nam primus sensus est qui habetur
per litteram, alius est qui habetur per significata per litteram.
Et primus dicitur litteralis, secundus vero allegoricus sive
moralis sive anagogicus. Qui modus tractandi, ut melius pateat,
potest considerari in hiis versibus: "In exitu Israel de Egipto,
domus Jacob de populo barbaro, facta est Iudea sanctificatio
eius, Israel potestas eius." Nam si ad litteram solam inspicia-
mus, significatur nobis exitus filiorum Israel de Egipto, tempore
Moysis; si ad allegoriam, nobis significatur nostra redemptio
facta per Christum; si ad moralem sensum significatur nobis
conversio anime de luctu et miseria peccati ad statum gratie:
si ad anagogicum, significatur exitus anime sancte ab huius cor-
ruptionis servitute ad eterne glorie libertatem. Et quanquam
isti sensus mistici variis appellentur nominibus, generaliter
omnes dici possunt allegorici, cum sint a litterali sive historiali
diversi. Nam allegoria dicitur ab "alleon" grece, quod in
latinum dicitur "alienum," sive "diversum." [6]

and the Letter continues directly as follows:

Hiis visis, manifestum est quod duplex oportet esse subiectum,
circa quod currant alterni sensus. Et ideo videndum est de
subiecto huius operis, prout ad litteram accipitur; deinde de
subiecto, prout allegorice sententiatur. Est ergo subiectum
totius operis, litteraliter tantum accepti, status animarum post
mortem simpliciter sumptus; nam de illo et circa illum totius
operis versatur processus. Si vero accipiatur opus allegorice,
subiectum est homo prout merendo et demerendo per arbitrii
libertatem iustitie premiandi et puniendi obnoxius est.

Now this, to return to the distinction made in the *Convivio*, is,
beyond the shadow of a doubt, the "allegory of theologians."
It is their kind of allegory not only because Holy Scripture is
cited to illustrate it, but because since Scripture is cited, the
first or literal sense cannot be fictive but must be true and, in
this instance, historical. The effects of Orpheus' music on
beasts and stones may be a poet's invention, setting forth under
a veil of fiction some hidden truth, but the Exodus is no poet's
invention.

All medievalists are familiar with the classical statement of
the "allegory of theologians" as given by St. Thomas Aquinas
toward the beginning of the *Summa Theologica*:

> Respondeo. Dicendum quod auctor Sacrae Scripturae est Deus, in cuius potestate est ut non solum voces ad significandum accommodet, quod etiam homo facere potest, sed etiam res ipsas. Et ideo cum in omnibus scientiis voces significent, hoc habet proprium ista scientia, quod ipsae res significatae per voces, etiam significant aliquid. Illa ergo prima significatio, qua voces significant res, pertinet ad primum sensum, qui est sensus historicus vel litteralis. Illa vera significatio qua res significatae per voces, iterum res alias significant, dicitur sensus spiritualis, qui super litteralem fundatur et eum supponit.[7]

St. Thomas goes on to subdivide the second or spiritual sense into the usual three: the allegorical, the moral, and the anagogical. But in his first division into two he has made the fundamental distinction, which St. Augustine expressed in terms of one meaning which is *in verbis* and another meaning which is *in facto*.[8] And, in reading his words, we have surely recalled Dante's in the Letter to Can Grande: "nam primus sensus est qui habetur per litteram, alius est qui habetur per significata per litteram."

An allegory of poets and an allegory of theologians: the Letter to Can Grande does not make the distinction. The Letter is speaking of the way in which a poem is to be understood. And in choosing its example of allegory from Holy Scripture, the Letter is clearly looking to the kind of allegory which is the allegory of theologians; and is thus pointing to a poem in which the first and literal sense is to be taken as the first and literal sense of Holy Scripture is taken, namely as an historical sense.[9] The well-known jingle on the four senses began, one recalls, "Littera *gesta* docet. . . ."

But, before going further, let us ask if this matter can have more than antiquarian interest. When we read the *Divine Comedy* today, does it matter, really, whether we take its first meaning to be historical or fictive, since in either case we must enter into that willing suspension of disbelief required in the reading of any poem?

Indeed, it happens to matter very much, because with this poem it is not a question of one meaning but of two meanings; and the *nature* of the first meaning will necessarily determine the nature of the second—will say how we shall look for the second. In the case of a fictive first meaning, as in the "allegory of poets," interpretation will invariably speak in terms of an outer and inner meaning, of a second meaning which is conveyed but also, in some way, deliberately concealed under the "shell" or the "bark" or the "veil" of an outer fictive meaning. This allegory of the poets, as Dante presents it in the *Convivio*, is essentially an allegory of "this *for* that," of "this figuration in order to give (and also to conceal) *that* meaning." Orpheus and the effects of his music yield the meaning that a wise man can tame cruel hearts. Please note, incidentally, that here we are not speaking of allegory as expressed in a personification, but of an allegory of action, of event.

But the kind of allegory to which the example from Scriptures given in the Letter to Can Grande points is not an allegory of "this *for* that," but an allegory of "this *and* that," of this sense *plus* that sense. The verse in Scripture which says "When Israel went out of Egypt," has its first meaning in denoting a real historical event; and it has its second meaning because that historical event itself, having the Author that it had, can signify yet another event: our Redemption through Christ. Its first meaning is a meaning *in verbis*; its other meaning is a meaning *in facto*, in the event itself. The words have a real meaning in pointing to a real event; the event, in its turn, has meaning because events wrought by God are themselves as words yielding a meaning, a higher and spiritual sense.

But there was a further point about this kind of allegory of Scriptures: it was generally agreed that while the first literal meaning would always be there, *in verbis*,[10] the second or spiritual meaning was not always to be found in all the things and events that the words pointed to. Some events yielded the second meaning, some did not. And it is this fact which best shows that the literal historical meaning of Scriptures was not necessarily a sense *in the service of* another sense, not therefore a matter of "this for that." It is this that matters most in the interpretation of the *Divine Comedy*.

The crux of the matter, then, is this: If we take the allegory of the *Divine Comedy* to be the allegory of poets (as Dante understood that allegory in the *Convivio*) then we shall be taking it as a construction in which the literal sense ought always to be expected to yield another sense because the literal is only a fiction devised to express a second meaning. In this view the first meaning, if it does not give another, *true* meaning, has no excuse for being. Whereas, if we take the allegory of the *Divine Comedy* to be the allegory of theologians, we shall expect to find in the poem a first literal meaning presented as a meaning which is not fictive but true, because the words which give that meaning point to events which are seen as historically true. And we shall see these events themselves reflecting a second meaning because their author, who is God, can use events as men use words. *But,* we shall not demand at every moment that the event signified by the words be in its turn as a word, because this is not the case in Holy Scripture.

I, for one, have no difficulty in making the choice. The allegory of the *Divine Comedy* is, for me, so clearly the "allegory of theologians" (as the Letter to Can Grande by its example says it is) that I can only continue to wonder at the efforts made to see it as the "allegory of poets." What indeed increases the wonder at the continued effort is that every attempt to treat the first meaning of the poem as a fiction devised to convey a true but hidden meaning has been such a clear demonstration of how a poem may be forced to meanings that it cannot possibly bear as a poem.[11]

It seems important to illustrate the matter briefly with a single and obvious example. All readers of the *Comedy*, whatever their allegorical credo, must recognize that Vergil, for instance, if he be taken statically, in isolation from the action of the poem, had and has, as the poem would see him, a real historical existence. He was a living man and he is now a soul dwelling in Limbus. Standing alone, he would have no other, no second meaning, at all. It is by having a role in the action of the poem that Vergil takes on a second meaning. And it is at this point that the view one holds of the nature of the first meaning begins to matter. For if this is the allegory of poets, then what Vergil does, like what Orpheus does, is fiction devised to convey a hidden meaning which it ought to convey all the time, since only by conveying that other meaning is what he does justified at all. Instead, if this action is allegory as theologians take it, then this action must always have a literal sense which is historical and no fiction; and thus Vergil's deeds as part of the whole action may, in their turn, be as words signifying other things; but they do not have to do this all the time, because, being historical, those deeds exist simply in their own right.

But can we hesitate in such a choice? Is it not clear that Vergil can not and does not always speak and act as Reason, with a capital initial, and that to try to make him do this is to try to rewrite the poem according to a conception of allegory which the poem does not bear within itself?

If, then, the allegory of the *Divine Comedy* is the allegory of theologians, if it is an allegory of "this and that," if its allegory may be seen in terms of a first meaning which is *in verbis* and of another meaning which is *in facto*, what is the main outline of its allegorical structure?

In the simplest and briefest possible statement it is this: the journey to God of a man through three realms of the world beyond this life is what is given by the words of the poem. This meaning is *in verbis* and it is a literal and historical meaning. It points to the event. The event is that journey to God through the world beyond. "Littera *gesta* docet." The words of the poem have their first meaning in signifying that event, just as the verse of Psalms had its first meaning in signifying the historical event of the Exodus.

And then, just as the event of the Exodus, being wrought by God, can give in turn a meaning, namely, our Redemption through Christ; so, in the event of this journey through the world beyond (an event which, as the poem sees it, is also wrought by God) we see the reflection of other meanings. These, in the poem, are the various reflections of man's journey to his proper end, not in the life after death, but here in this life, as that journey was conceived possible in Dante's day—and not only in Dante's day. The main allegory of the *Divine Comedy* is thus an allegory of action, of event, an event given by words which in its turn reflects (*in facto*) another event. Both are journeys to God.[12]

What, then, of the *Convivio*? Does not its "allegory of poets" contradict this "allegory of theologians" in the later

work? It does, if a poet must always use one kind of allegory
and may not try one in one work and one in another. But shall
we not simply face this fact? And shall we not recognize that in
this sense the *Convivio* contradicts not only the *Divine Comedy* in its allegory, but also the *Vita Nuova* where there is no
allegory? [13] The *Convivio* is Dante's attempt to use the "allegory of poets." And to have that kind of allegory and the
kind of figure that could have a role in it—to have a Lady
Philosophy who was an allegory of poets—he was obliged to
rob the "donna pietosa" of the *Vita Nuova* of all real existence.
And in doing this he contradicted the *Vita Nuova*.

The *Convivio* is a fragment. We do not know why Dante
gave up the work before it was hardly under way. We do not
know. We are, therefore, free to speculate. I venture to do so,
and suggest that Dante abandoned the *Convivio* because he
came to see that in choosing to build this work according to the
allegory of poets, he had ventured down a false way; that he
came to realize that a poet could not be a poet of rectitude and
work with an allegory whose first meaning was a disembodied
fiction.

St. Gregory, in the Proem to his Exposition of the Song of
Songs, says: "Allegoria enim animae longe a Deo positae quasi
quamdam machinam facit ut per illam levetur ad Deum," [14]
and the Letter to Can Grande declares that the end of the
whole *Comedy* is "to remove those living in this life from the
state of misery and lead them to the state of felicity." A poet of
rectitude is one who is interested in directing the will of men
to God. But a disembodied Lady Philosophy is not a *machina*
which can bear the weight of lifting man to God because, in
her, man finds no part of his own weight. Lady Philosophy did
not, does not, will not, exist in the flesh. As she is constructed
in the *Convivio* she comes to stand for Sapientia, for *created*
Sapientia standing in analogy to uncreated Sapientia Which is
the Word.[15] Even so, she is word without flesh. And only the
word made flesh can lift man to God. If the allegory of a Christian poet of rectitude is to support any weight, it will be
grounded in the flesh, which means grounded *in history*—and
will lift up from there. In short, the trouble with Lady Philosophy was the trouble which Augustine found with the Platonists:

"But that the Word was made flesh and dwelt among us I did not read there." [16]

Dante, then, abandons Lady Philosophy and returns to Beatrice. But now the way to God must be made open to all men: he constructs an allegory, a *machina*, that is, in which an historical Vergil, an historical Beatrice, and an historical Bernard replace that lady in an action which is given, in its first sense, not as a beautiful fiction but as a real, *historical* event, an event remembered by one who was, as a verse of the poem says, the scribe of it.[17] Historical and, by a Christian standard, beautiful [18] as an allegory because bearing within it the reflection of the true way to God in this life—a way given and supported by the Word made flesh. With its first meaning as an historical meaning, the allegory of the *Divine Comedy* is grounded in the mystery of the Incarnation.[19]

In his commentary on the poem written some half century after the poet's death, Benvenuto da Imola would seem to understand the allegory of the *Divine Comedy* to be the "allegory of theologians." To make clear to some doubting reader the concept by which Beatrice has a second meaning, he points to Rachel in Holy Scripture:

> Nec videatur tibi indignum, lector, quod Beatrix mulier carnea accipiatur a Dante pro sacra theologia. Nonne Rachel secundum historicam veritatem fuit pulcra uxor Jacob summe amata ab eo, pro qua habenda custodivit oves per XIIII annos, et tamen anagogice figurat vitam contemplativam, quam Jacob mirabiliter amavit, sicut autor ipse scribit Paradisi XXII capitulo, ubi describit contemplationem sub figura scalae. Et si dicis: non credo quod Beatrix vel Rachel sumantur unquam spiritualiter, dicam quod contra negantes principia non est amplius disputandam. Si enim vis intelligere opus istius autoris, oportet concedere quod ipse loquatur catholice tamquam perfectus christianus, et qui semper et ubique conatur ostendere se christianum.[20]

Dr. Edward Moore once pointed, in a footnote, to these remarks by the early commentator and smiled at them as words that throw "a curious light on the logical processes of Benvenuto's mind." [21] But Benvenuto's words have, I think, a way of smiling back. And to make their smile more apparent to a modern reader I would transpose them so:

Let it not seem improper to you, reader, that this journey of a
living man into the world beyond is presented to you in its
first sense as literally and historically true. And if you say:
"I do not believe that Dante ever went to the other world,"
then I say that with those who deny what a poem asks be
granted, there is no further disputing.

Notes

1 *Convivio*, II, i, 2–4, in the standard edition with commentary by G.
Busnelli and G. Vandelli (Florence, 1934). Concerning the lacuna and the
reasons for filling it as this has been done (words in brackets in the
passage above) see their notes to the passage, Vol. I, pp. 96–97 and 240–
242. The "penultimo trattato" where Dante promises to explain the
reason for the "allegory of poets" was, alas, never written.

2 *Convivio*, II, i, 15: "Io adunque, per queste ragioni, tuttavia sopra
ciascuna canzone ragionerò prima la litterale sentenza, e appresso di quella
ragionerò la sua allegoria, cioè la nascosa veritade; e talvolta de li altri sensi
toccherò incidentemente, come a luogo e tempo si converrà."

3 One recalls, of course, that Boccaccio and many others have preferred the *theologian*. On Dante as theologian one may now see E. R.
Curtius, *Europäische Literatur und lateinische Mittelalter* (Bern, Switzer-
land, 1948), pp. 219 ff. To see the poet as *theologian* is to see him essentially as one who constructs an "allegory of poets," hiding under a veil the
truths of theology—a view which has a long history in Dante interpretation.

4 By no means all commentators of the poem who discuss this matter
have faced the necessity of making a choice between the two kinds of
allegory distinguished by Dante. More often than not, even in a discussion
of the two kinds, they have preferred to leave the matter vague as regards
the *Divine Comedy*. See, for example, C. H. Grandgent's remarks on
Dante's allegory in his edition of the poem (revised, 1933), pp. xxxii–
xxxiii, where the choice is not made and where allegory and symbolism are
lumped together.

5 This, to be sure, is only *one* of the several arguments that have
been adduced in contesting the authenticity of the Letter; but whenever
it has been used, it has been taken to bear considerable weight. The most
violent attack on the authenticity of the Letter was made by D'Ovidio in
an essay entitled *L'Epistola a Cangrande*, first published in the *Rivista
d'Italia* in 1899 and reprinted in his *Studi sulla Divina Commedia* (1901),
in which his remarks on the particular point in question may be taken
as typical (*Studi*, pp. 462–463): "Il vero guaio è che l'Epistola soffoca la
distinzione tra il senso letterale meramente fittizio, poetico velo d'un
concetto allegorico e il senso letterale vero in sè, storico, da cui però o
scaturisce una moralità o è raffigurato un fatto soprannaturale. Dei tre
efficacissimi esempi danteschi ne dimentica due (Orfeo e i tre Apostoli),
e s'attacca al solo terzo, stiracchiandolo per farlo servire anche al senso
morale e all'allegorico; nè riuscendo in effetto se non a modulare in tre
diverse gradazioni un unico senso niente altro che anagogico. Non è nè
palinodia nè plagio: è una parodia. La quale deriva da ciò che, oltre la
precisa distinzione tomistica e dantesca del senso allegorico dal morale e
dall'anagogico, era in corso la dottrina agostiniana che riduceva tutto alla

sola allegoria. Dante ne fa cenno, dove, terminata la definizione del senso allegorico, prosegue: 'Veramente li teologi questo senso prendono altrimenti che li poeti; ma perocchè mia intenzione è qui lo modo delli poeti seguitare, prenderò il senso allegorico secondo che per li poeti è usato.' Nè, si badi, avrebbe avuto motivo di mutar intenzione, se si fosse posto a chiosar il Paradiso, che, se Dio vuole, è *poesia anch'esso"* (italics mine).

It is worth noting in this respect that Dr. Edward Moore, in an essay entitled "The Genuineness of the Dedicatory Epistle to Can Grande" (*Studies in Dante*, Third Series, pp. 284–369) in which he undertook a very careful refutation, point by point, of D'Ovidio's arguments, either did not attribute any importance to the particular objection quoted above or did not see how it was to be met. For a review of the whole dispute, see G. Boffito, *L'Epistola di Dante Alighieri a Cangrande della Scala* in *Memorie della R. Acad. delle scienze di Torino*, Series II, Vol. 57, of the *Classe di scienze morali*, etc., pp. 5–10.

6 *Opere di Dante* (ed. Società Dantestca Italiana, 1921), Epistola XIII, 20–25, pp. 438–439.

7 *Summa Theologica*, I, i, 10.

8 *De Trinitate*, XV, ix, 15 (*PL*, XLIII, 1068): "non in verbis sed in facto." On the distinction of the two kinds of allegory in Holy Scripture see *Dictionnaire de théologie catholique* (Vacant, Mangenot, Amann), t. I (1923), col. 833 ff. s. v. *Allégories bibliques*. On St. Thomas' distinctions in particular, consult R. P. P. Synave, *La Doctrine de s. Thomas d'Aquin sur le sens littéral des Écritures* in *Revue Biblique*, XXXV (1926), 40–65.

9 *Literal* and *historical* as synonymous terms for the first sense are bound to be puzzling to modern minds. In the discussion of allegory by St. Thomas and others we meet it at every turn. Perhaps no passage can better help us focus our eyes on this concept as they understood it than one in Hugh of St. Victor (cited by Synave, *op. cit.*, p. 43, from ch. 3 of Hugh's *De scriptoris et scripturibus sacris*): "*Historia* dicitur a verbo graeco ἱστορέω historeo, quod est video et narro; propterea quod apud veteres nulli licebat scribere res gestas, nisi a se visas, ne falsitas admisceretur veritati peccato scriptoris, plus aut minus, aut aliter dicentis. Secundum hoc proprie et districte dicitur historia; sed solet largius accipi ut dicatur historia sensus qui primo loco ex significatione verborum habetur ad res."

10 It may be well to recall on this point that, in St. Thomas' view and that of others, a parable told by Christ has only *one* sense, namely that *in verbis*. This is true of the Song of Songs, also, and of other parts of Scripture. But in such passages there is no allegory, because there is no *other* meaning *in facto*, i.e., no historical facts are pointed to by the words.

11 Michele Barbi sounded a warning on this matter some years ago, but in so doing appealed to a solution (the poem as *vision*, as *apocalypse*, which needs, I think, further clarification: ". . . Io ho un giorno, durante il positivismo che s'era insinuato nella critica dantesca, richiamato gli studiosi a non trascurare una ricerca così importante come quella del simbolismo nella Divina Commedia: oggi sento il dovere di correre alla difesa del senso letterale, svilito come azione fittizia, come bella menzogna, quasi che nell'intendimento di Dante l'importanza del suo poema non consista già in quello che egli ha rappresentato nella lettera di esso, ma debba andarsi a cercare in concetti e intendimenti nascosti sotto quella rappresentazione. Non snaturiamo per carità l'opera di Dante: è una

rivelazione, non già un'allegoria da capo a fondo. La lettera non è in
funzione soltanto di riposti intendimenti, non è bella menzogna: quel
viaggio ch'essa descrive è un viaggio voluto da Dio perchè Dante riveli in
salute degli uomini quello che ode e vede nel fatale andare." (*Studi
danteschi*, I, 12–13.) This is all very well and very much to the point. But
the problem which Barbi does not deal with here and which calls for
solution is how, on what *conceptual* basis, is an *allegory* given in a poem
in which the first meaning is not a "bella menzogna"—the question, in
short, which the present paper is trying to answer.

12 It is essential to remember that I am concerned throughout this
paper with the main allegory of the *Divine Comedy*; otherwise this can
appear an oversimplification to any reader familiar with the concrete detail
of the poem, and certainly many questions concerning that detail will
arise which are not dealt with here. How, for example, are we to explain
those passages where the poet urges the reader to look "beneath the veil"
for a hidden meaning (*Inferno*, IX, 62; *Purgatorio*, VIII, 19–21)? Do
these not point to an "allegory of poets"? I believe that the correct answer
can be given in the negative. But, however that may be, we do not meet
the main allegory of the poem in such passages.

Likewise, finer distinctions in the allegory of the poem will recognize
that the allegory of the opening situation (*Inferno*, I, II) must be distinguished from the main allegory of the poem, and of necessity, since at
the beginning the protagonist is still in this life and has not yet begun to
move through the world beyond. For some considerations on this point
see the author's article in *RR*, XXXIX (1948), 269–277: "Sulla fiumana
ove'l mar non ha vanto: *Inferno* II, 108."

13 For a discussion of the absence of allegory in the *Vita Nuova* see
the author's *Essay on the Vita Nuova* (Cambridge: Harvard University
Press, 1948), pp. 110 ff. and *passim*.

14 PL, LXXIX, 473. In interpreting the Song of Songs, St. Gregory
is not speaking of the kind of allegory which has an *historical* meaning as
its first meaning (see n. 10 above)—which fact does not make his view
of the *use* of allegory any less interesting or suggestive with respect to
Dante's use of it.

15 On *created wisdom* and the distinction here see Augustine, *Confessions*, XII, XV.

16 *Confessions*, VII, 9.

17 *Paradiso*, X, 22–27:

> Or ti riman, lettor, sovra'l tuo banco,
> dietro pensando a ciò che si preliba,
> s'esser vuoi lieto assai prima che stanco.

> Messo t'ho innanzi: omai per te ti ciba;
> chè a sè torce tutta la mia cura
> quella matera ond'io son fatto scriba.

As every reader of the *Commedia* knows, a poet's voice speaks out frequently in the poem, and most effectively, in various contexts. But these
verses may remind us that when the poet does come into the poem, he
speaks as *scribe*, as one remembering and trying to give an adequate account
of the event which is now past.

18 Cf. Menendez y Pelayo, *Historia de las ideas estéticas en España*,
ch. V, Introduction: "No vino a enseñar estética ni otra ciencia humana

el Verbo Encarnado; pero presentò en su persona y en la unión de sus dos naturalezas el protótipo más alto de la hermosura, y el objeto más adecuado del amor. . . ."

19 Those who refuse to recognize this "mystery" in the allegory of the *Divine Comedy*, who view it instead as the usual "allegory of poets" in which the first meaning is a fiction, are guilty of a *reader's* error comparable in some way to the error of the Manicheans concerning the Incarnation, as set forth by St. Thomas in the *Summa contra Gentiles*, IV, XXIX: "They pretended that whatever He did as man—for instance, that He was born, that He ate, drank, walked, suffered, and was buried—was all unreal, though having some semblance of reality. Consequently they reduced the whole mystery of the Incarnation to a work of fiction."

20 *Comentum* (Florence, 1887), I, 89–90.

21 *Studies in Dante* (Second Series, 1889), p. 86, n. 1.

Erich Auerbach

8 · Typological Symbolism
in Medieval Literature

IN DANTE'S third heaven, the heaven of Venus, the soul on
whom Dante apparently wishes to focus our attention is introduced to him, by one of her companions, in this manner: "Now,
I will satisfy the ultimate desire which this star has suggested
to you; you wish to know who is hidden in this light which
shines about me like a sunbeam in pure water: this soul is
Rahab, and her splendor gives to our ranks the seal of supreme
beatitude; she was the first to be received into this heaven when
Christ liberated the souls from hell; it was most fitting that she
should be in one of the heavens as a trophy of the victory that
was won with both hands; and this because she contributed to
the first conquest made by Joshua in the holy land, a remembrance which means little to the Pope." And then, the speaker
continues with a violent attack against the avarice of the clergy.

This passage is full of problems. Rahab, in the second and
sixth chapters of the book of Joshua, is the harlot who hides
in her house the two spies sent by Joshua into the town of
Jericho—who saves them by deluding their pursuers, declares
to them her faith in the God of Israel, helps them to escape by
means of a red cord through the window of her house which is
on the town wall, and makes them swear that the Jews would
spare her and her parents and all her family in the house. The
men asked her to bind to the window, as a sign, the scarlet rope
by which she had let them down; and thus only Rahab the

Reprinted by permission from *Yale French Studies* (9, 1952).

harlot and her house were spared when all of Jericho, men and women, were put to death by the victorious Jews entering the town.

Now, why does the splendor of this harlot confer on the third heaven the highest degree of beatitude, why is the explanation of her position able to fulfill the ultimate desire which the star of Venus has suggested to Dante, why was Rahab the first to be received in this star when Christ liberated the souls of the old Covenant, what is meant by the victory won with both hands, and what has the avarice of the Pope to do with his forgetting the glory of Joshua in the Holy Land?

All these problems are easily resolved if you consider the figurative or typological interpretation of the book of Joshua which, in a constant tradition, fully developed already in the writings of Tertullian, is explained or alluded to in an infinite number of commentaries, sermons, hymns, and also in Christian art. The book of Joshua, especially its first chapters, has always been one of the most popular objects of figurative interpretation; Joshua was regarded as a figure of Christ (the identity of the names of Jesus and Joshua is emphasized as early as Tertullian), and when he leads his people over the Jordan (just like Moses leading his people out of Egypt) he figures Christ leading mankind out of the slavery of sin and perdition into the true Holy Land, the eternal kingdom of God. Concerning Rahab, all ancient commentators consider her as a type of the church; her house alone, with all its inhabitants, escapes perdition, just as the church of the faithful will alone be saved when Christ appears for the last judgment; she found freedom from the fornication of the world by way of the window of confession, to which she bound the scarlet rope, the sign of Christ's blood, *sanguinis Christi signum.* Thus she is *figura Ecclesiae,* and the scarlet rope, like the posts struck with the blood of the Lamb in Exodus, becomes the figure of Christ's redeeming sacrifice. The conceptions of Jericho as eternal perdition was supported by the parable from Luke 10, 30 (a certain man went down from Jerusalem to Jericho, and fell among thieves) generally interpreted as a figure of the fall of Man. In the same manner, the victory gained with one and the other hand alludes to Joshua's victory won with the help of Moses' outstretched

hands, the figure of the victory of Christ on the cross with his
hands outstretched on the *arbor vitae crucifixae*. Thus, Rahab,
or the Church, stands, in our passage of the Paradiso, as a
trophy of both victories, that of Joshua, and that of Christ;
of the victory of Joshua inasmuch as Joshua prefigures Christ,
and of that of Christ inasmuch as Christ is the fulfillment of
Joshua (*implere*); both entities in the figurative relationship
are equally real and equally concrete; the figurative sense does
not destroy the literal, nor does the literal deprive the figured
fact of its status as a real historical event. Obviously, the last
sentence of our passage, namely, that the Pope has forgotten
Joshua's glory in the Holy Land, is also to be understood in a
two-fold and typological manner. It is not only the Holy Land
in its concrete and geographical sense which the Pope neglects by fighting against Christians instead of liberating it; he
has also, for the sake of the *maledetto fiore*, the golden florin
of Florence, lost all memory of the city to come, *eterna Jerusalem*. And now, the meaning of the passage has become completely clear: the first elect soul in the heaven of Venus is
Rahab, a figure of the Church, that is of the bride in the Song
of Songs, in love of her bridegroom who is Christ—a symbol
of the highest form of love—and this view, as Folchetto says,
will satisfy the ultimate desire the star of Venus has prompted
in Dante's mind.

The method used here for the interpretation of the first
chapters of the book of Joshua does, of course, not apply only
to this text, but is part of an entire system which embraces the
whole of the Old Testament. When Saint Paul came to the
conviction that a man is justified by faith alone, not by action
according to the Jewish law, and that God is not the God of the
Jews alone, the character of the Old Testament was changed
completely—this was no longer the law and the particular history of the Jews, because "all these things happened to them
in figura": thus the Old Testament became a series of prefigurations of Christ, of his incarnation and passion, and of
the foundation of the Christian Church. Saint Paul himself gave
a few figurative interpretations (the conception of figurism as
such was not unknown to the Jewish tradition), and the whole
system developed so rapidly that we find it completely worked

out, with an incredible abundance of details, in the earliest patristic literature. You will realize that this method of interpretation involves an approach to human and historical phenomena entirely different from ours. We are apt to consider the events of history and the happenings of everyday life as a continuous development in chronological succession; the figurative interpretation combines two events, causally and chronologically remote from each other, by attributing to them a meaning common to both. Instead of a continuous development, the direction and ultimate result of which is unknown to us, the figurative interpreter purports to know the significance and ultimate result of human history, because this has been revealed to mankind; in this theory, the meaning of history is the fall and redemption of Man, the Last Judgment, and the eternal Kingdom of God. We, on the other hand, are able to explain to a certain extent every single historical fact by its immediate causes and to foresee to a certain extent its immediate consequences, moving so to speak on a horizontal plane; with the figurative approach, on the contrary, in order to explain the significance of a single historical event, the interpreter had to take recourse to a vertical projection of this event on the plane of providential design by which the event is revealed as a prefiguration or a fulfillment or perhaps as an imitation of other events. In view of the facts that education and culture were almost entirely ecclesiastical up to the fourteenth century, that the conception of human history, as taught by the Church, was dominated by the interpretation of the scriptures, and that this interpretation was entirely figurative and based on the trilogy fall of man, incarnation of Christ, last judgment—in view of all these facts it is evident that the figurative conception of history had to exert a deep and lasting influence on medieval spiritual life even on laymen. Sermons, religious poetry (lyrical and dramatical), Church sculpture, that is to say the three most important means of popularizing knowledge in the Middle Ages, were entirely impregnated with figurism. May I draw the attention of my readers to the important difference which obtains between figurism and other similar forms of thinking such as allegorism or symbolism. In these patterns, at least one of the two elements combined is a pure sign, but in a figural relation both the signifying and the signified facts are real and concrete historical events. In an allegory of love or in a religious symbol at least one of the terms does not belong to human history; it is an abstraction or a sign. But in the sacrifice of Isaac considered as a figure of the sacrifice of Christ, it is essential, and has been stressed with great vigor, at least in the occidental tradition, that neither the prefiguring nor the prefigured event lose their literal and historical reality by their figurative meaning and interrelation. This is a very important point.

Dante's mind was deeply rooted in this tradition, and I believe that not only many particular passages in the Commedia can be explained in this manner, but that the whole conception of the great poem has to be considered from this angle. It is not difficult to prove that the community of the blessed in the Empireo, in which Dante's Paradiso culminates, is arranged according to a figurative pattern. Not only the world of the Christian religion, but also the ancient world is included in Dante's figural system; the Roman empire of Augustus is for Dante a figure of God's eternal empire, and the prominent part Vergil plays in Dante's work is based on this assumption. Dante is not the first to subject all the material of human history to the figural conception; biblical history, Jewish and Christian, came to be seen as universal human history, and all pagan historical material had to be inserted and adapted to this framework. Especially Roman history was interpreted by Saint Augustine and other patristic authors as a path of Christian universal history and of the plan of providence. Medieval authors followed this tradition, and very often used it for political purposes, in the long struggle between imperium and sacerdotium. So did Dante, and most of his figures taken from Roman history are connected with his political ideas, as the following example shows.

At the foot of the mountain of the Purgatorio, Dante and Vergil meet a venerable old man, who, with severe authority, teaches them how to prepare for the ascent, as the guardian who controls access to purification. It is Cato of Utica. The choice of this particular character for such a function is very astonishing. For Cato was a pagan; he was an enemy of Caesar and the monarchy; his allies, Caesar's murderers Brutus and Cassius, are put by Dante in the deepest hell, in Lucifer's mouth by the side of Judas; moreover, Cato committed suicide, a crime for which horrible punishment is meted out in another circle of the Inferno. And yet Cato has been appointed as guardian of the Purgatorio! The problem becomes clear to us by the words with which Vergil addresses him: "I pray you, allow my companion to enter; he is in search of liberty, that precious good you know so well—you who have despised life for it; you know it well, because death was not bitter to you in Utica, where you abandoned your body that will be so radiant on the last day." From these words, it becomes obvious, that Cato is a figura, or better still, that the historical Cato is a figura of the Cato in Dante's Purgatorio. The political and earthly freedom for which he died was only a shadow, a prefiguration of Christian freedom from evil which leads from the bondage of corruption to true sovereignty over oneself, the *libertas gloriae filiorum Dei* —a freedom which Dante finally attains at the top of the Purgatorio, when Vergil crowns him as master over himself. Cato's choice of voluntary death in order to avoid slavery is obviously considered by Dante not as a crime, but as a figura of this liberation. Of course Dante was inspired in the choice of Cato for this part by Vergil's sixth book, where Cato is represented as a judge of the righteous in the netherworld (*secretosque pios, his dantem jura Catonem*) and he was encouraged to treat Cato in a special manner by the universal admiration expressed for him even by authors who were his political opponents. Cato was one of the classical examples of Roman virtue on which Dante based his political ideology of universal Roman monarchy. But the manner in which he introduced Cato and justified his part is independent of Vergil and is clearly figurative. Both forms of Cato are real and concrete, the historical and the eternal form; his function in the beyond presupposes the reality of his historical role. Cato is not an allegory nor a symbol of liberty, but an individual personality: he is raised from his preliminary status, where he considered political freedom as the highest good, to the final perfection of his form, in which civil virtue or law have lost their value, and in which the only thing of importance is the *"ben dell'intel-letto,"* the true highest good, the liberty of the immortal soul in the sight of God.

In striking contrast to earlier poets who dealt with the other world, the inhabitants of Dante's three realms have not lost the individual shape and strength of their earthly character; on the contrary, their individual character presents itself with an intensity and concreteness superior to what it was during the various stages of their earthly careers; and this realism in the beyond is allowed to survive in spite of the fact that they have left history for an eternal, and eternally unchanging, situation. This powerful realism is based on Dante's conception, that God's judgment develops and fixes the complete and ultimate form of the individual—a conception which is in concordance with Thomistic anthropology—and which at the same time is figuralistic: in that God's judgment endows an earthly figure with its own final and absolute perfection.

Earlier poets never used figurism in such a universal and audacious manner; they confined figuralistic treatment in most cases to the poetical illustration of sacred history; figurative interpretation of other events or of life in general was mostly unconscious.

From the very beginning of Christian art and poetry, the figurae have a tendency to appear in series. These series of figures can be found already on the early Christian sarcophagi; we find for example the liberation of Joseph from the pit, the liberation of Jonah from the belly of the whale (after three days) and the resuscitation of Lazarus (also after three days) represented side by side as figures of Christ's resurrection. But the full development of figurative series in Christian poetry is rather a medieval phenomenon than one of late antiquity. So far as I can see, the Latin hymnologists of the Carolingian period, especially the inventor of the sequences, Notker Balbulus, were the first to use this form consciously; and the great master of what I may call figurative eulogies is Adam of St. Victor; the twelfth century is the apogee of figurism and especially of figurative series. The praise of the Virgin, for instance, in many of the sequences of Adam and his imitators, consists of just such series; she is represented successively as Sarah laugh-

ing at Isaac's birth, Jacob's ladder, the top of which reaches
to heaven, Moses' burning bush which is not consumed by the
flames, Aaron's rod that budded, Gideon's fleece soaked with
dew, the ark of the Covenant that contains the celestial Manna,
the throne or the bed of the true Solomon who is Christ,
Isaiah's rod coming out of the stem of Jesse, Ezekiel's gate looking toward the East which shall be shut because the Lord has
entered by it; she is the garden enclosed, the fountain sealed,
the fountain of gardens, the well of living waters from the Song
of Songs, and so forth.

A student of medieval French literature may remember
here the figurative series in the mystery plays, especially the
most famous of them, the Jeu d'Adam, with its procession of
prophets. These prophets are not prophets in the restricted
sense in which we normally use this word, but Old Testamen-
tary personalities in general: besides Isaiah, Daniel and Jeremiah, there appear Abraham and Moses, David and Solomon,
Balaam and Nebuchadnezzar and others. Each of them begins
with one Latin sentence isolated from the text of the Bible, and
then goes on to explain the sentence in French as an announcement of Christ. Isaiah, for example, will not present the whole
of his prophecy concerning the future of Jerusalem and the king
of Babylon, but is introduced exclusively for the sake of one
sentence: *egredietur virga de radice Jesse* etc., which was considered as a prediction of the Virgin and Christ; just as Abraham is introduced for the sake of the promise God made to
him, and Aaron for his budding rod. This is pure figurism; as
I have mentioned before, the Old Testament becomes a succession of isolated prefigurations, or, if you prefer, figural prophecies of Christ. In this system even Adam may become not only
a figura but a figural prophet of Christ. His sleep during which
Eve, the mother of mankind in the flesh, was created out of
one of his ribs, prefigures Christ's death or sleep before his
resurrection, when one of the soldiers with a spear pierced his
side, and forthwith came there out blood and water, symbols
of the sacraments of the Church, the mother of mankind in
the spirit. Adam's sleep is the mystical sleep of contemplation
or ecstasy; when he awakens he starts prophesying: "therefore
shall a man leave his father and his mother and shall cleave

unto his wife, and they shall be one flesh"; this passage has been constantly interpreted as a figure of the union of Christ and the Church. This is one of the most ancient and venerable figures, one of the few introduced by Saint Paul himself (Eph: 5, 29–32): "sacramentum hoc magnum est, ego autem dico in Christo et in ecclesia." This interpretation of Adam as a figurative prophet predicting Christ and the Church has become an unbroken tradition. I became aware of it for the first time when reading a sermon of Saint Bernard, the second in Septuagesima. The Jeu d'Adam, it is true, does not present Adam in the procession of the prophets, but in another passage of the play he outspokenly predicts Christ. After his fall, when he gives himself up to despair and long-winded self-accusations, he sees one ray of hope: "There will be no salvation for me except by the son who will be born of the virgin—"Deus . . . ne me ferat ja nul aïe, fors le fils qu'istra de Marie." In his deepest despair, he becomes conscious of the future redemption; he has knowledge of the future. This blithe anticipation of the future may appear to us as medieval naiveté, as a lack of historical perspective—the same historical naiveté with which Adam and Eve or in other plays other biblical personalities are realistically depicted as Frenchmen of the twelfth and the thirteenth centuries. And, of course, there is indeed implied, in such phenomena, a naiveté and lack of historical perspective; but such an evaluation would not be exhaustive. The figurative interpretation, in spite of its stress on historical completeness derives its inspiration from the eternal wisdom of God, in whose mind there does not exist a difference of time. In His sight, what happens here and now, has happened from the very beginning, and may recur at any moment in the flow of time. At any time, at any place, Adam falls, Christ sacrifices himself, and humanity, the bride of the Song of Songs, faithful, hopeful, and loving, searches for Him. A personality who is a *figura Christi*, as Adam is, has knowledge of the providential future— Christ knew that Judas would betray him, just as another figure of Christ, Charlemagne, "*Charles li reis, nostre emperere maignes,*" in the Chanson de Roland, knows from the very beginning that Ganelon is a traitor. The eternal coexistence in God's mind of all historical events is a conception best expressed by Saint Augustine's doctrine that God keeps present in his mind all things past and future in their true reality—that therefore it is not correct to speak of God's foreknowledge, but simply of his knowledge—"scientia Dei non praescientia sed tantum scientia dici potest." Figurism gives the basis for the medieval fusion of realistic naiveté and otherworldly wisdom.

IV. Themes and Episodes

9·*On the* Personae *of the* Comedy

THE FIBER of Dante's *Comedy* is woven of human flesh and blood. His doctrinal and philosophical homilies emerge through dialectic; his *exempla* are drawn from the actual personalities of his experience or his reading. Even in the poet's most abstract lucubrations the reader rarely loses sight of the *persona* which is the vehicle of their expression, and even his similes more often than not—the tailor peering through the needle's eye, the shepherd leading his flock to pasture, the girls pausing in their dance—are fortified by the presence of living and breathing humanity. More than any other poem the *Comedy* teems with human characters; his gallery is better stocked than that of Ariosto, for example, and infinitely more varied.

One can legitimately, I think, distinguish various levels, or perhaps more accurately, degrees of plasticity; even as in sculpture we might find full figures or bas reliefs or simple line carving. I believe the investigation of the poet's use of these various styles may be of interest, particularly perhaps as illustrative of the different natures of the three *cantiche*. Possibly such a study will merely confirm what we sense already as significant in the characterization of the realms but it may be not without value as revealing the means by which the poetic ends are achieved.

For my purposes here I have chosen to divide the *nomina* —not so much the *consequentia* as the *substantia rerum* of the

Reprinted from *Italica* (XLII, 1, 1965) by permission of the American Association of Teachers of Italian.

poem—into the three general categories suggested above: 1) the characters of the narrative itself, figures whom the poet meets or sees in the course of his journey; 2) figures of reference, by which I mean those mentioned within the framework of the narrative either by Dante the *personaggio* or any of his inter-locutors, including Vergil and Beatrice; and 3) characters not strictly *in* the fiction itself but alluded to by Dante the poet; one could call them, perhaps, figures of secondary reference or simply (if slightly inaccurately) figures of ornament.

To begin, then, with the first category. For the *Inferno* my census of figures actually met or seen by the poet shows a total of 162. This is not, of course, the total population of the *Inferno*.[1] I have taken no account of such phrases as "più di mille," and have not considered in my total even specific names unless Dante actually sees the individuals who bear them. My count does not include Frederick the Second or Mordred, for instance, although we know they are there; on the other hand I include anyone with a distinct identity or some visual impact, either a name alone, as in the catalog of Canto IV, or a dis-tinguishing phrase, such as "colui che fece per viltà il gran rifiuto" or "un anzian di santa Zita."

Some details of the census should be mentioned, with reference to their relationship to the figures for the succeeding *cantiche*. A sizeable number is made up of guardians or officials or what one might call attendant monsters. (I include here such characters as Charon, the Malebranche and the centaurs: such purely animal types as the *cagne* and the *arpie* of Canto XIII I have not included; in any case they are not individualized.) The number of such figures, from Charon to Satan himself, runs to 35; one could, I suppose, add to this group the heavenly messenger of Canto IX but I have not done so in my census. I count him as the one celestial of the *Inferno*. Aside from such functionaries we are left with 126 distinctly identified *dannati*. The number is impressive in itself; it averages out to almost four per canto. It is true that the catalog of Canto IV accounts for 30 and one could argue that aside from a few figures—Homer, Caesar, Saladino, Aristotle—the names in the catalog are hardly individualized. On the other hand Dante's plan obliges him to give us two *canti* (II and XI) with no *personaggi* on the immediate narrative level; so if one were to make a new calculation ignoring completely Canto IV and considering only the *canti* of the journey itself (i.e., without the expository II and XI) the average is still better than three per canto. This succession of new and varied personalities is certainly one of the secrets of the appeal of the *Inferno*. And the variation is as important as the number. Aside from the 35 monsters one might break down the *personae* into three large groups: classical figures, contemporary Italians, and others. There are 53 classical figures (again, even excluding the Limbo catalog, more than a score are brought before us in our progress through the circles), 56 Italians (23 fellow townsmen of the poet) and no less than 5 Arabs, 3 Old Testament figures and assorted specimens from late Roman history, the Romance tradition and a few non-Italian contemporaries.

In the *Purgatory* the number of figures "in the round" actually met in the ascent of the Mount is considerably smaller. I make it 77, excluding such groups as the carvings on the terrace of pride, lifelike though they be, and the visions seen among the wrathful, but including all the members of the Beatrician procession, even though they could be considered pure allegory and certainly do not have the same substance as Pia or Forese or even Cato. (Structurally and perhaps even culturally they balance the catalog of *Inferno* IV, though of course comparison would be out of order.) Yet even including these it is noteworthy that the total is much smaller than the "first plane" *personae* of the *Inferno*. The average, indeed, works out at barely two per canto. It is much smaller if we omit the figures in the procession. In this total, also, the number of "officials" (i.e., the functionaries corresponding to the guardians and monsters of the *Inferno*) is quite large: if we include the members of the procession in that group, as I think we must, we shall have a total of 31 (beginning with the *angelo custode* but not counting Cato, whose humanity transcends his functional character), thus leaving us a mere 46 characters of our own human sort met in the course of 33 *canti* as against 109 of like sort in the 34 *canti* of the *Inferno*. There is much less variation too; inevitably in view of the restricted character of *Purgatory*. Dante does manage to get in two figures from the classical tradition (Cato and Statius, both with important roles) but the remaining 42 are largely from the "contemporary" world: 33 are Italians, a smaller number but a higher proportion than the colony of Dante's compatriots in the *Inferno*. The relative paucity of Florentines is interesting: even including Beatrice we have only four. (Perhaps I should say here that I do not count Matelda as a Florentine; her identity is to me a little uncertain and indeed her status is ambiguous too; I have counted her as a resident rather than as an official but I am not sure that I should.)

The trend continues in the *Paradiso*, which gives us only 72 figures actually in the narrative. In fact the relative rarity of this group is much greater than a simple census of those present would indicate. Many of the figures encountered in the *Paradiso* are merely names in catalogs; it is true that there are catalogs in the *Inferno* and the *Purgatory* too but the proportion of such items is much higher in the *Paradiso* where the catalogs are more numerous; one has but to think of the Dominican and Franciscan rings, the champions of the Cross pointed out by Cacciaguida, the spirits of the Just in the eye of the eagle and the ultimate choir in the petals of the Rose. These make up the great majority of the souls seen by Dante in the course of his celestial ascent. Another way of bringing out the progression of rarefaction of the truly participant element in the narrative is by counting the speaking parts; undeniably a character that speaks has a more lasting impact, a more effective realism than one merely observed. (Professor Gilbert has remarked on this point in his recent *Dante and his Comedy*.) There are over 50 "speaking parts" in the *Inferno*, 38 in the *Purgatory* and only 23 in the celestial realm (this counting the eagle as six, on the assumption that the identified stalwarts of justice have their share of his voice). Or again, it is worth remarking that in the *Paradiso* there are no less than 16 *canti* in which the narrative presents us with no new character at all; there are only two such in the *Inferno* and but six in the *Purgatory*. One category has disappeared entirely in the Supreme Realm, for here we find no wardens, such as the various monsters in charge of the circles of hell or the successive angels on the purgatorial terraces, practically all with a line or so of speech. The absence of such officials has its own significance in setting paradise apart from the other kingdoms, but being here concerned only with its effect on our census we shall simply note that as the narrative proceeds from *cantica* to *cantica* the number of *personaggi* grows less. We may add for purposes of comparison with the other *cantiche* that the celestial residents include 40 recognized Saints (i.e., figures officially accepted as saints; of course all the residents of paradise are saints but some, like Charles Martel and Cunizza, have been canonized only by our poet), 15 Old Testament figures, seven Italians, including the Florentines Piccarda and Cacciaguida, three classical figures, and four miscellaneous.

The first category, however, is only a fraction (though a large one) of the names cited in the poem. Very copious indeed is the classification of names of reference, as I have called them. Such names have, of course, varying degrees of impact or of immediacy; I include here, for example, the "buon Augusto" mentioned by Vergil and the Federigo mentioned by Farinata. Clearly there is a considerable difference, for the latter is *there* as the former is not. But Dante doesn't actually see him and he is in the narrative only as it were by hearsay (no matter how reliable the witness) so he cannot be counted in the group of the fully and visibly participant. By my count (which I am not sure is entirely accurate) there are 99 such names in the *Inferno*, 189 in the *Purgatorio*, and 172 in the *Paradiso*. It seems to me worthy of note that as the number of actual presences decreases from *cantica* to *cantica* (with a fairly sharp drop between the *Inferno* and the *Purgatory*) so the characters of reference increase, with the sharp rise coming as we move from the first to the second realm. One might almost suspect that subconsciously —but did Dante do anything without full awareness?—the poet felt a need for a certain number of personal allusions and where the narrative was relatively sparse resorted to tangential reference to fill up the quota. This strategy becomes very evident, I think, if we look somewhat more closely at the figures for certain elements. Classical figures appear in the narrative of the *Inferno* to the number of 35 as we have seen; they are for obvious reasons very scantily represented in the upper realms. But among the figures of reference as against 26 such in the *Inferno* I count 69 in the *Purgatory* and 54 in the *Paradiso*. I think Dante must have composed *Purgatory* XXII and *Paradiso* VI—to mention the most striking examples—with purposeful consideration of his syncretistic intent. Perhaps that is why he gives us one angel even in hell. I am sure that is one reason why the Italian colony of the *Paradiso*, otherwise rather scanty, is reinforced by the catalog of family names on the lips of Cacciaguida.

Let us glance briefly at our third category, to which, as I have said, I assign the references that do not occur in the narrative proper, even at second hand, but are made by the poet himself, standing outside his work; such cases as the appeal to "Ovidio" in the *Inferno* or the allusion to Guinivere in *Paradiso* XVI. These are not in the narrative nor on the lips of any who play a part therein; they are voiced by the poet as he sits at his desk, transcribing his vision and permitting himself an offstage comment on its development. Such references, which we may call allusions of embellishment or reflection, are much less numerous than the other two categories. By my count there are 37 such in the *Inferno*, 41 in the *Purgatory*, and 34 in the *Paradiso*. I find it interesting that of these figures, the author's private gallery as it were, the classical names make up the great majority: there are 75 in all and the numbers are very consistent from *cantica* to *cantica*: 27 in the *Inferno* and 24 in each of the other two *cantiche*. The proportion is strikingly large in the *Paradiso* where the third category totals only 34—another attempt at syncretism?

Grand totals are then as follows: figures actually appearing in the fabric of the narrative, 408; appearing in the narrative by reference, 426; cited by the poet outside the narrative, 112. Perhaps here is the place to say that I have not counted groups but only individuals (thus, for example, the family names of *Paradiso* XVI are not included nor such names as "le Piche" or "le Naiade"); I have not included any figures not identified by name or recognizable by the reference; I have omitted classical names that clearly refer to the star or the planet rather than the god or goddess, and I have not counted a name more than once within a *cantica*—I count Vergil once in the *Inferno* and Beatrice once in the *Paradiso*, for example. Of course some names appear in all three of my categories and so may appear two or three times within the same *cantica*: thus Constantine appears in the narrative in *Paradiso* XX and as a character of reference on the lips of Justinian in Canto VI; I count both appearances in the appropriate categories. Likewise he appears twice in the *Inferno*, once in a reference of Guido da Monte-feltro and once in Dante's apostrophe in Canto XIX, and so would appear in my second and third categories. There are, of course, a number of such personalities.

The grand total of the *nomina* which go to make a good deal of the *substantia* of the poem is impressive; if my figures are at least approximately right they run close to a thousand (more, of course, if I were to add the group names). At least ten to a canto, then, or better than one to every five *terzine*. But we may go a little farther here and see just what kind of personalities Dante used to pack his comedy with flesh and blood. Counting the representatives from all categories, the largest single colony is the classical; I make a total of 272 figures from pagan antiquity—this not counting the infernal "monsters" such as the Minotaur, Cerberus, etc., of classical origin. The next largest bloc is the Italian one; even though it falls off sharply in the *Paradiso* there are yet 203 Italians in the *Comedy*. Old Testament figures come next with 85, and the group of saints, in which I include New Testament figures, comes to 80. Other categories are far behind although the catalogs of Kings— presences in the *Purgatory*, references in the *Paradiso*—make a tolerably large group.

Such a census as I have here undertaken to make is in itself only the first step in the study of Dante's choice of elements for his world and his manipulation of them. Groupings, relations within and between groups, lines assigned to speaking characters or dedicated to specific description of individuals: an analysis of such aspects of the poet's technique, which is not merely technique, would certainly be rewarding. They have yet, I believe, to be explored and analyzed. Meanwhile I hope the

outline figures as here given will serve as documentation of the
human realism of the *Comedy* and of the poet's persistent syncretistic purpose.

Note

1 I have dealt at somewhat greater length with this topic in "Hell:
Topography and Demography," *Essays on Dante*. Bloomington, Ind.,
Indiana Univ. Press, 1964, 76–93.

Theodore Silverstein

10·Rex Iustus et Pius: *Henry's Throne and Dante's Christian Prince*

NOWHERE has Dante offered more ample evidence of his faith in the Roman *imperium* and admiration of the Emperor Henry VII than in a brief passage of six lines in the thirtieth canto of the Paradiso. There, beyond the limits of the corporeal spheres in the heaven which is pure light, surrounded by the saintly splendors of the City of God, Beatrice directs the poet's gaze to a vacant seat among the thrones of the blessed:

> On that great seat thine eyes are drawn unto
>> By the crown hung already over it
>> Ere at this wedding-feast thyself art due,
> The soul, on earth imperial, shall sit
>> Of the high Henry, coming to enforce
>> Right ways on Italy, though she is yet unfit.
>> (vv. 133–138) (transl. Binyon)

And the power of these lines is consolidated by contrast with the bitter condemnation of Pope Clement V, which directly follows them. During his flight through the spheres Dante had frequently been reminded by the celestial inhabitants of the political affairs of earth below. But this, after all, is the very yellow of the eternal rose, the goal of the poet's journey. Yet Beatrice's words—the last spoken by her in the poem—are of temporal pope and emperor.

For at least one recent critic, moreover, the homage to

Reprinted by permission from *The Harvard Theological Review* (XXXII, April 1939). Copyright 1939 by the President and Fellows of Harvard College. Title has been changed, and quotations are in translation.

Henry acquires tremendous force from another striking element
in the passage. This is what is conceived to be the "unfitness
of a symbol of mundane sovereignty in Paradise." [1] The motif
of the vacant seat in Heaven, in Dante's peculiar use of which
the discordance apparently lies, stems, it is true, from ancient
Christian tradition,[2] but the instances of its occurrence in medieval popular lore to which the commentators have pointed, seem
on first glance to intensify rather than dissipate the incongruity.
For the *sedes vacua mirae pulchritudinis et gloriae* (empty
throne of a marvelous beauty and glory) described by Caesarius
of Heisterbach in the Dialogus miraculorum,[3] the *sedile mira-
biliter ornatum in quo nemo sedebat* (wonderfully ornate chair
on which no one was sitting) of the Vision of Tundale,[4] and
the *sedes ceteris dignoir, pretiosis ornata lapidibus et omni
gloria refulgens* (throne nobler than the others, tricked out with
precious stones and glittering with every glory), seen according
to St. Bonaventura, in a vision by the Franciscan brother
Pacificus,[5] are all destined, not for kings or emperors, but for
humble friars and simple monks.[6] This is true also of what is
surely among the most elaborately set occurrences of the motif
in the West, the account in the Long Latin text of the Apocalypse of St. Paul—a work almost certainly known to Dante and
used by him [7]—of the jewelled thrones stored up in the City
of Christ for God's foolish: "And turning about I saw golden
thrones and set upon them diadems and jewelled girdles. And
I looked again and saw within the twelve walls another row of
thrones, which appeared in so much glory that no one would
be able to adumbrate their praise. 'Who are they who are to
sit upon the thrones?' And the angel answered and said unto
me, 'These are the thrones of them who have goodness and
innocence and understanding of the heart, who made themselves foolish for God's sake; not knowing many passages of
Scripture nor many Psalms, but remembering a single chapter
of God's precepts and mindful of them, they acted in respect
to them with minute diligence, having a right intent before the
Lord.' " [8]

Amidst so pre-Raphaelite a brightness as this which en-
compasses the eternal reward of Christian simplicity, it might

indeed seem a violation of poetic justice that even the memory should remain of mundane power.

But any view of the incongruity—however supposedly intentional—of Dante's image is formed without proper understanding of the two fundamental elements on which the passage is grounded. The first is the general eschatological motif of thrones and crowns, of which the medieval instances where they are vacant constitute but a single and, as dwelt on exclusively by the commentators, even a misleading aspect. The other is the traditional conception of Christian kingship, especially in its association with the throne motif. Seen in the increased light cast by these two elements, the fancied incongruity of the image in the Paradiso disappears entirely. With its disappearance the passage becomes, not a less, but a more powerful tribute to Henry VII from a new profundity that may be detected in its meaning.

The vision of the *sedes* seen by Brother Pacificus *in quadam ecclesia deserta* is the dramatic climax of a discourse on the practical idealism of the Franciscan Order which furnishes the clue to the traditions that we are seeking. "For this reason, as a model of humility," St. Bonaventura tells us by way of introduction to the incident, "Francis wished his Brothers to be named *Minores* and the prelates of his Order to be called *ministros*, both that he might use the words of the Gospel which he had promised to observe, and that from the name itself his disciples might learn that they had come as Christ's humble to teach their followers humility," and he quotes Matthew xx, 26–27 in confirmation: "Indeed the Master of humility, Jesus Christ, in order to mould his disciples to perfect humility, said: 'Whosoever will be great among you, let him be your minister, and whosoever will be chief among you, let him be your servant.'" [9]

The point of the quotation as regards the heavenly seat of the vision lies in the fact that in the Gospel Jesus, making response to the request of the mother of the sons of Zebedee that they "may sit, the one on thy right hand, and the other on the left, in thy kingdom," takes the opportunity to deal briefly

with the entire problem of material and spiritual power. Together with its counterparts in Mark x and Luke xxii this discourse furnished the Middle Ages with the basis for its theory
of the function of leadership in a Christian society and, furthermore, related this theory to the eschatological promise of the
glory of thrones and crowns. The language of Luke, which
varies somewhat from that of the others, is particularly significant for our purposes: "And there was also strife among them,
which of them should be accounted the greatest. And he said
unto them, The kings of the Gentiles exercise lordship over
them; and they that exercise authority upon them are called
benefactors. But ye shall not be so: but he that is greatest
among you, let him be as the younger; and he that is chief, as he
that doth serve. For whether is greater, he that sitteth at meat,
or he that serveth? is not he that sitteth at meat? but I am
among you as he that serveth. Ye are they which have continued with me in my temptations. And I appoint unto you a
kingdom, as my Father hath appointed unto me; That ye may
eat and drink at my table in my kingdom, and sit on thrones
judging the twelve tribes of Israel." [10]

The commentaries on these Scriptural passages do not
usually apply them directly to the problems of secular Christian kingship. When specific reference is made it is either to
the ecclesiastical hierarchy or, as in the discourse of Bonaventura, to the members of a religious brotherhood.[11] But the
words in Luke on the throne of judgment and the explicit
contrast in all three Gospels with kingship among the Gentiles
constantly kept before the eyes of the commentators the relevance of this passage within the narrower limits also of Christian monarchical authority.[12]

With the growth of Christianity into a civilization and
its universal extension in the Middle Ages, the exhortation of
Jesus which distinguished between the realms of God and
Caesar, now might be applied equally to both. Behind the numerous discussions of the qualities of the good king lie the
example of Christ's ministry and the spirit of his words to the
contending disciples, if not the words themselves, together with
various of the related passages in the Old Testament that express the ancient Hebrew conception of which the Christian is

the fuller development.[13] An arresting instance of such discussion appears in the treatise *De institutione regia* addressed by Bishop Jona of Orleans (ninth century) to Pippin: "Consider that the fear of God, and the keeping of His precepts, and humility, which does not permit him to raise himself above his brothers, and the rectitude of justice, cause not only the king but his sons also to reign for a long time. That the prince therefore should avoid exaltation Ecclesiasticus says by way of admonition: 'Have they made thee ruler of a feast? Be not lifted up, but be thou among them as one of them'" (*Eccle.* xxxii, 1). In Proverbs: "The king that faithfully judges the poor, his throne shall be established for ever" (*Prov.* xxix, 14). Likewise: "Mercy and truth preserve the king: and his throne is upholden by mercy" (*Prov.* xx, 28).[14] Jona confines his quotation here to the Old Testament, but the ideal Christian monarch so strikingly described by him is clearly the secular counterpart of the spiritual minister of the Gospels; just as the eternal throne with which, according to the Scriptural texts here adduced, royal justice and mercy are rewarded, corresponds to the seats of the just in Luke xxii.

Close enough to this tradition, moreover, to make a part of it and provide it with the force of additional distinguished illustration, stands the delineation, often repeated in the Latin West, of David as the type of the just and humble ruler. Thus, St. Zeno writes in the third, or perhaps the fourth century: "Humble, subservient and obscure, David made himself lowly in his father's house, always tending the sheep, almost as if a wanderer off the roads, an innocent, as it were, among the innocent. This was pleasing to God: anointed king and inspired to be a prophet, he does not grow insolent in his reign; he darkens no man's life with terror of the prophet; he does not avenge his injuries by means of the royal power; he counters with love those who hate him; he spares his enemies; he excuses his sons their parricidal plots; his persecutor and, what is more, a king given over by God into his hands, he prefers to fear forever rather than to kill; gentle and good in the inverse position, he was to please God when he held in his grasp God's world. A compassionate king, a merciful father, a modest prophet, he can do anything but dissimulates that power; and not changed by the great and wonderful things of the world, remains everywhere the mild and humble shepherd." [15] And Burchard of Worms some eight hundred years later, discoursing on the proper exercise of royal power, offers testimony to the unfaded survival of the portrait: "He who exercises royal power properly should so excel all men in his conduct that the more he shines in the brilliance of his honor so much the more should he keep a humble mind, proposing to himself as an example of humility David, who was not puffed up with his merits but, prostrating himself humbly, said: 'I began vile and shall appear vile before God who chose me.' He who exercises royal power properly should establish a model of justice by deeds rather than by words." [16]

We need not pause for all the references to the lowliness, justice, and compassion desirable in a king, to the Christian requirement that justice be accompanied by mercy and fair words by deeds of charity, which lie scattered in profusion through medieval thought and writing.[16a] Instead we may read what will serve as a summary of the tradition in the eloquent words of the Testament of Benjamin on the character of the good man and his heavenly reward. Written originally during the second century B.C. for a world quite different from that of the Middle Ages, this book had been freshly brought to the knowledge of Dante's generation by the influential Latin rendering of Robert Grosseteste: "Observe, my sons, the end of a good man: do ye in good mind imitate his mercy, so that ye also may put on crowns of glory. A good man hath not a darkling eye for he showeth mercy to all men even though they be sinners and devise with evil intent concerning him. For he who doeth good overcometh evil, being shielded by the good. The just moreover he loveth as his own soul. If a man be glorified, he envieth him not; if a man be enriched, he is not jealous; if a man be valiant, he praiseth him; believing him chaste, he praiseth him. As for him who hath the fear of God, he protecteth him; him that loveth God he helpeth; him that rejecteth the Most High he admonisheth that he change his ways; and him that hath the grace of a good spirit he loveth as his soul. On the poor man he hath mercy, on the weak compassion; and he feareth God and singeth praise of Him." [17] To

this we may add, by way of supplement from a strictly contemporary document, the account of royal charity and the art
of ruling in the *De regimine principum* of Tolomeo of Lucca,
a work which the poet vigorously opposed for its Papal politics
yet as deeply drew on for its view of the place of Rome in universal history: "Besides, kings and princes act on earth as God's
vicars, through whom God governs the world as if by secondary
causes. . . . But God's special care is the care of the poor, to
supply the defect of their nature. Because this is so, Divine
Providence acts to the indigent as a father towards his helpless
sons, concerning whom an ampler solicitude is required because
of an ampler necessity. . . . Therefore, to supply this defect of
the poor, princes and prelates are debtors as vicars of God acting
on earth and as fathers whose function is to be the helpers of
those beneath their control. . . ." [18]

There is a passage in the twelfth-century Vision of Tundale, important for its connection with this tradition, which
has been strangely neglected by the commentators on Paradiso
XXX. This is the description of the good King Cormach, seated
on a throne in his ornate dwelling in Paradise and attended by
priests and a group of laymen bringing gifts: "Now as that soul
was delighting in such lovely buildings, looking about he saw a
golden throne decorated with gems and silks and all sorts of
ornaments, and he saw the lord King Cormach sitting on that
throne dressed in such vestments as neither he nor any other
king could be invested with on earth. Now, as he stood a little
in wonder, there came many people into that house with gifts
to the king and each of them separately offered his offerings
with joy. And when he had stood a while before the lord his
king . . . , there came many priests and levites ceremoniously
dressed as if for mass with silk chasubles and other very fine
ornamental robes, and the royal house was hung about with
marvellous decorations. . . . Then the soul said to the angel:
I am confused, my lord, to conceive whence come here to my
lord so many ministers, among whom is not one of his own
when he was in the body. These, said the angel, are not of his
household which he had when he was in the body. . . . For
these whom you see are all the poor of Christ and wayfarers to
whom the king himself distributed worldly goods when he was

in the body; and therefore here at their hands he receives in return payment eternal and without end." [19] It is clear, I think, that the account owes something to the renowned passage on otherworld visions in the Dialogues of Gregory the Great, where Peter hears of a magnificent mansion being erected in Paradise and is told in explanation that, with each deed of charity on earth, the compassionate man helps piece by piece to build his house of gold in the life to come and that the builders are the souls of the former beneficiaries of his human sympathy.[20] But unlike Tundale, Gregory is talking of all men, not of royalty in particular. If we are to understand fully the significance of Cormach and his heavenly reward, it must be in the light of the long Judeo-Christian tradition of the compassionate and serviceable king. The passage from Tundale thus bears in large part the character of a literalization, in a piece of popular lore current during the thirteenth and fourteenth centuries, of the admonition and eschatological promise of Luke xxii: "he that is greatest among you, let him be as the younger; and he that is chief, as he that doth serve. . . . And I appoint unto you a kingdom, as my Father hath appointed unto me; That ye may eat and drink at my table in my kingdom, and sit on thrones, judging the twelve tribes of Israel."

And this, no doubt, is how Dante would have understood it.

With the Judeo-Christian tradition of kingly rule the medieval "idea of Rome," mistress of world peace and arbiter of universal justice, easily coalesced. The literary source of the idea may be said to be a single, famous phrase from Vergil:

Remember, Romans, you shall govern nations,
These your arts: to set the habit of peace,
To spare the beaten and beat down the proud.
parcere subiectis et debellare superbos

(*Aen.* vi, 851–853)

the magnificence of which dazzled the imagination of the Middle Ages, as its nobility has since captured our own. Thus when in the anonymous twelfth-century *Gesta per Imperatorem Fridericum Barbam Rubeam* the emperor seeks divine assistance to success, his prayer contains a paraphrase of these verses that is symptomatic of their pervasive influence: "To rule the subject and curb with sword the proud." [21] As for the coalescence of the two traditions, its pattern is foreshadowed by the opening sentences of St. Augustine's *De civitate Dei*, where Vergil's phrase is juxtaposed with Proverbs iii, 34, James iv, 6, and 1 Peter v, 5, to indicate the two-fold nature of divine justice— its repressive power and its protective grace: "God resisteth the proud, but giveth grace unto the humble." [22] Under the influence of St. Augustine the same juxtaposition likewise provides substance for a major theme of the ninth-century discourse on kingship by Bishop Jona.[23]

More directly relevant to Dante is the flowering of the idea of Rome in the pamphleteering controversy which accompanied the bitter struggle between Pope and Emperor during the thirteenth and fourteenth centuries. To this controversy, especially for their relationship to the *De monarchia*, Tolomeo of Lucca's *Determinatio compendiosa* and his continuation of Aquinas's *De regimine principum* [24] are not the least distinguished contributions. Tolomeo is guided to his position largely by St. Augustine also. His view that the rightfulness of Roman dominion rested in great part on their zeal for justice and the exercise of compassion (*pietas, civilis benevolentia, humanitas*) [25] touches both poles of the realm marked out in the introduction to the *De civitate Dei*. Similarly Dante begins his treatment of the subject in *De monarchia* II, v, with an assertion of the intense concern of the ancient Romans for *ius* and summarizes his view by quoting a renowned phrase about Roman compassion from the Christian legend of Constantine and St. Silvester: "The Roman *imperium* springs forth from the fount of pity." [26]

Justitia and *pietas*—the curbing, measuring quality of justice and its humanity—that these two elements constituted the strength of imperial authority, every man in the fourteenth century would have agreed, whatever his opinion of the relative power of court and curia. Of them the Christian Scriptures and the persistent medieval memory of ancient Rome wrought in literature and legend the portrait of an ideal king worthy of the noblest place in the Christian Paradise.

In the autumn of 1310 the Emperor Henry VII crossed the Alps into Italy, bringing new hope to his adherents on the

peninsula. His coming was doubly important for Dante, who
now at last might look forward to a return from exile to his
native Florence. And in his enthusiasm the poet wrote three
letters of flaming eloquence.

To Dante Henry was the ideal Christian king. He came to
Italy, not for his own ease, but for his people's.[27] He was of
the race of Aeneas, a second Moses, of the seed of Jesse, the
Lamb of God.[28] He would be stern with the iniquitous, the
impious, the backsliders, but compassionate to those who
sought mercy, "since he is Caesar and [and the phrase is that
same maxim attributed to Constantine] his majesty flows forth
from the fount of pity." [29] With a reminiscence at once of Vergil
and Lactantius,[30] the writer speaks of the approach of a new
Golden Age of peace and justice, delayed hitherto only by the
malice of the iniquitous. The intensity of Dante's joy, betrayed
in the eager impatience of these letters, is the fullest measure of
his profound despair when, three years later, Henry lay prema-
turely dead of fever at Buonconvento, his purpose unfulfilled.
For with him seemed to die all of Dante's hope on earth.

As the visionary in the thirtieth canto of the Paradiso
stands amidst the splendors of the Heavenly City, it is entirely
human that, for just a moment before immersion in the final
mystical experience, there should be a turning back, through
Beatrice's guiding speech, to all the old and poignant concerns
of earth below. The condemnation of the popes is sharpened
by a bitter irony, the irony that of the two great divisions of
authority in God's temporary realm, the one which might properly be the more worldly is destined to be prevented from achiev-
ing its divine mission [31] by the mundane greed of the more
spiritual power. For this interference with the workings of divine
justice Pope Clement will merit forever the torments of
Hell.

But as for Henry, his place, like that of the good king Cormach, is on a throne in Heaven among God's saints. His reward
—so the long line of Christian writings makes clear from the
Gospels to the Vision of Tundale—is not the divine recognition
of imperial *power*, but the accolade of kingly righteousness. For
the throne is the throne of Justice, and the crown is the crown
of Compassion.

Notes

1 *La Divina Commedia*, ed. C. H. Grandgent (revised ed., Boston, 1933), p. 942, n. 134.

2 See *Apoc.* iv, 4 *et passim* and *Psalms* ix, 7. Christian iconography, moreover, offers many instances of thrones, called *etimasia*, prepared for the Judgment with crown, cross, lamb, roll, and gospels: see, among other works on the subject, Cabrol and Leclercq, *Dictionnaire d'archéologie chrétienne et de liturgie*, art. Etimasie; and Kraus, *Realencyclopädie der christlichen Altertümer*, I, 432. These thrones appear to be an adaptation from similar pagan insignia, examples of which are found in connection with what the Romans called *sellisternium* and derived from the Greeks: see Lily Ross Taylor, "A Sellisternium on the Parthenon Frieze?" *Quantulacumque, Studies Presented to Kirsopp Lake* (London, 1937), especially pp. 262 ff. They are evidently related to the thrones used widely in Greek cult; for which see Furtwängler, *Masterpieces of Greek Sculpture*, ed. Sellers (1895), pp. 429 ff. For the association of the throne and other insignia of rank with kings, it is particularly important to note that, according to Diodorus Siculus (xviii, 61, 1) Eumenes, secretary to Alexander the Great, set up, after his master's death, a golden throne, adorned with the king's diadem, scepter, and armor before which Alexander's generals offered sacrifice, and that (xvi, 92, 5) at the marriage of Philip of Macedon's daughter an image of Philip seated on a throne was carried into the theatre among the twelve other thrones for the gods.

3 *Distinc.* VI, cap. x (Ed. J. Strange, Cologne, 1851, I, 364). See A. D'Ancona, "I precursori di Dante," in his *Scritti danteschi* (Firenze, 1912–1913), pp. 62–63, n. 3; F. D'Ovidio, "Fonti dantesche, I: Dante e san Paulo," *Nuova antologia*, 4to serie, LXVII (1897), 237–238 (reprinted in his *Studii sulla D. C. Milano-Palermo*, 1901, p. 355; and Caserta, 1931, II, 85); and *La D. C.*, ed. Grandgent, p. 942, n. 133.

4 *Visio Tnugdali*, ed. Albrecht Wagner (Erlangen, 1882), p. 54. Cf. D'Ancona, *loc. cit.*, D'Ovidio, *loc. cit.*, and Grandgent, p. 942, n. 133.

5 *Legenda sancti Francisci*, cap. vi, §6 (S. Bonaventurae opera omnia, Ad Claras Aquas: Ex type. Collegii S. Bonaventurae, 1898, VIII, 521). Cf. U. Cosmo, "Le mistiche nozze de Frate Francesco con Madonna Povertà," *Giornale dantesco*, VI (1898–1899), 101–102. The visionary is unnamed; for his identification as Pacificus, see Bonaventurae opera, *loc. cit.*, n. 6.

6 S. *Bonaventurae opera*, VIII, 521: "Sedes ista unius de ruentibus [id est angelis cadentibus—VIII, 521, n. 7] fuit et nunc humili servatur Francisco." In Caesarius the throne is for the simple friar Engilbert and the entire episode occurs in a section of praise *de virtute simplicitatis*. Similarly the throne in Tundale is intended for an unnamed and humble Irish friar; Wagner, p. 54.

7 See my article "Did Dante Know the Vision of St. Paul?" *Harvard Studies and Notes in Philology and Literature*, XIX (1937), 231 ff.; and "The Passage of the Souls to Purgatory in the Divina Commedia," *Harvard Theological Review*, XXXI (1938), especially 61–63.

8 The St. Gall Text (St. G.), §29: Silverstein, *Visio sancti Pauli*

(Studies and Documents, ed. Kirsopp and Silva Lake, no. IV, London, 1935), pp. 140–141. Grandgent, p. 942, n. 133, refers to the Syriac version, which, of course, Dante could not have known, but which provides us with assistance in solving a textual problem of some importance for this passage as it is related to the Divina Commedia. For the completer surviving form of the Latin Long Text (P), printed by M. R. James, Apocrypha anecdota, I (*Texts and Studies*, II, no. 3, Cambridge, Eng., 1893), pp. 26–27, varies significantly from the text quoted above, and James's emendations obscure further the empty throne motif: "Et conuersus me uidi tronos aureos positos per singulas portas, et super eos (uiros habentes) diademas aureas (et) gemas: . . . Et interrogaui angelum et dixi: Domine, quis est super tronum? Et respondens angelus dixit mihi: Ii troni eorum sunt qui bonitatem et intellectum habebant cordis et semetipsos stultos fecerunt propter dominum deum. . . ." The extant Greek text, which is abbreviated, omits this passage (C. Tischendorf, *Apocalypses apocryphae*, Leipzig, 1866, p. 54, §28), but the mutually independent testimony of the Syriac (Justin Perkins, in *Journal of the American Oriental Society*, VIII [1864], 201; G. Ricciotti, *L'Apocalisse di Paolo siriaca*, Brescia, 1932, I, 63, §29), the Coptic (E. A. Wallis Budge, *Miscellaneous Coptic Texts in the Dialect of Upper Egypt*, London, 1915, p. 536 and pp. 1055–56) and another late medieval Latin form (the "Vienna Fragment," in Silverstein, *Visio sancti Pauli*, p. 151) confirms the fact that P has suffered editorial modification. Moreover, there is conclusive evidence (Silverstein, p. 59) that it was the normal type of text represented by St. G. which circulated in the late Middle Ages and affected the history of the current abbreviations in Latin and the vernaculars.

Another work in which Dante might have found ample reference to empty thrones as seen by a living visitant to the Otherworld, is the *Ascension of Isaiah*, which circulated in the Middle Ages in two Latin versions (L¹ and L²); *The Ascension of Isaiah*, ed. R. H. Charles (London, 1900), Introduction, §6, pp. xviii–xxi. Only L² now survives for the pertinent passages: vii, 22; viii, 26; ix, 10–13, 18, 24–26; xi, 40 (ed. Charles, pp. 109, 117–118, 120, 122, 123–124, 138). Moneta, *Adversus Catharos et Waldenses*, ed. Riechlinius (1742), p. 218, discussing the heretical sect known as the Cathari, offers a hint as to the circle in which the book was especially used in Dante's time. See Charles, p. xi, n. 1.

9 S. *Bonaventurae opera*, VIII, 521.

10 xxii, 24–30. Cf. Mark x, 35–45.

11 For the line along which the commentaries chiefly moved see, among others, St. Jerome, *Comm. in Evang. Matth.*, III, xx (Migne, Patrologia latina, XXVI, 149–150); Paulus Diaconus, *Homilia* LXXXIV (Migne, XCV, 1251); Bede, *In Matth. evang. exposit.*, III, xx (Migne, XCII, 89); Rabanus Maurus, *Comm. in Matth.*, VI, xx (Migne, CVII, 1031–1032); S. Bruno Astens, *Comm. in Matth.*, IV, xxi, 83 (Migne, CVII, 1031–1032); S. Bruno Astens, *Comm. in Matth.*, IV, xxi, 83 CLXV, 239–240); Radulph Ardens, *Homiliae*, XXVI (Migne, CLV, 1403–1406), Peter Comestor, *Hist. schol.*, cap. cxiii, "In Evangelia"; Bede, *In Lucae evang. expos.*, VI, xxii (Migne, XCII, 598–599); Albertus Magnus, *In Marci evang., ad loc.*, and *In Matth., ad loc.*; St. Thomas Aquinas, *In Matth. evang. expos.* (ed. Parma, 1860, X, 188); Aquinas, *Catena aurea in Matth. evang.*, cap. xx (ed. Parma, XI, 401), and *Catena*

aurea in Luci evang., cap. xxii (XII, 229). St. Thomas's compilations provided easy access to relevant excerpts on these passages from several of the Greek fathers also, i.e., Theophylactus, Chrysostom, Basil, Origen.

12 See especially Albertus Magnus, *In Evang. secundum Lucam*, xxii, 25 (*Opera omnia*, ed. Borgnet, xxiii, 681–682), whose exposition is a tissue of relevant quotation and comment on the activities of kings in general: " 'Reges gentium.' Hoc est, qui secundum jura Gentium, quae tamen a Deo sunt, 'reges' sunt, hoc est, qui alios, leges utiles et honestas condendo, regunt: quia si aliter facerent, non reges sed tyranni vocarentur. Illi ergo tales reges 'dominantur eorum,' hoc est, dominium exercent superpositionis in eos. Dominus enim cum severitate coercet subditos. . . . 'Et qui potestatem habent super eos.' Jure ordinatam per gladium coercendi malos ad laudem bonorum, 'benefici vocantur,' quia ad litteram multis benefaciunt. Tamen quaedam Glossa dicit: 'Qui potestatem habent largiendi, benefici vocantur.' . . ."

13 In addition to the references to *Proverbs* in the passage next quoted in the text above from Bishop Jona, see especially the *Jewish Encyclopedia*, art. Compassion, for the ethical notions on which the Hebrew conception of leadership was based.

14 Cap. iii (Migne, CVI, 288). Cf. Hincmar of Rheims, Migne, CXXV, 833, 835.

15 *Tractatus*, I, vii, "De humilitate," Migne, XI, 320–321. Cf. St. Hilary, Migne, *loc. cit.*, note: "David enim et propheta et rex, erat humilis antea et abjectus, neque convivio patris sui dignus, sed Deo complacuit: unctus in regem est, aspiratus est in prophetam. Non insolescit in regno, non odiis commovetus, persequentem seamat, inimicorum mortes honorat, incestuosis et parricidalibus parcit. Imperator contemnitur, pater laeditur, propheta vexatur: ultionem non ut propheta orat, vindictam non ut pater sumit, contumeliam non ut imperator exsequitur."

16 *Decretorum libri XX*, XV, xxxix, Migne, CXL, 905–906.

16a Besides Jona and Hincmar, see particularly Abbo of Fleury (ca. 990), in *Recueil des historiens de France*, par les Bénédictins de Saint Maur (nouv. ed., L. Delisle, Paris, 1869 et seq.), X, 627; and the Sixth Council of Paris, canons, ii, I (P. Labbé, *Sacrosancta concilia*, Venice, 1729, IX, 746 ff., and Mansi, *Concilia*, Venice, 1769, XIV, 574 ff.), which incorporates Jona's treatise. For a twelfth-century picture of this continuing ecclesiastical-patriarchal conception of royalty, see John of Salisbury, *Policraticus*, iv, 2, 3, 5, 7, 8; v, 6; vi, 20, 24, 25, 27, *et passim*. Cf. John Dickinson, "The Mediaeval Conception of Kingship and Some of its Limitations, as Developed in the Policraticus of John of Salisbury," *Speculum*, I (1926), 308 ff.

17 Test. Benj., IV, in Fabricius, *Codex pseudepigraphis veteris testamenti* (2nd ed., Hamburg, 1723), I, 731; reprinted from J. E. Grabe, *Spicilegium ss. patrum*, vol. I (Oxford, 1698). Benjamin's words lose none of their relevance to the present inquiry from the fact that his figure is limited to the other element of our twofold eschatological motif, the crown of compassion rather than the throne of justice.

18 *De reg. princ.*, II, xv, S. *Thomae Aquinatis opuscula selecta* (Paris, 1881), III, 316–317. For the influence on Dante see my article, "On the Genesis of De Monarchia, II, v," *Speculum*, XIII (1938), 326 ff. The authorship and date of the work, the opening of which is ascribed to St. Thomas, are treated conclusively by Marius Krammer in the introduction

to his edition of the Determinatio compendiosa (*Fontes iuris germanici antiqui*, Hannover and Leipzig, 1909) and Martin Grabmann, 'Ein Selbstzeugnis Tolomeos von Lucca für seine Autorschaft an der Determinatio compendiosa de iurisdictione imperii,' *Neues Archiv*, XXXVII (1911–1912), 818–819.

19 *Visio Tnugdali*, ed. Wagner, pp. 43–44. Cf. the Latin poem, Wagner, p. 99, vv. 1256–1271, and the German Albers Tnugdalus, pp. 168–170, vv. 1597 ff. In the Latin text printed by P. Villari, *Antiche leggende e tradizione che illustrano la Divina commedia* (Pisa, 1865), pp. 16–17, the king is incorrectly named Tormac, t and c being readily confused in ms. The entire incident is omitted from Villari's Italian version; *Antiche leggende*, p. 44.

Here also may be mentioned the remarkable account in the tenth-century *Visio Karoli Crassi* of the "Roman" emperors seated on their jewelled thrones in Paradise: "Cumque cerneret comes meus in tanto pavore esse spiritum meum, dixit ad me: 'sequere me ad dexteram partem luculentissimae vallis paradisi.' Et gradientes contemplatus sum ingenti claritate cum gloriosis regibus sedere Hlotharium meum avunculum super lapidem topasion mirae magnitudinis, coronatum diademate pretioso, et juxta eum filium ejus Hludogvicum similiter corona ornatum; vidensque me cominus accersivit me, blanda voce magna dicens: 'Karole, succesor meus nunc tutius in imperio Romanorum, veni ad me. Sapio quoniam venisti per poenalem locum, ubi est pater tuus fraterque meus positus in thermis sibi destinatis; sed per misericordiam Dei citissime liberabitur de illis poenis, sicut et nos liberati sumus meritis sancti Petri sanctique precibus Remigii, cui Deus magnum apostolatum super reges et super omen gentem Francorum dedit.'" (Hariulf, *Chronique de l'abbaye de Saint-Riquier*, III, xxi, ed. F. Lot, *Collection de textes pour servir à l'étude et à l'enseignement de l'histoire*, Paris, 1894, pp. 147–148.) Though this passage contains no reference to the tradition of royal justice and compassion, the direct association of the incident with the Roman imperium would have made it particularly attractive to Dante. For Dante's possible knowledge of the *Visio* see my note, "Inferno, XII, 100–126, and the Visio Karoli Crassi," *MLN*, November, 1936, pp. 449–452.

20 *Dialogorum liber* IV, cap. xxxvi, Migne, LXXVII, 384–388. Edmund Gardner (ed.), *The Dialogues of Saint Gregory, surnamed the Great*, transl. P. W. 1608 (London and Boston: Philip Lee Warner, the Medici Society, n.d.), p. 274, nn., to pp. 223–226, observes briefly the ultimate connection of this passage with Dante but not with Cormach.

21 Ed. Ernesto Monaci, in *Fonti per la storia d'Italia* (Rome, 1887), p. 73.

22 *De civ. Dei*, Praefatio.

23 *De institutione regia*, Migne, CVI, 293–295.

24 See n. 18 above.

25 *Determ. compend.*, capp. xxi–xxiii (ed. Krammer, pp. 42 ff.). Cf. *De reg. princ.*, III, capp. iv–vi (*Opusc. select.*, III, 326 ff.).

26 Ed. Enrico Rostagno, in *Le opere di Dante* (Firenze, 1921), pp. 376–377. See my article, "On the Genesis of De monarchia, II, v," especially pp. 330 ff. To the discussion there of *pietas-humanitas* and the instances referred to especially on p. 331, nn. 3–5, and p. 332, nn. 1–3, should be added the following examples, which have particular interest for the history of the word, since those quoted in the DuCange Glossarium

and the Godefroy Dictionnaire are few and relatively late: St. Zeno (3rd or 4th century), *Tractatus*, I, iii, §iv (Migne, XI, 285): "in pauperos miserosque sua necessitate neglecta pietatis largitur et furtim semina spargit"; and *Tractatus*, I, x, §v: "Sed haec non ad vos, fratres, quorum largitas provinciis omnibus nota est, quorum pia semina totius quodam modo orbis per membra jactantur." The Merovingian epitaph of one Epaefanius, in E. Le Blant, *Inscriptions chrétiennes de la Gaule antérieures au VIIIe siècle* (Paris, 1856–1865), no. 407: "pius pauperibus." Petrus Damianus (11th century), *Opuscula*, LVII, De principiis officio in coercitione improborum (Migne, CXLV, 825): "noxiae pietatis imaginem a te procul exclude, et erga populum, qui tibi commissus est, satage semper justitiam custodire"; and (Migne, CXLV, 826–827): "et Deus illi non paternae, sed quod majus est, viscera maternae pietatis impendat? Ut qui stans pro pupillis et viduis adversus impiorum nequitias dimicat, ipse tanquam lacteola soboles sub confoventibus se divinae pietatis uberibus requiescat"; and: "Multi nempe falsae pietatis errore decepti, unde se Deo placere insipienter autumnat, inde adversus eum crudeliter pugnant; et ex eo merentur iram, unde se adepturos opinati sunt gratiam; et dum aliis veniam falsae pietatis impertiunt, ipsi motum divinae indignationis incurrunt." See also Hugutio of Pisa, *Magnae derivationes* (12th century), MS. Laud 626, f. 136: "Pius-a-um: religiosus, misericors, benignus, propitius. . . ." For Dante's knowledge of Hugutio, see Paget Toynbee, "Dante's Latin Dictionary," *Dante Studies and Researches* (London, 1902), pp. 97 ff.

27 *Epistole*, VI, vi, 25, ed. Ermenegildo Pistelli, in *Le opere di Dante* (1921), p. 425; "non sua privata sed publica mundi commoda sitiens. . . ."

28 VII, iv and v, ed. Pistelli, pp. 427–428; V, i, 4, p. 420; VII, viii, 29, p. 429; VII, ii, 10, p. 427.

29 V, iii, 7, ed. Pistelli, p. 420. See also V, ii, 6: "prope est qui liberabit te de carcere impiorum; qui percutiens malignantes in ore gladii perdet eos . . ."; and V, iii, 10: "nonne relapsorum facinora vindicabit . . . ?"

30 Vergil is directly referred to (Ep. VII, i, 6, ed. Pistelli, p. 426), but not Lactantius. Cf., however, the passages in the *Epistles* (particularly VI, iii) and Paradiso xxx with *Divin. inst.*, V, De justitia, capp. vi and vii, where the injustice of darker times is said to be the result of human cupidity and the return of the Golden Age to depend on the restoration of justice at the coming of Christ. Critics have been in doubt about whether Dante knew Lactantius, but this is from nothing more definite than the failure hitherto to discover satisfactory positive evidence.

31 Cf. Ep. V, iv, 14, ed. Pistelli, p. 420.

Joseph Anthony Mazzeo

11 · Dante's Conception of Love

LOVE in the Aristotelian tradition of the schools was conceived
as the natural inclination, the natural appetite of anything
whatsoever for its object. This inclination was found to operate
in different objects in different ways: in an intellectual nature it
is a function of the will, in sensible natures it is a function of
the sensitive appetite, and in natures devoid of any cognition,
it is a function of the nature being ordered to some end.[1]

This doctrine in the course of its development had come
to be related in various ways to the complementary Aristotelian
theory of weight as due to natural place. Strictly speaking, only
corporeal objects lacking in cognition had a natural place to
which they tended, and in their case alone was appetition
equivalent to weight or gravity. St. Thomas, for example, is
careful to point out that it is ridiculous to attribute natural
place to spiritual substances except by analogy.[2]

On the other hand, the notion of natural place was extended to the spiritual realm so that appetition or love became
simply the desire of all things, corporeal and spiritual, to attain
the "place" in the universe, material or immaterial that was
proper or "natural" to them. Thus as air and fire go up and
earth and water naturally go down, so all things seek their place
and man seeks his "true place" in heaven. It is in this form, not
in the more properly Aristotelian form that St. Thomas expounds, that we find the doctrine of love as a cosmic principle

Reprinted by permission from *The Journal of the History of Ideas* (XVIII,
2, 1957). Copyright 1957 by Journal of the History of Ideas, Inc.

in Dante; his "spiritual gravity" is the correspondence between
states of soul and their proper or natural place in the universe.
The equation of love equals weight, *amor* equals *pondus*, so
basic to the moral and physical cosmology of Dante's poem,
was no mere similitude to him or to St. Augustine, who may
have been a source for Dante in this matter. After pointing out
the manner in which all the orders of reality seek their own good
or their own place in the order of things, St. Augustine affirms
that weight is to body what love is to soul.[3] Even more explicitly, in a moving passage of the *Confessions*, St. Augustine
compares the soul's desire for rest in God with the manner
in which all bodies seek rest in their natural place in the universe.[4]

Boethius, in the *Consolation of Philosophy*, echoes this
augustinian conception and sings a song of praise to God who
creates souls and, scattering them throughout the universe,
afterwards calls them back to Himself, their Good and Origin.
They return to him as fire returns to its natural place.[5] In
Book III he points out that each thing must find its own proper
course again, and rejoices in its return to its own place. Nothing
can keep that order with which it is endowed unless in some
way it unites its rising (*ortum*) with its end (*finis*), and so
makes immutable its own circular course.[6] Thus the theory of
love as a generalization of the doctrine of natural place appears
as a process of outgoing and return. Man loves and desires because his home is heaven. In Plato and the neoplatonists, the
doctrine of "return" was associated with the pre-existence of
the human soul. For orthodox Christians like Boethius and St.
Augustine, the soul did not pre-exist, but it "returns" to God
as to its Creator.

In the thirteenth century the author of the *De intelligentiis*
echoes this augustinian equation of *amor* and *pondus*. The natural place of a nature is where it comes to rest. What lightness
and heaviness are to corporeal substances, love and fear are to
spiritual substances, for love "elevates" and fear "depresses." [7]

Thus, for the Christian, the neoplatonic doctrine of return
to the one is modified to free it from its emanationistic and
pantheistic consequences. The soul "returns" to God because it
came from a God who created it, not because it literally returns

to a supernatural world in which it pre-existed. It desires to return because of the *nisus* which God implants in all created things, a *nisus* which is not so much a yearning for a pre-existent state based on reminiscence of the bliss of that state, but a divinely implanted tendency to return to the Creator in Whose "presence" the soul was formed in the very moment of its creation.

In the *Convivio* Dante discourses at great length on love and defines it as nothing other than the spiritual union of the soul and the beloved object, a union the soul seeks by nature. If it is free it achieves this union sooner than if impeded, but the natural impulse is always present. Dante explains, citing the authority of the *Liber de causis*, that this natural impulse is present in the soul because it is created by God, and, as an effect of the First Cause, it partakes of the nature of that cause to the extent that it is able, and according to its own proper nature. Every form partakes of the divine nature not in the sense that the divine nature is divided, but in the same way that the other heavenly bodies partake of the nature of the sun. The nobler forms share to a greater degree in the divine nature, and the human soul, since it is the noblest of all the forms generated beneath the heavens, receives most of the divine nature.

Since the first cause is being, the source of existence, it is natural for anything to want to exist in God. The human soul desires with all its power to be, and because its being depends on and is preserved by God, it desires by nature to be united to Him in order to strengthen that being. Since God manifests Himself in different degrees in His creatures, and the human soul naturally desires union with God, it seeks to unite itself spiritually more strongly and quickly with an object the more perfect that object appears to it to be. This "appearance" depends on whether the judgment (*conoscenze*) is clear or impeded, and this union is love, the union of a soul with something else which fits that thing. It is what the soul finds fitting as an object of love which reveals what is within the soul, its state and quality. By discerning in the world without what the soul loves, we discover what is within. The lady in whom so much of the Divine light was revealed was the object of this kind of love.[8]

Every level in the order of creation has its own kind of love or desire. Simple bodies have a natural love for their own proper place. Thus earth always tends downwards to the center while fire has a natural love to ascend to the circumference adjoining the heaven of the moon. The primary composite bodies, such as minerals, have a natural love for that place which is suitable for their generation. Such is the place in which they grow and acquire vigor and power. Plants, which are the first of all creatures endowed with soul, i.e., the vegetative functions, more obviously manifest this love. They display a preference to grow in places adapted to the requirements of their natures, e.g., some plants grow well by water, others at the foot of mountains, and if they are transplanted either die or love, so to speak, sadly, like separated lovers. Animals not only more obviously love their own particular place but love one another; man, possessing a portion of the nature of every one of these lower creatures, can and does experience all of these kinds of love as well as his own specific love for all perfect and noble things, a kind of love he possesses by being the noblest of created things under the heavens.[9]

It is because he possesses love of the first kind, that of simple bodies, that man "loves" to sink downwards and is fatigued if he goes against this tendency, or upwards. By reason of the nature of mixed body he loves the season of the year and the place wherein he was generated. Hence everyone feels best physically when he is in the place of his birth, and at the time of year in which he was generated. By possession of the vegetative nature or soul, man has a natural desire and affinity for certain foods which will help to make him strong. This kind of desire for food is to be carefully distinguished from the kind arising from sensuous appetite, by which a man might eat foods that are bad for him. It is the animal soul in man, i.e., the sensitive soul or the unity of the faculties of sensation, which makes man feel desire following upon sensible apprehension. This is the love most in need of control because its activity is excessive, especially in regard to the pleasure of touch and taste.

The last faculty, the truly human or even angelic nature, is the rational soul by which man has a natural desire for truth and virtue. From this "affection" derives true and perfect friendship of the kind that Aristotle described in the eighth book of the *Ethics*. This nature is the mind, and Dante adds that when he spoke of love discoursing to him in his mind, he meant this kind of love for truth and virtue, the love springing from the noblest nature. He says this in order that no one might hold the false opinion that he was referring to the delights of sense. When in the poem on which he is commenting, he says "desiringly," he means to call attention to the intensity and continuing duration of this love. It was so powerful, so stirred his mind, that his intellect went awry. In thinking about his lady he wished to demonstrate things about her that he found himself unable to understand and was often so wrapped in thought and bewildered about her that his outward appearance was of a man out of his mind (*alienato*).[10]

It is important here to observe that the contemplation of the beauty of the lady led him to the perception of truths about her which he could not understand. The effort to understand so dominated him that he seemed as one outside of himself. This "alienation" is nothing else than the description of the "madness" of ecstasy or rapture, a rapture which involves the intuition of truth not fully understood.

So far there are only two differences between the scale of love expounded by Dante and the common Aristotelian doctrine of the schools typified by St. Thomas. First, in applying the doctrine of natural place, Dante does not attempt to distinguish between corporeal and spiritual substances. The equation of gravity (*pondus*) and love (*amor*) is carried right through the whole scale of creatures. Secondly, Dante places *special* emphasis on the fact that man is a microcosm of all these loves; as we shall see, Dante makes fruitful use of this idea, and culminates his discussion by describing the effect of the beauty of the "lady" in terms of rapture, madness, or ecstasy.

The most important difference between Dante and the doctrines of the schools is that the union of loves in man is *dynamically* and not statically conceived. Dante accepted the commonplace that the human soul possessed all of the faculties of the lower souls, but he set these souls and their "loves" in a dialectical motion. An objective ladder of "goods" or objects of love corresponds to this ladder of desires, and desire restlessly pursues Absolute Good and Beauty through a hierarchy of objects. The soul has its origin in God and is impelled to return to Him. It is eager for the Highest Good at the very beginning of its mortal course, a course which it never traveled before. It is like the pilgrim who travels along an unknown road and believes each house that he sees to be the inn he is looking for and, disappointed in each one in turn, puts his faith in the one further on until he finds the right one. The soul similarly directs her eyes toward the goal of the Supreme Good, but it is not fully aware of it, and because of this often mistakes a lesser good for its goal. Because the pilgrim soul has little knowledge and experience she magnifies things of little value, and she first of all begins by desiring such things. So it turns to one beautiful thing after another, always expecting to achieve supreme joy and always disappointed. Thus in the infant years we see children desiring an apple above all things, then a little bird, a horse, a woman, and greater and greater degrees of riches, always seeking and hoping, not finding what it seeks and driven on to something else further on.[11]

Elsewhere in the *Convivio* (IV, xxiii, 3 and xxviii, 2) Dante refers to this natural desire to return to God as a return to the most high and glorious power of nobility, or to the port from which the soul set out on the journey over the sea of this life. The gift of nobleness finally returns to safe harbor in God, together with that most noble part of the soul which cannot die.

In the *Purgatorio* he develops this doctrine of a natural desire in man to return to God more explicitly and with an interesting and significant addition. The restless dialectical movement up the ladder of love is a true eros, for the soul fixes its eyes on the Supreme Good, without being fully aware that it is doing so. Its restless yearning is compounded of unconscious knowledge and what we might call "conscious ignorance," the true platonic love-nostalgia, the yearning for a beauty once seen and then in part forgotten. Plato explained this state as the result of a "fall" from a pre-existent state in which the disembodied soul saw the plain of truth. In Dante the sight of the plain of truth is replaced by the instantaneous contact of the soul with God, at the moment of its creation. In the moment that it issued from God, the soul experienced a supreme ineffable happiness and joy. After entering the body it became oblivious of this divine happiness except that it constantly carried within itself a vague longing to experience what it once felt. Dante compares it to an imprinted passion as we have upon awakening from a dream whose content we have forgotten but whose joy lingers on.

The state of "forgetfulness," which Dante describes as the state of every human being when it enters this world, is actually the same state that the mystic has after he has descended from his instantaneous and brief contact with God. He experiences a failure of intellectual and visual memory but the joy of the experience lingers.

> From that moment my vision was greater than our speech, which fails at such a sight, and memory too fails at such excess. Like him that sees in a dream and after the dream the passion wrought by it remains and the rest returns not to his mind, such as I; for my vision almost wholly fades, and still there drops within my heart the sweetness that was born of it.[12]

It is thus that the snow loses its stamp when it is melted by the rays of the sun and the Sibyl's utterances were lost when the leaves on which they were written were scattered by the wind.

> So doth the snow unstamp it to the sun, so to the wind on the light leaves was lost the Sybil's wisdom.

Thus the *Paradiso* points back and clarifies the past journey. The state he describes here is not as "unknowing" as the state of ordinary human beings, for Dante has had a second contact with God given to few men. He thus has "forgotten," but he can identify the source of his indwelling joy. He can no longer mistake a lesser good for the Supreme Good which alone can satisfy the desire to re-experience that joy.

Shortly afterward, in the final canto, he calls our attention again to this same state when he identifies what he saw, not by calling it to mind—that is impossible—but by "recollecting" and re-experiencing the joy and happiness which attended the vision. He *believes* he saw the transcendent unity of substance and accidents because his joy expands. Yet the experience as *comprehended*, as *immediate*, went into a deeper oblivion than that which twenty-five centuries cast on the exploits of Jason:

> I think I saw the universal form of this complex, because in telling of it I feel my joy expand. A single moment makes for me deeper oblivion than five and twenty centuries upon the enterprise that made Neptune wonder at the shadow of the Argo.[13]

Similarly, in *Par.* XXXIII,[14] after Christ appears to him, Dante has a rapture, and he cannot recall what became of his mind. He hears the voice of Beatrice in a state similar to that of one trying to recall a forgotten dream:

> As fire breaks from a cloud, swelling till it has not room there, and against its nature falls to the earth, so my mind, grown greater at that feast, was transported from itself and of what it became has no remembrance.
> "Open thine eyes and look at me as I am; thou hast seen such things that thou hast gained strength to bear my smile." I was like one that wakes from a forgotten dream and strives in vain to bring it again to mind when I heard this invitation, worthy of such gratitude that it can never be blotted from the book that records the past.

The important point about Dante's dream psychology is that the emotional content remains even when the conceptual content of the dream-vision cannot be recalled. Thus like the joy of a dream, a mystical vision and prenatal contact with God all remain as desire, a desire impelling the soul to experience again its original pleasure. It fixes on one object or another, always unsatisfied but always in hope, unaware exactly of what it seeks but always able to judge the lesser good as inadequate because of the "imprinted passion" in its soul. This process is nothing else than the search for the divine beatitude and with proper guidance of human experience and judgment on the one hand and law on the other, it reaches its goal:

> From His hand, who regards it fondly before it is, comes forth, like a child that sports, tearful and smiling, the little simple soul that knows nothing, but, moved by a joyful maker, turns eagerly to what delights it. At first it tastes the savour of a trifling good; it is beguiled there and runs after it, if guide or

curb do not divert its love. Therefore there was need for law to be set as a curb; there was need for a king who should discern at least the tower of the true city.[15]

In the characteristic manner in which the same themes appear and reappear as he sees more and more truth, and achieves greater understanding as he approaches his goal, Dante refers in the *Paradiso* [16] to the implanted love for the Creator which the soul acquires in that moment of contact with God when it was created:

> The angels, brother, and the pure country where thou art may be said to be created just as they are in their entire being; but the elements thou hast named and those things that are made from them are given their form by created power. Created was the matter that is in them, created was the informing virtue in these stars that wheel about them. The soul of every beast and of the plants is drawn from a potential complex by the shining and motion of the holy lights; but your life the Supreme Beneficence breathes forth immediately, and He so enamours it of Himself that it desires Him ever after.

Thus Dante, having experienced a true platonic love-nostalgia, found an equivalent for the platonic notion of *anamnesis* in the doctrine of the special creation of each individual soul. The previous contact with the absolute came in the moment of its creation—not in a vision in a pre-existent state, itself one of an infinite series of such states interrupted by reincarnations.

Love in Dante thus appears not only in terms of the Augustinian doctrine of the weight of love (*pondus amoris*) fused with the Aristotelian doctrine of natural place, but it appears as nostalgia, the truly platonic note in love speculation. The kinds of love are not statically classified and distinguished but are in a dynamic and dialectical relationship to one another. Man is the focal point of every kind of love, including the love he derives from his status as a part of nature, and the love which impels him dialectically through and beyond the lower forms of love and springs from that moment of contact with God in the creation of his immortal and supernatural part. This love leads man to use creatures in order to ascend to a transcendent God through a natural process guided by judgment and law, forms of volitional discipline which order desire. The ascent through the scale of creatures arranged in a hierachy of good and beautiful is nothing other than the dynamic nature of love itself, each grade in the ladder helping the pilgrim regain that half-remembered supreme beauty. Love carries intellect with it in this journey, expanding and enriching it, while intellect in turn feeds the flame of love.[17]

The main discourse of love is elaborated in the *Purgatorio* (XVI–XVIII) at the very center of the Divine Comedy. It is at the center because love itself is the "central" revealer of the universe, it is the heart of things in both the actual universe and the universe of the poem. In Canto XVIII Dante explains how implanted love operates on the natural level. Every soul is potentially capable of love, a love which can be actualized by perception of an object which is pleasing. This notion is already present in the tenth sonnet of the *Vita Nuova:* "Amor e 'l cor gentil sono una cosa," in which Dante describes the love of a gentleman for a lady and how she actualizes the potentiality of love in her lover.

Dante in the following passage fully explains how the process takes place. The intellect abstracts from the sensible forms conveyed to it through the senses, the form or species (i.e., *intenzione,* l. 23) of a true or real being in the outside world (*esser verace,* l. 22). The intellect, after this process of abstraction takes place, presents this form to the will which is free to incline itself to the object or not.

> The mind, created quick to love, is readily moved towards everything that pleases, as soon as by the pleasure it is roused to action. Your perception takes from outward reality an impression and unfolds it within you, so that it makes the mind to turn to it; and if the mind, so turned, inclines to it, that inclination is love, that is nature, which by pleasure is bound on you afresh.[18]

This love is natural, not supernatural, as Vergil points out when he refers Dante to Beatrice for an explanation of that love to which reason cannot attain (ll. 46–48). The will is "bound again," in the sense that when it was in a potential state in regard to love it was "bound" the first time. After the potentiality of love has been actualized and the will has freely made its choice, it is "bound again" in that the will is fixed on the object of its desire. It wants the thing itself and cannot rest in pursuit of it. Dante emphasizes the naturalness of this process by comparing this kind of love to the natural movement of fire seeking its place.

> Then, as fire moves upward by its form, being born to mount where it most abides in its matter, so the mind thus seized enters into desire, which is a spiritual movement, and never rests until the thing loved makes it rejoice.[19]

This impulse to love and the knowledge of primary ideas are in men as the impulse to make honey is in bees. There is no further explanation possible, in the sense that it cannot be deduced from man's rational essence. This primary natural love is innocent in its impulse and a man is not guilty in terms of a natural impulse. We possess, however, a faculty of judgment which counsels the impulse of natural desire by assenting or denying. "This is the principle in which is found the reason of desert in you according as it garners and winnows out good and guilty loves." Natural impulses of desire arise from necessity, but the will is free and it is in man's power to control it.

> Therefore, whence come the knowledge of primary ideas and the bent to the primary objects of desire, no man knows; they are in you just as in bees zeal to make honey, and this primal will admits no deserving of praise or blame. Now in order that to this will every other may be conformed there is innate in you the faculty which counsels and which ought to hold the threshold of assent. This is the principle in which is found the reason of desert in you according as it garners and winnows out good and guilty loves. Those who in their reasoning went to the root recognized this innate freedom and therefore left ethics to the world. Admitting then that every love that is kindled in you arises of necessity, the power to control it is in you; that noble faculty Beatrice means by freewill and therefore see thou have it in mind if she would speak of it to thee.[20]

The description of the process we find here is substantially the same as that common in the schools and described by Aquinas. Love is something which pertains to the appetite and can be classified according to the kinds of appetites. There is the kind of appetition which does not follow its own apprehension, namely, the simple natural impulse. This is the natural appetite of creatures without knowledge, directed to their ends by a higher knower or "by the apprehension of another." There is the kind of appetition which follows immediately upon apprehension and this is sensitive appetition. It is of necessity and not of free will, the possession of dumb animals. In man, however, this same sensitive appetition appears in a different form, where it participates in a kind of freedom to the extent that it may obey reason. The third and highest kind of appetition is that following upon the apprehension of a creature possessing free choice (*secundum liberum arbitrium*) and this is rational, intellective appetition or will (*voluntas*). In each and every case, love may be called the principle of motion tending toward the goal that is loved (*principium motus tendentis in finem amatum*). St. Thomas goes on to explain that the principle of this motion in natural love or appetition is a certain "connaturality." In the higher forms, the appetition of the sensitive nature or of the faculty of will, the principle of motion is a certain "coaptation" or "complacency" of and in the good. We might perhaps express this "complacency" as a singular and particular affinity for a particular good, as distinct from generalized desire for goodness.[21]

St. Thomas gives a further explanation of what he means by these terms in a discussion of whether or not love is a "passion." A passion is the affect of an agent in the patient or that upon which it acts. This agent confers both form and the motion consequent upon that form, so that, for example, in the process of generation the agent gives to a body its weight and the motion following upon that weight. This principle of weight (*gravitas*) is the principle of motion of a body to a place which is "connatural" to it because of the kind of weight it has. Thomas says, with his usual suspicion of anything that suggests the metaphorical use of language, that this may be called natural "love" in a manner of speaking (*quoddammodo dici amor naturalis*), just as he was willing to grant to the metaphysicians of light their use of metaphors of light to describe spiritual and intellectual matters so long as they were aware they were using figurative language. Analogously, the object of appetition first gives to the faculty of appetition a kind of "co-aptation" which is complacency in the object of appetite (*complacentia appetibilis*) and, second, motion toward it.

Thus appetition acts in a pattern which may be described as circular. The object of appetite acts as the efficient cause when the faculty receives the form which assimilates it to the object, and as the final cause because the object elicits motion towards itself. This reception of the form, species, or "intention" of the object of appetite in the faculty of appetition is the first change brought about by the object of desire in the subject. It is the result of "complacency" in the object of appetition. The motion following upon this is desire, and the ultimate rest which follows upon attainment of the object is joy.[22] This whole analysis, it becomes clear, is an attempt to explain why we like some things, how we come to feel an affinity for what we actually in each instance want.

St. Thomas' language here is quite technical, and I have expounded him in his own terms before explaining the relevance of these texts to the passage from the *Purgatorio* (XVIII, 19ff.) because his meaning will become clearer if we see the way in which Dante rendered these concepts. The term "piacere" in line 27 (cf. Provençal *plazer*, "attraction," "charm") often translated as "pleasing impression" is actually a translation of the Latin *complacentia*. In the lower kinds of substances there is the implanted natural affinity for them to seek their proper place. This affinity, which follows upon the apprehension of a higher knower who directs them to their ends, St. Thomas calls connaturality. The higher analogue in the realm of appetition is *complacentia*, not active desire but what might be called *awareness of desirability*, a certain coaptation of the appetite for its object, the necessary presupposition of motion towards it or of desire for it. *Complacentia* is the first change which the object of appetition induces in the subject and consists of the reception in the subject of the "intention" (l. 23) or form. This reception creates an affinity in the subject for the object, it "coapts" him to the object. The same thing which is the cause of creating this affinity is also its final cause, inducing active desire. Thus the circularity of the process of love, the closing of the circle being accompanied by rest and joy.

The pattern of love in Dante is also circular, or perhaps spiral, each step in the ladder to God closing one circular movement and initiating another—increase of good and beauty increasing love which in turn demands a higher good.

The analogous process takes place on every level of reality. Active desire is the higher analogue on the conscious level of motion to natural place on the lower level. Conscious affinity, accompanied by pleasure, is the higher analogue of natural unconscious affinity of insentient creatures for their natural place. In the insentient order natural appetition is unconscious and unwilled; in the order of sensation without rationality, it is conscious and unwilled; in man it is willed and conscious.[23]

But desire in man has a further peculiarity precisely because it is the desire of a rational being. Man, by nature, desires the eternal, or immortality, in which alone the higher faculties can find the rest and joy which is the goal of all desire. A sign of immortality is that the natural desire for it cannot be in vain. The will of any rational creature naturally desires the eternal because reason, unlike sense, is not confined to the "here and now" but knows without being confined to either time or place. It knows "absolutely" and, in a sense, "timelessly." Its mode of existence being thus spaceless and timeless it naturally desires eternal existence.[24]

Dante makes significant use of this doctrine of desire for the eternal. Speaking of the beauty of the angelic lady, he says that he intends to speak of her in the aspect in which the goodness of her soul reveals itself as sensible beauty. This beauty is such that things are revealed through it which demonstrate some of the joys of Paradise. The noblest of joys is to be content, which is nothing less than to be blessed. This kind of blessedness or contentment is found in the sensible beauty of the lady who is perfect in her species, but it is different from what would be felt in Paradise because it is interrupted and not everlasting.[25]

So in *Paradiso* XXIV, Beatrice invokes the blessed as those eternally satisfied:

> O FELLOWSHIP elect to the great supper of the blessed Lamb, who feeds you so that your desire is ever satisfied, since by God's grace this man has foretaste of that which falls from

your table, before death appoints his time, give heed to his measureless craving and bedew him with some drops; you drink always from the fountain whence comes that on which his mind is set.[26]

As the beauty of the lady in the *Convivio* fed the eyes of her beholders giving them a foretaste of the joys of Paradise, so Beatrice in Paradise asks for more food from the supper of the lamb for Dante, who is having a foretaste of the joys which his measureless craving desires.

This measureless craving, this desire for eternal possession of good or beauty, is a function of the rational soul, of man's natural desire for possession of eternal good in an eternal existence. So much is common to both Dante and the schools. The important difference between them on this matter is that for Dante sensible human beauty is the highest temporal analogue of the perpetual joys and contentment of the eternal existence man desires. This satisfaction which is the goal of man's desire is a union of peace and ardor, tranquility and passion, a passionate tranquility in which desire finds rest without in some sense ceasing to be desire—a state which in Paradise cannot be lost and which requires no effort to retain.

Notes

1 St. Thomas Aquinas, *Summa theologiae*, 1, q. 60, a. 1. All citations from the *Summa theologiae* are from the Leonine edition (*Opera omnia*, 15 vols., Vols. 4–12, Rome, 1882–1930).

2 *Ibid.*, 1, q. 102, a. 2, ad 2.

3 St. Augustine, *De civitate Dei*, XI, 28; *P.L.* 41, col. 342.

4 St. Augustine, *Confessiones*, XIII, 9; *P.L.* 32, cols. 848–9. Cf. the general introduction to the *Obras de San Augustin*, by P. Victorino Capanaga, I (2nd ed., Madrid, 1950), 66ff., for a discussion of this doctrine of *amor* as *pondus*. In the *De Trinitate* (X, 1, 3; *P.L.* 42, col. 474) St. Augustine relates love to knowledge. Love follows upon knowing, but it is a desire to know more. Because a man loves what he knows, he desires to know what he does not yet know. Knowledge generates love which in turn demands more knowledge and so on in a spiral. This pattern of circularity is an important motif in the *Paradiso* in which increase of knowledge generates love which in turn demands more knowledge.

5 Boethius, *Consolatio philosophiae*, III metrum, 9, 18–25 in *Boethius, The Theological Tractates, The Consolation of Philosophy* by H. F. Stewart and E. K. Rand (London and Cambridge, Mass., 1918 [Loeb Classical Library]). The poem cited is an excellent paraphrase of the first part of the *Timaeus*.

6 *Ibid.*, III, metrum 2, 34–38.

7 *Liber de intelligentiis*, LII, ed. by C. Baeumker in *Witelo, ein Philosoph und Naturforscher des XIII Jahrhunderts* in *Beiträge zur Geschichte der Philosophie des Mittelalters* (Münster, 1908), III, 2.

8 *Convivio* III, ii, 3–9. All references to the *Convivio* are to the edition of G. Busnelli and G. Vandelli, 2 vols. (2nd ed., Florence, 1954). According to Bruno Nardi, love in Dante's *Convivio* is no longer a "disio che vien dal core" as in the *Vita Nuova*, but a *virtus unitiva*, a notion which Dante may have derived from Dionysius (*De div. nom.* IV, 12, 15, 17) and which is a neoplatonic definition of love. This idea coupled with Boethius' notion of *mentibus hominum veri boni naturaliter inserta cupiditas* (*De cons.* III, pr. 2 and 3) is, according to Nardi, the source of the dialectic of love passage in *Conv.* IV, xii, 14–19 and the "Esce di man" passage in *Pur.* XVI, 85–93. For Boethius this inborn natural desire to return to the Creator which exists even in animals is a vague sentiment existing in the manner of a dream, of their origin and their goal (*ibid.*, pr. 8). Nardi also traces the idea of the natural motion of the soul to God in *Conv.* III, ii, 4–7, to the *Liber de causis*. Bruno Nardi, *Dante e la cultura medievale* (Bari, 1949), 47–55.

9 *Conv.* III, iii, 2–5.

10 *Conv.* III, iii, 6–7 and 9–13.

11 *Conv.* IV, xii, 14–17. For one form of the subjective ladder of love cf. *Conv.* IV, xxii, 4–8, where Dante expounds the various forms of self-love culminating, through purification, in the love of the highest or intellectual self. The natural appetite of the mind which the Greeks call *hormen* is infused in us from the source of our generation by divine grace. At first it seems like the ordinary forms of appetition, the purely natural forms. Later, however, it differentiates itself from them, in a manner similar to the way in which various grains look alike at first but change and differ as they grow. So all animals, rational and dumb, begin by behaving alike in their basic self-love which is physical in nature and necessary for survival. There is, later on, a differentiation between the appetite of men and of dumb animals and, in the human species, between the various forms and directions which this self-love may take. If this self-love of humans takes the right path, it eventually culminates in love of the best part of the self, the intellect, and in the life of contemplation of God, in this life only through His effects, in the afterlife directly.

12 *Par.* XXXIII, 55. Translations and citations in the original from the *Divine Comedy* are from *The Divine Comedy*, with translation and commentary by J. D. Sinclair, 3 vols. (New York, 1948).

13 *Par.* XXXIII, 91.

14 *Par.* XXXIII, 40.

15 *Pur.* XVI, 85.

16 *Par.* VII, 139.

17 Nancy Lenkeith refers to *De vera religione*, III, nn. 3–5, P.L. 34, cols. 123ff., as a possible source for Dante's version of love nostalgia, although she acknowledges that the explicit statement that the soul comes forth from God is lacking in the passage in question and that it is present in Petrarch's allusion to the augustinian passage to be found in the *Secretum* (I, W. H. Draper trans. [London, 1911], 41). She also points out that the purification of the soul from sense, necessary so that the soul can wake from the sleep which makes it forget its first splendor

and its Creator, is a description of the mystic way. It is not the use of creatures to ascend to God but a purely subjective process of progressive purification of the love uniting the individual with God. N. Lenkeith, *Dante and the Legend of Rome*, Medieval and Renaissance Studies of the Warburg Institute, Supplement II (University of London, 1952), 47–48.

I cannot suggest an explicit source, but the Boethian notions of the outgoing and return of all things from and to God and of the implanted desire for the Supreme Good whose attainment is happiness, suggest a possible context. Boethius, in the *Consolatio* (*op. cit.*), also expounds the notion that men are deceived by lesser goods and seek to amass them, ignorant of their true goal (Bk. II, prose 2). In the passage which affords the closest parallel to Dante, even to the extent of adopting a dream image, he says: "Vos quoque, o terrena animalia, tenui licet imagine vestrum tamen principium somniatis verumque illum beatitudinis finem licet minime perspici qualicumque tamen cogitatione prospicitis eoque vos ad verum bonum naturalis ducit intentio et ab eodem multiplex error abducit. Considera namque an per ea quibus se homines adepturos beatitudinem putant ad destinatum finem valeant pervenire." (III, pr. 3) All of the elements of the divine origin of the soul, its implanted desire to return to its creator, the restless unconscious pursuit of a half-forgotten Supreme Good through lesser goods, the image of the dream are present in Boethius. Dante describes the recollection of God as the imprinted passion of a dream that is over, while Boethius describes it as a kind of actual dream state. Boethius emphasizes how men err by remaining fixed in their desire on some finite rung in the hierarchy of objects of desire, while Dante emphasizes a more positive sense of the *use* of creatures to attain the Supreme Good. It is rather a question of emphasis than of difference.

18 *Pur.* XVIII, 19. It is important to remember that for Dante as for St. Bernard certain ideas are not to be reached except through love and its maturing flame (*Par.* VII, 20). The notion rests on the idea that beauty is a harmony and the most excellent harmony is that of the virtues. To know the virtues is to have pleasure and to acquire thereby the desire of practicing them. This desire, or love, restrains the passions, breaks up vicious habits, and gives rise to internal happiness of the kind which must necessarily accompany the proper activity of the soul.

19 *Pur.* XVIII, 28. Cf. St. Thomas Aquinas, *Summa theologiae*, 1–2, q. 10, a. 2 ad resp., 1–2, q. 26, a. 3; 1–2, q. 77, a. 2 on the "binding" of the will in loving.

20 *Pur.* XVIII, 55.

21 St. Thomas Aquinas, *Summa theologiae*, 1–2, q. 26, a. 1.

22 Ibid., loc. cit.

23 The Aristotelian doctrine of "complacentia" was used to formulate conceptually the Provençal conceit that the immediate perception of one's lady was a prerequisite to the birth of love. Love comes into being *upon* the eyes of the lady when encountered by those of her future lover. The love thus generated is conveyed on bright beams of *light* from her eyes to his. It passes through them to take up its abode in his heart. Cf. *Vita Nuova* XX, sonnet 10. Cf. also Sections XIX, XXI, XXVI.

24 St. Thomas Aquinas, *Summa theologiae*, 1, q. 75, a. 6.

25 *Conv.* III, viii, 3–5, esp. 5.

26 *Par.* XXIV, 1. The goal and dialectical nature of love is also expressed in the image of a "sweet fruit" sought through the boughs of a tree. There is almost certainly an allusion to the "tree" of Porphyry, the diagram illustrating the logical and ontological structure of reality, a commonplace in medieval teaching of logic. *Par.* XXVII, 115: " 'That sweet fruit which the care of mortals goes to seek on so many boughs shall today give peace to thy cravings.' Such were Vergil's words to me. . . .' "

Porphyry's tree is a representation of the scale of forms and according to the fundamental principle of Greek idealistic thought, every higher form contains virtually whatever belongs to the lower, i.e., repeats the lower on a higher level while transcending it. Thus Vergil says of spiritual love what Francesca had said of carnal love in *Inf.* V, 103ff. *Pur.* XXII, 10: "When Vergil began: 'Love kindled by virtue always kindles another, if only its flame appear without. . . .' "

Giuseppe Antonio Borgese

12 · The Wrath of Dante

EVEN MORE than by the burning pinnacles of the city of Satan, the eighth canto of Dante's *Inferno* is dominated by the episode of Filippo Argenti. Out of the dark marsh of Styx, allotted to the wrathful, which Dante and Vergil are crossing on the Devil Phlegyas's boat, one inmate, "full of mud," rises before the visitor:

> "Who art thou that comest before thy time?" And I to him: "If I come, I remain not; but thou, who art thou, that hast become so foul?" He answered: "Thou seest that I am one who weep." And I to him: "With weeping, and with sorrow, accursed spirit, remain thou! for I know thee, all filthy as thou art." Then he stretched both hands to the boat, whereat the wary master thrust him off, saying: "Away there with the other dogs!" And he put his arms around my neck, kissed my face, and said: "Indignant soul! blessed be she that bore thee. In your world that was an arrogant personage; good there is none to ornament the memory of him; so is his shadow here in rage. How many above there now think themselves great kings, that shall lie here like swine in mire, leaving behind them horrible reproaches!" And I: "Master, I should be glad to see him dipped in this swill, ere we quit the lake." And he to me: "Before the shore comes to thy view, thou shalt be satisfied; it is fitting that thou shouldst be gratified in such a wish!" A little after this, I saw the muddy people make such rending of him that even now I praise and thank God for it. All cried: "At Filippo Argenti!" The passionate Florentine spirit turned with his teeth upon himself. Here we left him, so that of him I tell no more.

Reprinted from *Speculum* (XIII, 1938) by permission of the Medieval Academy of America.

Contemporary or early testimonies provide us with a consistent although sketchy picture of this antagonist, however difficult or even hopeless it may be to draw a clear-cut line between authentic information and such variations on the Dantean source as the portrait of Filippo Argenti in *Decameron* IX, 8. They tell us that he was an overbearing and reckless nobleman of the Neri faction, opposed to Dante's. The nickname Argenti, which superseded the well-known family names of Cavicciuli and Adimari, was suggested by the bumptious extravagance which made him shoe his horse with silver instead of iron. Legend and chronicle mix inextricably in the story that he, a hater of his fellow-citizens, had a horse which he called the horse of the Florentine people and which he generously offered for use to each and all who wanted it. Then, of course, he was unable to lend it save to the one who was lucky or brisk enough to appear at the stable first; the others, the late comers, were saluted by the gentleman with insulting laughter.

This is, so far, not much of a criminal record, considering circumstances and times. Fits of anger and unpleasant jokes might have been seen more leniently, from the angle of the picturesque, by a judge more easy-going than Dante; and such is the treatment to which the Argenti theme was to be subjected in the passage of the *Decameron*. Dante, however, for his own good reasons, thought that eternal mud was fit retaliation for the insolent flash of those silver hoofs. Filippo, who indeed had been a man on horseback, is dismounted forever; neither does he seem to enjoy the strange privilege by which he, a rather obscure commune-baron, is picked by the poet to herald in sight of Pandemonium the parade of Centaurs, monsters, and Titans, who will be overtowered by the stature of Capaneo and overcrowed by the blasphemy of Vanni Fucci.

II

The novelty of the Argenti episode is at least twofold. Structurally, Dante proves able for the first time to handle three persons at once: Argenti, Vergil, and himself. Thus far he had not surpassed the flat or Byzantine technique of straight dialogue between himself and Vergil, or between himself and a shade, or between Vergil and an official of the underworld. Even in the most elaborate episode of the preceding cantos, Vergil acted simply as stage director, introducing the Dante-Francesca dialogue, during which the most pertinent reason for the famed silence of Paolo is the inability of the poet to manage a third personage. Now, in the eighth canto, it is as if he at one stroke had achieved in his dramatic technique a transition like that from the two-actor to the three-actor performance in Greek tragedy. Together with the other enrichments in landscape, movement, language, and rhythm, this change implies a profound allotropy in the poet's imagination, and points to a gap between the composition of the seventh and of the eighth canto, the extension of which in chronology might be of years or of weeks, but the depth of which bears the significance of a mental conversion, and marks the transition from Dante's youthful style to his poetic maturity, from apprenticeship to masterhood. A partial analogy might be found, e.g., in the transition in painting from golden ground to perspective and chiaroscuro, with all the spiritual values involved in the difference. The change in Dante's style belongs, in fact, to the series of individual and collective phenomena which lead from medieval taste to Renaissance.

Psychologically, the Argenti episode offers the first instance of an outburst of violent passion in Dante's heart. Strange as it may seem, the only prelude, so far, to such moods had been ascribed to Vergil, the gentle Sage, when he addressed Pluto: "Be silent, cursed Wolf!" Dante himself had never dared and the limited range of his emotions had been contained between fear and pity: fear, perhaps, occasionally relieved by such puerile nonchalance as the wanderer's delight at the leopard's gay skin, but usually assuaged by the pupil's no less childlike confidence in Vergil's guidance; pity so conventionalized that Dante's quavering words and flowing tears are the same before the glutton Ciacco as they had been in the presence of Francesca the heroine of love. Both feelings repeatedly stretched to the extreme expression of swooning and falling like a dead body, which however must be taken partly as a mannerism or convention of medieval sentimentality rather than as a statement of actual happening. Now, suddenly, a third set of emotions, as red-hot as the city of Dis, breaks the monotony of the long prelude. As the first seven cantos—and not the fifth alone—had been the cantos of pity, so the eighth is the canto of rage.

To be sure, *si vis me flere flendum est ipsi tibi,* which also means that the poet wanting to stage a mad dog like Argenti must inject a quantum of madness into his own brain. The contagion of dramatic passion had been observed at least as early as Plato, and Dante himself, later in the *Inferno,* will exclaim with exceptional flippancy, "In church with saints, and with guzzlers in the tavern." Yet the eighth canto gives a probably unique instance of such a sweeping assimilation or symbiosis. With a chorus of rioting devils behind the scene, all four actors of the play build a Laokoöntian group under the sign of wrath. That Phlegyas, the infernal boatman, should be as furious as the damned souls, seems rational. Far less intelligible, in the field of rational behavior, is the fact that Vergil, the sweet master, indulges three times successively in the condemned passion: first when he, thrusting back Argenti, cries, "Away there with the other dogs!"; second, when he enthusiastically approves Dante's violent heart and promptly grants him the pleasure of contemplating the torture of Argenti; third, when he self-complacently admits that the resistance of the devils at the entrance of the city of Dis has made him "angry." Dante, however, tops everybody and everything, while the meekest of all is the supposedly mad dog Argenti. His approach to the passer-by is as beggarly and humble as could be: "Who art thou? . . . I am one who mourn." It is Dante's unprovoked insult that maddens him to a miserably impotent threat; whereupon the expiation is frightful, and more frightful is Dante's grinning thanksgiving to the justice of God.

This savagery is only matched in the nethermost pit of Hell when Dante, a traitor among traitors, thumbs his nose, so to speak, at friar Alberigo, whom he has cheated, or when, shortly before, he has actually struck at Bocca degli Abati, pulling some locks of hair from his eternally frozen head. Rightly another inmate of the penitentiary, hearing Bocca's howling and unaware of the traveling poet, asks him: "Who is the devil who is tormenting thee?"

III

The readers' reactions to the Argenti episode have varied according to their personal tempers. Kind souls have shrunk before the horror; more hardy ones, less numerous, have cheerfully applauded Dante's scorning "justice."

An historic and poetic interpretation would amount to more than mere favor or disfavor toward Dante's attitude.

If Dante had become conscious of his change, if he had tried to justify his allotropy with teachings and examples drawn from classical antiquity, he hardly would have found valid support in pagan poetry or philosophy. Juvenal, whom he knew, suggested, rather theoretically, that "indignatio facit versus"; his *indignatio*, at any rate, was moralizing diatribe, not fury opposed to fury. Greek poetry was to the Christian poet a sealed book; had he been able to open it, he would have realized how constantly for ten centuries or more it deprecated ire and urged moderation and forgiveness. Wrath was occasionally supposed in gods, with a mixture of stupor and awe; it was not allowed to men. This attitude is grounded in the very first foundation of classical culture, the *Iliad*. Achilles knows the sweetness of wrath, "far sweeter than trickling honey," as well as he knows the joy of battle. He also knows, however, that gentleness is the better part, and wishes that strife and wrath may "perish utterly among gods and men." The barbaric *Iliad* is the poem of the Wrath of Achilles, with the poet and Achilles himself against it. The Christian *Comedy* is, partly at least, the poem of the Wrath of Dante, with the poet for it.

The Greek attitude did not change with Vergil and all other Latin poets and moralists. Such fits of temper as occurred in Catullus as well as in Archilochus were openly autobiographical without any attempt at ethical rationalization. Seneca's *De Ira*, which Dante may have read, is an elaborate, nay, punctilious, argument against any justification whatsoever of any kind of anger. This tide, undoubtedly, may surge within a noble soul, battering the dykes of reason. The example to follow in such predicaments is offered by Socrates, who (as though he already had intuited the discoveries of Darwin and James on emotion and expression) when wrath swelled in his breast, lowered his voice and restrained his speech, thus starving the monster. Unbridled anger is barbaric; it belongs, Seneca says, to Germans and Scythians. From these and such other outcasts of culture decadent Romans learned it.

If Seneca had known the Jewish God, this thunderer without the Olympian catharsis of the reigning Zeus, he probably would have considered him as the product of a barbaric imagination. This could nowise be the point of view of a medieval Christian. Of hypotyposes of the furious God there was no scarcity in the Pentateuch, in the Prophets, in the Psalms, in Job, in nearly all the books of the old Testament; they were to a Christian of those times anything but myths. Had the new Covenant allayed the divine wrath and modified God? Is God modifiable? Cautiously, yet dangerously, Fathers of the Church and doctors approached the problem. Lactantius' treatise *De ira Dei*, the issues of which were exemplified in the same author's *De morte persecutorum*, is unlikely to have been familiar to Dante. He would have cherished it. Its point is that *qui non odit nec diligit*; hence the unbreakable tie of love and anger in the loving Christian God, to whom three affections and none more may and must be ascribed, namely, mercy, wrath, and pity. Augustine, more deeply impressed by classical philosophy, tried to square the circle by describing an undescribable anger of God, which does not inflame His mind, nor disturb His unchangeable tranquility. More safely, Aquinas, while stating that "in willing justice God wills punishment" (*Summa*, I, Q.19, A. 9) shuns the troubling issue of divine anger, too impure, perhaps, for his Pure Being.

But cold-minded punishment, or judicial aloofness—let alone the radiant laxity of the imperturbable deity which we shall meet some centuries later in Gothe's *Faust*—was inadequate to Dante, the most tragic of Christians. By a logic of the heart, which the logic of the mind does not know, the horror of eternal punishment, which orthodoxy forced him to admit, in turn forced him to postulate a proportionate passion of God, whose anger was the lightning of Justice. The tide of violence, first released from the mud of Styx, not only floods the cone of Hell. It besprinkles, and more than that, the slopes of Purgatory despite all hymns and rites to mansuetude. It mounts to

Heaven, where the saints, the blessed, are flushed with unani-
mous wrath as if—says Dante—the ruddy planet Mars and the
white planet Jove were birds and had changed their feathers
(a dazzling absurdity at which Boccaccio and Ariosto were slyly
to smile in their caricatures of the angels Gabriel and Michael
as boxers and bravoes), until it reaches, invisible but unmistakably present, the throne of God, its alleged source. Not
wrath alone, revengefulness is attributed to God, with its delight
in fulfillment postponed. "O my Lord, when shall I rejoice to
see thy vengeance, which, hidden, maketh sweet thine anger in
thy secret?" True, there is no throne of God in Dante. His God
has neither beard nor hand; a Point, the Point, metaphysical
and metamathematical, He is flawlessly above any residue of
anthropomorphism. Yet He is strongly anthropopathic, a hopeless contradiction, though it is with contradictions that poetry
lives or dies, and nothing is peculiar to those of Dante save their
magnitude.

Whatever, for the rest, he may have thought or felt of
God's wrath does not carry any validity of exoneration for
Dante's own. The prophets, in behalf of God, had used violence
of words rather than of deeds, and against living armed sinners,
not against helpless shades of the underworld. As a rule they had
been tortured, not torturers. Christ had known at times the
urge of indignation, not only when scourging the money-
changers. But apart from the superhuman character which any
faithful should have acknowledged in His exceptional anger, all
the weight of His teaching and doing reposes on meekness and
leniency. Lactantius, indeed, had granted to men a certain
amount of anger, adding the explanation, quite interesting to
a modern reader, that this passion, opening a natural, or, as
we would say, physiological outlet to the humors of the spleen,
cannot be taken as wholly sinful. This concession, however,
was made under the restriction that moral anger should never
grow inexorable and irreconcilable.

The most imperative authorities to whose judgment Dante
might have subjected the particular quality of his wrath were,
as usual, Aristotle in the *Nicomachean Ethics*, and Aquinas in
the *Summa*. Aristotle, whose assertions in this regard were to

be disputed by the radical negation of Seneca, bent somehow from the ordinary course of Greek feeling, also in this field adopting his cherished middle way. In respect of anger—the Aristotelian word for which is at any rate ὀϱγή and not Achilles' μῆνις—(ɪɪ, 7): "Here too there is excess, defect, and a mean state; but since they may be said to have really no proper names, as we call the virtuous character meek, we will call the mean state meekness" (Medieval Latin translators more appropriately rendered πϱᾶον and πϱαότητα with *mansuetus* and *mansuetudo*), "and of the extremes, let the man who is excessive be denominated Passionate, and the faulty state Passionateness, and him who is deficient Angerless, and the defect Angerlessness." The passage is expanded in Book ɪv, 5, where "the notion represented by the term 'meek man' is that of being imperturbable, and not of being led away by passion, but of being angry in that manner, and at those things, and for that length of time, which Reason may direct." This concept of a reasonable and managed anger, nay, of an anger unperturbed and "meek" or at least gentle and calm was developed and systemized in several passages of Aquinas, especially in *Prima Secunda*, Q. 46–48 and *Secunda Secundae* Q. 158. The gist of the discussion is that "si . . . aliquis irascitur secundum rationem rectam, tunc irasci est laudabile," but anger becomes a sin "si nimis ardenter irascatur interius, vel si nimis exterius manifestet signa irae" and a mortal sin "in illo casu in quo ira contrariatur charitati."

Clearly enough, neither Aristotle nor Aquinas, had they traveled in Hell, would have behaved with Filippi Argenti or Bocca degli Abati as Dante did. Agreement with the decrees of justice does not imply that he who agrees should add, while visiting a penitentiary, the crack of this extra whip to the punishment of the offenders, nor that he should otherwise volunteer for jobs which pertain to executioners upon the earth and to devils below. Dante's outbursts and violences, rather than under the Thomistic heading of *De Iracundia*, belong to the following: *De Crudelitate*.

Obviously enough, there is no ethical or theological level at which his wrath could meet poetic acquittal.

IV

Glimpses of biographical explanation appear in early commentators. We are told that there had been personal as well as political enmity between Dante and Argenti: a grudge, e.g., which had followed the fine assessed by Dante as a magistrate on the ruthless horseman, who, in his "hybris," had madly ridden through the city with legs apart. More surely, we know that a relative or brother of Filippo, Boccaccino degli Adimari, had taken hold of Dante's estate after the latter's exile. This is the information of which a recent interpreter, Giovanni Ferretti, takes most stock. It is at once explanatory and ennobling. By cursing Filippo, Dante wants to warn and intimidate the living brother, thus protecting as best he can his wife and children, whom he has left behind in cruel Florence. We are dealing with a horseman. We are warranted to use an old metaphor of horses and say that, according to the far-fetched hypothesis of this otherwise very stimulating interpreter, Dante is beating the saddle to beat the horse; or, as the Italians put it, he is talking to daughter-in-law in order that mother-in-law may listen.

One isolated early commentator suggested that the retortion is more direct. He assumes that once in his earthly life Filippo Argenti had actually slapped Dante in the face. Of course, we shall never find documentary evidence of this commentator's truthfulness or falsehood.

A story like this displeases the regular Dante scholar. Dante scholars usually are balanced, dignified, irreprehensible people. They feel as if Dante had been a Dante scholar.[1]

Such attitude was and is particularly striking in the endless dispute about the tenzone of insults between Dante and Forese Donati, the only stain in the pink and blue idealism of the poet's youth. When it proved impossible to throw away those evil sonnets as apocryphal stuff, Dante scholars ordinarily have clung to the opinion that they were clear fun, or mere training in the art of writing jocular verse.

They were no fun, no joke, as any unbiased reader must directly realize. They staged a real fight, in which Dante was the loser. His charges against Forese sound comparatively weak and vague. Forese's against Dante disclose, indeed, not that

Dante was an embezzler and barrator, but how and why it could happen that some years later Dante was sentenced in absentia for embezzlement and barratry, and perhaps also why he was to deal with barrators (*Inferno*, xxi and xxii) in that particular way, high-spirited, and yet half-consciously self-conscious. Above all—and this is what is pertinent to our topic—Forese hammers and hammers on Dante's cowardice. They are fighting, but one of the two mercilessly denies the opponent's fighting qualities, should they pass from words to deeds. Not only is Dante accused of neglecting to take revenge for some obscure shame upon his father's and his family's honor; more generally and conclusively he is pilloried as a coward. "Him who lavishly thrashes thee thou takest for brother and friend." These are Forese's final words, and we do not know of any Dantean retort. It seems as though he had shrunk back into his private Paradise. Conciliation—of a chivalric sort—comes much later, in the second canticle of the *Comedy*, when the two, meeting in the light of Eternity, make to each other equally allusive but equally generous apologies.

Whether in Dante's youth the propensity to endure abuse and injury was cowardice or piety is no real problem. Orphanhood, poverty, repression, and the insecurity of the rather lonesome déclassé living for long years on the margins of Florentine society combined with the radically Christian doctrine of Franciscan humility, turning the other cheek. As there is no reason for trusting blindly the commentator according to whom Filippo Argenti had slapped Dante in the face, there is no sufficient reason either for discarding indignantly whatever probability his statement may contain. Supposing that Dante really endured the outrage, he may have rationalized—or even justified—his behavior not only with words of Christ, but with the words, more unequivocal, of the Franciscan tradition which crowned as the friar of perfect bliss, of *perfetta letizia*, him who, left out in the cold, and affronted and struck and *dragged in the snow*, nevertheless unbeatably beaten, exults in the thought of the cross.

At any rate it would be inadequate to mark the difference between the first seven cantos of the *Inferno* and the Argenti scene as a change from an early attitude in the *Divine Comedy*

to a later one. It is much more than that. An undertow of re-
pressed ire ran before the beginning of the poem, through all
the *Vita Nuova*; Dante, enthralled in visionary meekness, constantly triumphed, a Franciscan lamb, over its suffocated
rumble. He did not mind the cruel mockery of the young ladies
and of Beatrice herself at the wedding party, he candidly pictured himself as the laughing stock of the Florentine girls, and
the strongly pre-Freudian interpretation of his dream in a lewd
sonnet of his friend Dante da Maiano proves, together with the
sonnets of the other friend Forese, how easy it was to scoff at
him and get away with it. "I say," he wrote, "that whenever
she [Beatrice] appeared in any place, in the hope of her marvelous salutation there no longer remained to me an enemy; nay,
a flame of charity possessed me, which made me pardon every
one who had done me wrong; and had any one at that time
questioned me of anything, my only answer would have been
'Love,' and my face would have been clothed with humility."
She "humbled him till he forgets all wrong." "Anger and pride
away before her fly."

Now pride and anger are unmistakably present, to remain,
however ably the latter may be surnamed disdain, and together
with them, most probably, is revengefulness, of the most personal and passionate kind. Even if it were possible, as it is not,
to explain the outburst on the base of Aristotelian or Thomistic
ethics, even if it were warranted to apply to the present case
St. Gregor's or Bishop Butler's eulogies of righteous anger and
to reject the unqualified disapproval uttered by Buddhism or
Tolstoyanism, the dubiousness of the moral issue would not
curtail by any means the significance of the emotional and
poetic change: a real conversion involving the whole of Dante's
personality. Whether or how much the conversion impinged
on Dante's actual behavior and how deep or superficial is the
historic foundation for the legends of *Dante furens*,[2] lies beyond
the boundaries of our present purpose, and we do know that
what Dante did to Argenti or Bocca degli Abati or Frate Alberigo he did not actually do but simply dream. Nevertheless his
psychic attitude became thoroughly different, and the pre-
Raphaelite poet of the sweet new style, whose work had extended
from the early poems to the seventh canto and whose provisory

masterpiece had been achieved in the Francesca scene, was superseded by the master of the grand and not seldom violent style, by the one who might be called the "Michelangelesque" Dante (only so to speak, since, as is obvious, elements of this kind came to Michelangelo largely through Dantean imitation), and who was and remains the Dantean Dante. In no other artist, before or after Dante, did the release of anger play such a part as in him,[3] and this passion appears as a decisive component in the structure of his originality. It is not surprising that, together with the inner proportion of feelings, his poetic taste and technique of expression also underwent a metamorphosis; the primitivist draftsman yielded to the Renaissance painter, with a stupendous increase of realistic color and dramatic power.

V

The long dispute about the dating of the *Divine Comedy* seems to be in a hopeless deadlock. The latest contribution, a weighty and brilliant book by Giovanni Ferretti on *I due tempi della composizione della Divina Commedia* (Bari, 1935),[4] was saluted by the leading Dantist Michele Barbi [5] with the most gratifying praises to its scholarship and shrewdness, and in the same breath with the curtest rejection of its conclusions, minimized, despite all toil, as sheer hypotheses.

This proves again that the external evidence in this problem is weak and crippled, and as such is bound to remain unless unpredictable miracles happen in unexplored archives.

Until that day, it is linguistic, metaphorical, psychological, and aesthetic analysis alone which can supply the internal evidence apt to tip the scales.

One instance may be taken from the famed invective to Madonna Pietra (Rime ciii). It starts with the line: "Cosí nel mio parlar voglio esser aspro." The similarity of this exordium with the first line of *Inferno* xxxii, "S'io avessi le rime aspre e chiocce," striking as it is, remains unconvicing as long as it remains isolated. But if, reading further in the canzone, we meet the image of the poet violently and well nigh sadistically catching the tresses of the woman, and reading further in *Inferno* xxxii we meet the same Dante tearing the locks of hair of

Bocca degli Abati, the second coincidence lifts more than geo-
metrically the meaning of the first, and the evidence that the
two compositions belong to the same period becomes almost
commanding.

Analogous results should be yielded by careful tests of the
tissue of Dante's poetry. And if the external evidence does not
irreparably conflict, the aesthetic-psychological analysis should
provide us with probability at a degree approaching certitude.

VI

The problem of the dating of the *Divine Comedy* is not
indeed a trivial one; so deep-going and wide-spread are its implications concerning the biography of a great poet, the meaning of a great monument, the history of an age, and our
intelligence—in general—of the poetic process.

What has been said about the release of anger in *Inferno*
VIII authorizes us, in the learned confusion of a dispute which
is aging without maturing, to propose for further investigation
the following scheme.

It is certain that between the seventh and the eighth canto
there is a gap, a stylistic and moral interval, which postulates
a decisive crisis of the personality with, most probably, an adequate interruption in time. It is quite possible that the first
seven cantos were composed on inspirations, plans, or even
sketches and drafts reaching as far back as Dante's Florentine
period, or even as far back as the *Vita Nuova* and "Donne che
avete intelletto d'amore." It is highly unlikely—and not on
account of Ciacco's prophecy alone—that they were written,
such as we have them now, in a past so remote. It might seem
plausible to place them sometime during the early stage of
Henry VII's expedition, when collaboration with the papacy and
a happy political outcome still appeared conceivable. This part
of the *Inferno*, extant before 1313, may suffice to explain the
mention of Dante's work in Francisco da Barberino, the so-
called Barberinian argument in favor of an early dating of the
Comedy.

It is little short of absurd to suppose that when Dante
wrote his epistle Amico Florentino, in 1315, he had finished the
Inferno, nay the *Purgatorio*. "Hocne meruit . . . sudor et labor

continuatus in studio? . . . Absit a viro phylosophie domestico
. . . Nonne dulcissimas veritates potero speculari ubique sub
celo?" Even if one grants what must be granted to his termi-
nology and poetics, it is clear, notwithstanding, that in the
epistle he speaks rather like a philosopher than a poet, as if the
Convivio still were in his opinion his greatest asset. Had he had
in hand the thirty-four cantos of the *Inferno,* nay, the sixty-seven
of the two first canticles, the poetic vaunt would hardly have
been avoided. It is not absurd to suppose that with the vanish-
ing of the last hope, the *Divine Comedy* really and at last began.
The epistle to the Florentine friend, which shatters all chance
of conciliation and return, strikes, for that matter, the same
string as the Argenti episode. "Absit a viro phylosophie domestico temeraria tantum cordis humilitas, . . . ut quasi vinc-
tus ipse se patiatur offerri." This seems to be the announcement
of the great wrath.

Now, all earthly hope and earthly love spent, with old age
and death at his heels, and on the other hand sheltered in more
comfortable hospitalities, he could ply his work, in the concentration and continuity without which the intensity of the result
would be nearly unthinkable. Thirteen hundred thirteen, the
year of Henry VII's failure and death, might be one of the op-
tional dates for the end of the Middle Ages, and not the least
fitting of all, since thenceforth all planning for the world unity
of Church and Empire was to be mere daydream.[6] In the wake
of that catastrophe Dante writes his book, and dies. The *Divine
Comedy* is the swan-song of the Middle Ages.

VII

Thus, in irretrievable defeat and unbending poetic self-
justice, the Argenti episode is the Dantean "Fluch vor allem
der Geduld." A physician of our time would say, perhaps, that
a powerful release of adrenalin has balanced a morbid personality and completed its frame.

Not that pity or even morbidity disappear. The old Dante
lives forth, but bridled and spurred at once by the new. The
Comedy, essentially a tragedy, is made of pity and terror; but
Dante, medievally extreme, was unable to even the two elements in the continuous harmony of classical poetry. Hence,

one excess was counterpoised by the other; utmost humility
and tremor by utmost anger and pride, according to the gothic
technique, which does not tame the opposing stresses of the
material in the straight line or soothe them in the round arch,
but frankly avows them, baring the struggle. The eighth canto
itself, half outburst against the damned, half fear of the devils
forbidding the entrance to Dis, is perfectly a pointed arch.

Pride soars on the wings of wrath. Almost stooping, Dante
had said: "Io non Enea, io non Paolo sono." Now suddenly he
promotes himself to justiciar and helper of God's wrath: God-
like. His Dies Irae has dawned. Vergil's salutation, borrowed
from the Ave Maria: "blessed be she that bore thee" hints, unaware of sacrilege, at a symbolic equalization of Dante with
Christ, and the canto is not closed ere a replica is more than
sketched in the scene of the devils defending the gates of Hell
against the intruder who, Christ-like, will vanquish them.

However dangerous, the allotropy in pride and anger now
has lifted Dante to the height of his power. It is no political or
sacerdotal power; neither will he rebuild the Empire or reform
the Church. But he has acquired the inner freedom in plenitude
which we call poetic genius.

Notes

1 E.g., Barbi, *Studi Danteschi*, ix, p. 130: "Possibile tanta viltà in
un'anima di quella tempra?" Or Zingarelli, *Dante*, p. 919, apropos of the
Argenti episode: "Chi crede che egli sfogasse una vendetta personale non
può onestamente conciliarlo con la lode di Virgilio, e la serietà del Poeta,
che non avrebbe esposto la sua opera, facendola strumento di privati
rancori, al sospetto e discredito, e distrutto ogni buon effetto."

2 See them perspicuously collected by Hayward Keniston, *The Dante
Tradition in the XIV and XV Centuries*, in the Report of the Dante
Society (Cambridge, Mass., 1915).

3 The example of the "harsh rhymes" in troubadouric poetry may lie
behind such exertions as the Dantean Sordello's invective; but, strictly
conventional and oratorical as they are, they hardly offer a significant
precedent for a passional upheaval involving all the personality of a great
poet.

4 He had been preceded by Henri Hauvette, *Etudes sur la D.C.: la
composition du poème et son rayonnement* (Paris, 1922), and Hauvette
in turn by Constanza Agostini, *Il racconto del Boccaccio e i primi sette
canti della Commedia* (1908): a forerunner who, like so many others,
had passed either unheeded or minimized. A valuable contribution to the
problem of the date is in Luigi Pietrobono, *Saggi Danteschi*, (Rome, 1936)

"Sulla data di composizione della *D.C.*," pp. 185–220, which essay, however, had been written several years before Ferretti's book.

5 *Studi Danteschi*, xix, 172 f.

6 As 1313 seems to be the most significant date for the end of the Middle Ages, 313, the date of the Edict of Milan, which established the world-unity of Empire and Church, might be adopted for their beginning. The Middle Ages would be contained in a span of exactly one thousand years, while the Classical Age from the Trojan War to Constantine the Great would comprise approximately fifteen hundred years, and the third age—or Revival, or Transition, or Era of the Nations —would run for exactly six hundred years, from the failure of Henry VII and the real Hegira of Dante to the eve of the World War. The symmetry of the figures would be countenanced in this case by their appropriateness to the decisive features of the epochs concerned.

13 · Voices of the Divine Comedy

I

The dramatic power of the Divine Comedy is due largely to Dante's extensive and masterly use of direct discourse: more than half of the more than fourteen thousand lines of the poem are spoken.[1]

There are in all more than eight hundred passages that are in direct discourse. They vary greatly in length, but they are predominantly very short, their brevity contributing greatly to the total dramatic effect. Nearly a hundred are less than a full line in length; nearly half of them all are less than three lines in length; and only about twenty-five are over fifty lines in length.[2]

The number of spoken passages of less than a full line in length is very striking, as is the number of those that are less than a full tercet in length. Most of the half-line passages are questions, or replies thereto, or exclamations. Many of them consist of three words or less. The passage length that occurs most frequently is that of two and a half lines: these passages are introduced, typically, by a half line that is not spoken, followed by the rest of the tercet as spoken, as in the case of *Inf.* III 76–78:

> And he to me: "The things shall be known to thee, when
> we stay our steps upon the joyless strand of Acheron."

Reprinted by permission from *The Seventy-Ninth Annual Report of the Dante Society of America*, published by the Dante Society of America in 1961.

Similarly, the many passages consisting of five and a half lines are introduced, typically, by a half line that is not spoken, followed by the rest of the two tercets (there are five cases in *Inf.* VI).

The great majority of all the spoken passages, whatever their length, begin in the middle of a line, after an introductory phrase: the procedure is frequently varied, however, by placing the first spoken words at the beginning of a line, and following them by explanatory words that are not spoken. Nearly all spoken passages end at the end of a line; but there are a very few cases in which the end of a spoken passage is carried over to the beginning of a new line (as in *Inf.* VIII 73).

The hundred cantos of the poem vary greatly in the amount of spoken material that they contain. No canto is entirely without spoken lines, but there are a few in which the number of spoken lines is twenty or less. There are twenty-five cantos in which the number of spoken lines is over a hundred.

Dante, Vergil, and Beatrice of course speak very often. Well over a hundred other individuals speak once or twice or oftener in a single canto or in two or more successive cantos, and then recede into memory; and a considerable number of larger or smaller groups of persons speak in virtual unison.

Brief spoken passages are often combined to form a continuous or virtually continuous series of verbal exchanges of various kinds. The longest such series are that in *Purg.* XVI, containing eleven passages spoken by Dante and Marco Lombardo, that in *Purg.* XXI, containing twelve passages spoken by Statius, Vergil, and Dante, and that in *Par.* XXIV, containing fifteen passages spoken by St. Peter and Dante.

In a dozen cases the speaker quotes words previously spoken by himself or someone else. The most remarkable of these cases is the first, in *Inf.* II, in which Vergil quotes Beatrice, who quotes Mary and Lucia. Other notable cases occur in *Inf.* XVII, XXVI, XXVII, and XXXIII and in *Purg.* V and IX.

Linguistic variation is attained by the use of occasional lines in Latin, such as Pope Hadrian's

> Scias quod ego fui successor Petri,

or Arnaut Daniel's several lines in Provençal, or the unintelligible utterances of Pluto and Nimrod.

The spoken passages vary marvellously in tone and temper, and in their effect upon the persons to whom they are addressed.

Dante contrives, furthermore, to make his readers aware that a great many words were spoken in the course of his journey in addition to those that he quotes as spoken. References to such additional words occur, for instance, in *Inf.* XXI and *Purg.* VI.

Certain differences between the *Inferno* and the *Purgatorio* on the one hand and the *Paradiso* on the other may be noted briefly. In each of the first two *cantiche* the number of lines that are spoken is a little less than half of the total number of lines in the *cantica:* in the *Paradiso* considerably more than half of all the lines are spoken. In each of the first two *cantiche* the number of spoken passages is about three hundred and fifty: in the *Paradiso* it is about one hundred and fifty. In each of the first two *cantiche* the spoken passages average about six lines in length: in the *Paradiso* they average about twenty lines in length. In each of the first two *cantiche* the number of individual speakers is somewhat more than fifty: in the *Paradiso* it is less than twenty.

Dante of course had ample precedent in the *Aeneid* for the extensive use of direct discourse; but Dante's use is more extensive and much more dramatic than Vergil's. More than half of the lines of the Comedy are spoken; of the roughly ten thousand lines of the *Aeneid* less than half are spoken (even if one includes in the count the 1500-line narrative of Aeneas that fill Books II and III). There are about eight hundred passages of direct discourse in the Comedy, as against less than three hundred in the *Aeneid*. Nearly a hundred of the spoken passages of the Comedy are of less than a full line in length: there are only two such lines (V 166 and VII 116) in the *Aeneid*. Nearly half of all the spoken passages of the Comedy are of less than three lines in length: less than fifty of all the spoken lines of the *Aeneid* are of such brevity.

II

Supplementary, in dramatic effect, to the passages that are spoken by persons of the Comedy are certain other vocal passages that are not so spoken: the mysterious voices suggested or heard in Purgatorial circles, and, more particularly, the voices that are heard not in speech but in song.

Nearly all of the singing heard in the poem is the singing of familiar psalms or hymns, or of beatitudes or other scriptural verses; and in such cases Dante, even when intending his readers to understand that the psalm or hymn or verse is to be sung in its entirety, gives in his text only its opening line or half line.

In the first such case his intention is made perfectly clear. As the angelic vessel bearing "più di cento spirti" approaches the shore of purgatory,

> "*In exitu Israel de Aegypto*," sang they all together with one voice, with what of that psalm is thereafter written.

That the song is to be heard in its entirety is made explicit in *Purg*. VIII 16–17 and XXV 127, and is clearly implied in other cases. In one case, however, *Purg*. XXX 83–84, we are told that only the first part of a hymn was sung.

So also when Casella sings Dante's own *canzone*,

> "*Love that in my mind discourseth to me*,"

he certainly sings the whole *canzone*, and not only its first line, which alone appears in the text of the poem.

Even when beatitudes or other scriptural verses are sung Dante gives only their opening words.

The only passages in which the text appears to give all that is sung are the three lines sung by Justinian at the opening of *Par*. VII and the six lines that are sung in *Purg*. XXXI by four nymphs who represent the cardinal virtues.

The singing is nearly always in Latin. The only cases in which it is entirely in Italian are the case just mentioned and Casella's singing of the *canzone*. There are two cases, *Purg*. XV 38–39 and XXIX 85–87, in which Latin and Italian both appear. The implication of *Par*. XXIV 113,

> God *we praise* rang through the spheres,

is not that the *Te Deum* (already sung in Latin in *Purg*. IX) was here sung in Italian, but simply that there was a singing of that hymn (certainly in its Latin form). Similarly, Dante certainly thought of the *Gloria patri* as sung in Latin (in *Par*. XXVII).

In almost all cases the singing is choral, not individual. The only persons who sing as individuals are Casella, the spirit, presently joined by others, who begins the *Te lucis ante* in *Purg.* VIII, some of the angelic guardians, Matelda, the singer of *Purg.* XXX 11, Piccarda, and Justinian. Four nymphs sing together in *Purg.* XXXI; three nymphs sing together later in the same canto; and the two groups sing alternately in Canto XXXIII. In all other cases the singing is by large groups: "più di cento spirti" in the first case. The final "gloria!" is sung by the entire host of the redeemed.

Still other vocal sounds are to be heard in the poem: the "sospiri, pianti e alti guai" that are heard immediately on entrance through the gate of Hell, and repeatedly thereafter. The entire pit is called a

> dolorous Valley of the Abyss, which gathers thunder of endless wailings.

The sound of sighing is characteristic of the Limbus in particular. Paolo weeps so bitterly that Dante faints from pity. In the sixth circle of the Purgatory song and weeping mingle:

> in tears and song was heard: "*Labia mea Domine*," in such manner that it gave birth to joy and grief.

There is no singing in the *Inferno,* and no weeping in the *Paradiso.*

III

I venture finally to suggest that any group of students of the Divine Comedy may derive pleasure and gain understanding through a cooperative reading of spoken passages from the poem. A program consisting of such reading was designed for use in the 1959 Annual Meeting of the Dante Society of America; and it is the impressiveness of that program that has led me to make the present suggestion. In such a program some one member of the group reads words spoken by some one person of the Comedy; another member of the group reads words spoken by some other person of the Comedy; and so on. No words of the Comedy that are not spoken are read. If the group is large, or if some of its members are relatively unfamiliar with the Comedy, one member of the group may well serve as leader, providing brief introductory or linking statements as may seem advisable. Desirably, each reader should read his or her part as if being in fact the person whom he or she represents. It is possible that such a program would be successful even if the reading were done in a good translation.

A copy of the program used in the meeting of 1959 is given herewith, by way of making the suggested plan more definite. Variations would naturally be called for in order to adapt it for use by any other group. The reading of this particular program took a little less than an hour.

Inferno I
Leader: The first voice heard in the Divine Comedy is that of a man in dire peril, to whom a rescuer appears.
Dante: 65 (omitting *gridai a lui*)—66.
Vergil: 67 (beginning *Non*)—78.
Dante: 79–80 and 82–90.
Vergil: 91, 93, and 112–123.
Dante: 130 (beginning *Poeta*)—135.

Inferno II
Leader: The first words spoken by Beatrice had been spoken to Vergil, urging him to rescue Dante.
Beatrice: 58–74.

Inferno V
Leader: In the Second Circle Dante beholds a host of spirits swept through the air, among them two who go together.
Dante: 73 (beginning *Poeta*)—75.
Vergil: 76 (beginning *Vedrai*)—78.
Dante: 80 (beginning *O*)—81.
Francesca: 88–107.
Vergil: 111 (only the words *Che pense?*).
Dante to Vergil: 112 (beginning *O*)—114.
Dante to Francesca: 116 (beginning *Francesca*)—120.
Francesca: 121 (beginning *Nessun*)—138.

Inferno X
Leader: In the Sixth Circle a spirit rises in his burning tomb.
Farinata: 22–27.
Vergil: 31 (beginning *Volgiti*)–33 and 39 (beginning *le*).
Farinata: 42 (beginning *Chi*).
Leader: After Dante's reply, Farinata says:
Farinata: 46 (beginning *Fieramente*)—48.
Dante: 49–51 (omitting *rispuosi lui*).

Leader: At this moment a spirit rises beside Farinata.
Cavalcanti: 58 (beginning *Se*)—60.
Dante: 61 (beginning *Da*)—63.
Cavalcanti: 67 (beginning *Come*)—69.
Leader: Cavalcanti sinks out of sight, and Farinata resumes.
Farinata: 77 (omitting *disse*)—84.
Dante: 85 (beginning *Lo*)—87.
Farinata: 89 (omitting *disse*)—93.

Inferno XXVI
Leader: In the Eighth Circle, in response to a request from
Vergil, Ulysses tells his story.
Ulysses: 90 (beginning *Quando*)—142.

Inferno XXXII–XXXIII
Leader: In the ice of the Ninth Circle Dante sees a spirit
gnawing another's head.
Dante: XXXII 133–139 (omitting *diss'io*).
Ugolino: XXXIII 4 (beginning *Tu*)—75.

Purgatorio V
Leader: On the lower slopes of the Mountain of Purgatory
several spirits desire to speak with Dante, among them
Buonconte, who in response to a question from Dante
tells the story of his death.
Buonconte: 94 (omitting *rispuos'elli*)—129.
Leader: Then another spirit speaks.
Pia: 130–131 and 133–136.

Purgatorio XXVI
Leader: Among the spirits on the Eighth Ledge is a Proven-
çal poet who speaks in his own tongue.
Arnaut: 140–147.

Purgatorio XXVII
Leader: The last words spoken by Vergil are these:
Vergil: 127 (beginning *Il*)—142.

Purgatorio XXX and XXXI
Leader: Beatrice has appeared; but before Dante may attain
felicity there must be indictment and confession.
Beatrice: XXX 55–57 and (after a brief pause) 73–75.
Leader: Indictment follows, and Dante is bidden to confess.
Beatrice: XXXI 1 and 5–6 and (after a brief pause) 10 (begin-
ning *Che*)—12.
Dante: XXXI 14 (the one word *sì*).

Paradiso III
Leader: Among the spirits faintly visible in the Heaven of
the Moon is one to whom Dante speaks.

Dante: 37–41.
Piccarda: 43–51.
Dante: 58 (beginning *Ne'*)—66.
Piccarda: 70–72 and 82–87.

Paradiso XVIII

Leader: Among the words spoken by Beatrice to Dante are these:
Batrice: 5 (beginning *Muta*)–6 and (after a brief pause) 20 (beginning V*olgiti*)—21.

Paradiso XXXI

Leader: In the Empyrean Dante turns to speak to Beatrice, but finds that she has been replaced by a venerable spirit, St. Bernard.
Dante: 64 (only *Ov' è ella?*).
St. Bernard: 65 (beginning A)—69.
Leader: Dante then looks upward toward Beatrice, and speaks his last words to her.
Dante: 79–90.
Leader: From afar Beatrice bestows a last smile on Dante; and St. Bernard speaks again.
St. Bernard: 94 (beginning *Acciò*)–102 (omitting *disse* in 95) and 112–117 (omitting *cominciò elli*).

Paradiso XXXIII

Leader: The last words spoken in the poem are those spoken by St. Bernard on behalf of Dante.
St. Bernard: 1–39.

Notes

1 The Comedy contains 14,183 lines, of which, by my count, 7,532½ are spoken. Many lines are in part spoken and in part not spoken (as for instance *Inf.* I 65 and 67): I have counted each such line as a half line, regardless of the exact proportions of its two parts. I have not counted as spoken lines the instances of the *visibile parlare* of the first Purgatorial circle, or the disembodied voices of the second and sixth circles, or voices heard in dreams, or thoughts formulated but not uttered, or lines that are sung rather than spoken.

2 The exact figures, if my count is correct, are as follows:

Lines	Passages	Lines	Passages
½	97	11–20½	95
1, 1½, and 2	116	21–30	26
2½	168	31–50½	27
3–5	88	51–75	15
5½	86	76–100	5
6–10	111	101–142	7

Charles Speroni

14· Dante's Prophetic Morning-Dreams

IN THE *Divine Comedy* Dante makes reference to two sorts of prophetic dreams: (1) the prophetic dream of the pregnant mother, and (2) the prophetic morning-dream. The former has been thoroughly investigated by Francesco Lanzoni.[1] Since the subject of the prophetic dream has not received the attention it deserves,[2] the present article is an attempt to explore the subject in greater detail and thus show how interesting and widespread is the folklore of the morning-dream.

Dante alludes five times to the morning-dream in the *Divine Comedy*. Twice in the *Inferno:* in the invective against Florence at the beginning of the canto of Ulysses:

> But if the truth is dreamed of near the morning, thou shalt feel ere long what Prato, not to speak of others, craves for thee.[3]

and in the episode of Count Ugolino:

> when I slept the evil sleep that rent for me the curtain of the future.

> When I awoke before the dawn, I heard my sons who were with me, weeping in their sleep, and asking for bread.

> They were now awake, and the hour approaching at which our food used to be brought us, and each was anxious from his dream.[4]

Reprinted from *Studies in Philology* (XLV, 1, 1948) by permission of the University of North Carolina Press. Copyright 1948 by the University of North Carolina Press.

Three times in the *Purgatorio*: in the description of the Poet's awakening at the door of Purgatory:

> At the hour when the swallow begins her sad lays nigh unto the morn, perchance in memory of her former woes,
>   and when our mind, more of a wanderer from the flesh and less prisoned by thoughts, in its visions is almost prophetic;
> in a dream methought. . . .[5]

in the dream of the "femmina balba":

> In the hour when the day's heat, overcome by Earth or at times by Saturn, can no more warm the cold of the moon;
>   when the geomancers see their Fortuna Major, rising in the East, before the dawn, by a way which short time remains dark to it,
> there came to me in a dream, a stuttering woman,[6]

and, finally, in the beautiful dream Dante has of Leah:

> As I was thus ruminating, and thus gazing at them, sleep fell on me, sleep which oft doth know the news ere the fact come to pass.
>   In the hour, methinks, when Cytherea, who seemeth ever burning with fire of love, first beamed from the east on the mount,
>   meseemed to behold in a dream, a lady, young and fair. . . .[7]

We see then that Dante has a morning-dream at the end of each of the three nights he spends in Purgatory. The poet also refers to a morning-dream in the first sonnet of his *Vita Nuova*: "*Già eran quasi che atterzate l'ore / del tempo che onne stella n'è lucente, / quando m'apparve Amor subitamente.*" We gather from the prose commentary to this sonnet that the dream came true: "*Lo verace giudicio del detto sogno non fue veduto allora per alcuno, ma ora è manifestissimo a li più semplici.*"

There seems to be no doubt that Dante really believed in the prophetic quality of morning-dreams. Actually, in the first of the three passages from *Purgatorio* the Poet goes so far as to try to explain why morning-dreams are prophetic: "*presso a la mattina . . . la mente nostra, peregrina / più da la carne e men da'pensier presa, / a le sue vision quasi è divina.*"

The fact that Dante's belief in divination by morning-dreams seems firmly established—a point further proved by an oft-quoted passage in the *Convivio* [8]—, poses the question as to how far back this belief can be traced. Other questions of interest to the scholar are: Was Dante influenced by earlier writers? Are there other references to this belief in literature? and Is this belief still alive?

Judging by the numerous references to prophetic dreams which we find in the Bible, in the books of the Chaldeans and of the Egyptians, in the sagas of northern Europe, in Greek and Roman literature, etc., divination is as old as the world. To quote from A. Bouché-Leclercq's well-known work *Histoire de la divination dans l'antiquité:* [9] *"il n'est point de peuple et, dans l'antiquité, presque point d'individus qui n'aient cru à une révélation divine par les songes."* Indeed, so great was the importance attached by the ancients to dreams, that many technical treatises were written on the interpretation of dreams, and numerous people made a profession of the interpretation of dreams. Typical of the ancient treatises on dreams and their interpretation is Artemidorus' *Onirocritica*, a work which became so popular as to obscure the names of its predecessors. [10] It must be said at once that Artemidorus does not mention morning-dreams. [11] However, morning-dreams *were* considered prophetic in antiquity, as some well-known writers unmistakably indicate. These writers are: Moschus:

> Εὐρώπῃ ποτὲ Κύπρις ἐπὶ γλυκὺν ἧκεν ὄνειρον
> νυκτὸς ὅτε τρίτατον λάχος ἵσταται, ἐγγύθι δ' ἠώς,
> ὕπνος ὅτε γλυκίων μέλιτος βλεφάροισιν ἐφίζων
> λυσιμελὴς πεδάᾳ μαλακῷ κατὰ φάεα δεσμῷ,
> εὖτε καὶ ἀτρεκέων ποιμαίνεται ἔθνος ὀνείρων. [12]

Horace:

> Vetuit me tali voce Quirinus,
> Post mediam noctem visus, cum somnia vera. [13]

Ovid:

> Namque sub aurora, iam dormitante lucerna,
> Somnia quo cerni tempore vera solent. [14]

Philostratus the Elder:

οἱ γοῦν ἐξηγηταὶ τῶν ὄψεων, οὓς ὀνειροπόλους οἱ ποιηταὶ
καλοῦσιν, οὐκ ἂν ὑποκρίνοιντο ὄψιν οὐδεμίαν μὴ πρότερον
ἐρόμενοι τὸν καιρόν, ἐν ᾧ εἶδεν. ἂν μὲν γὰρ ἑῷος ἦ καὶ τοῦ
περὶ τὸν ὄρθρον ὕπνον, ξυμβάλλονται αὐτὴν ὡς ὑγιῶς
μαντευομένης τῆς ψυχῆς.[15]

And Tertullian:

> Certiora et colatiora [= clariora] somniari
> affirmant sub extimis noctibus, quasi iam
> emergente animarum vigorem, prodacto sopore.[16]

These five seem to be the only clear-cut references to
morning-dreams to be found in classical writers, but they are
undoubtedly sufficient to establish that the ancient Greeks and
Romans were well acquainted with the value of morning-
dreams.[17] Just how wide-spread and deep-rooted this belief was,
however, is impossible to say. It certainly is odd that such technical writers on dreams as Aristotle, Artemidorus, and Cicero
have nothing to say about this particular kind of dream.

We note that Christianity during the Middle Ages had
inherited many of the beliefs and practices of classical antiquity,
and among these not an inconspicuous place was occupied by
divination. In the Middle Ages the church condemned most
arts of divination as the work of demons; it admitted, however,
divination by dreams, as long as dreams had the character of
divine inspiration.[18] In other words, the *somnium naturale* had
little, if any, significance, whereas the *somnium coeleste* always
had some significance.[19] Thus, Saint Thomas Aquinas believed
—and he had the authority of the Bible [20]—that men are
instructed by God in dreams, and that divination by dreams is
lawful.[21] Albertus Magnus believed that certain dreams are
prophetic, and he had the testimony of experience to prove it.[22]
There is a passage in one of Albertus Magnus' works that is of
very great interest to the student of Dante and of morning-
dreams:

> illae quidem imaginationes ad organum sensus
> communis deferuntur et per eosdem futuros
> effectus ad quos disponunt coelestes motus advertere
> possunt praecipue si ab occupationibus quieti fuerint
> et carnis deliciis . . . Et ideo huiusmodi praecipue
> sentiuntur in dormiendo et maxime in nocte et
> circam horam digestionis completae.[23]

After reading this explanation, especially if one bears in mind how well acquainted Dante was with the works of Albertus Magnus, one cannot but wonder whether Dante had it in mind when he wrote the passage in *Purgatorio* IX, 13–18.[24] At any rate, Albertus Magnus was not entirely original in his explanation; for, before him, not only had Gregory the Great said that certain dreams can be accounted for by a full or empty stomach,[25] but already as early as Plato [26] the conclusion had been reached that the state of the physical organism during sleep is very important in divination by dreams, and that whereas temperance produces clear and divine dreams, excess in food and drink produces untrustworthy ones.[27]

Close to Dante's time, Michael Scot also wrote about morning-dreams. According to him, a dream which occurs before digestion has started, either has no significance, or has to do with the past. A dream which comes during digestion has to do with the present, while a dream occurring after digestion concerns the future.[28]

After Dante's time, we encounter several references to the morning-dream in Italian literature. In his *Trattato de' sogni* Passavanti—although he himself did not have any faith in such dreams—gives us what we might call a "time-table" of prophetic dreams, and from his comment, we are led to conclude that the belief was popular in his day:

> dicono che 'l sogno fatto dalla prima ora della notte infino alla terza ha il suo tempo infra'l quale dee intervenire quello che significa: venti anni, venti mesi, o venti settimane, o venti dì, o venti ore. Il sogno fatto dalla terza ora insino alla sesta, verificherà la sua interpretazione infra quindici anni, o, il più che si possa indugiare, infino a diciessette. Quello sogno che si fa dalla sesta ora della notte infino alla nona, si compierà sua interpretazione ne' quattro o ne' cinque anni. Il sogno che si sogna dalla nona ora della notte insino al principio dell'aurora, dicono che si dee compiere insino a uno anno, o sei mesi o tre, o 'nfra 'l termine di dieci dì. E questi sogni, che si fanno intorno all'alba del dì, secondo che dicono, sono i più veri sogni che si facciano, e che meglio si possono interpretare le loro significazioni.[29]

Petrarch referred to a morning-dream in one of his *Triumphs*. In the night following the day of her death, Laura appears at dawn to the poet in a dream, and tells him that death is frightful to the wicked, but sweet to the good:

> *La notte che seguì l'orribil caso*
> *che spense il sole, anzi 'l ripose in cielo,*
> *di ch'io son qui come uom cieco rimaso,*
> *spargea per l'aere il dolce estivo gelo,*
> *che con la bianca amica di Titone*
> *suol da' sogni confusi tôrre il velo.*[30]

In Frezzi's *Quadriregio* [31] the author, just before dawn, dreams that the nymph Jonia, who has promised him her love, is lying with a faun; when he awakens, he starts through the woods and finds that his dream was, alas, too true.

In Trissino's *Sofonisba* we read:

> *Appresso un duro sogno mi spaventa*
> *Ch'io vidi innanzi l'apparir dell'alba.*[32]

In Aretino's *L'Ipocrito:*

> *I sogni, che presso al dì ho sopra ciò fatti,*
> *mi inducono a creder ogni mio sinistro.*[33]

And at the beginning of Monti's poem *I ritratti dei quattro Poeti:*

> *Nell'ora che più l'alma è pellegrina*
> *Dei sensi, e meno delle cure ancella*
> *Segue i sogni che il raggio odian del sole. . . .*[34]

But references to prophetic dreams occurring in the morning are not wanting in other literatures. In early Spanish literature, for example, the morning-dream is to be found not only in the *Crónica General escrita en 1344* and, as one might expect, in Lope de Barrientos' *Tractado del dormir é despertar*, but also in other works.[35] And in English literature, besides Michael Bruce, who speaks of morning-dreams in his well-known *Elegy Written in Spring*:

> Oft morning-dreams presage approaching fate,
> And morning-dreams, as poets tell, are true,

other writers have hinted at the belief: Dryden (*Cock and Fox*, 205), Pope (*Temple of Fame*, 7), Tennyson (*Morte d'Arthur*, 341), etc.[36] In England, moreover, there seems to be this saying: "Dreams at night are the devil's delight; dreams in the morning are the angel's warning." [37]

Like many another bit of folklore, the popular belief in the morning-dream is not confined to the descendants of the Greeks and Romans, or even to Europe. In fact, one finds it also in Asia and Africa. In Somadeva's *Kathā Sarit Sāgara*, for instance, Naravāhanadatta, son of the King of Vatsa, dreams before daybreak that his father is being dragged away by a black female toward the southern quarter. He awakens, and the personification of Science, Prajnapti, informs him about the death of his father.[38] For the Hindus the moment of accomplishment of morning-dreams depends on the hour at which the dream occurs: a dream in the first watch of the night takes a year to come true; one in the second watch, six months; one in the third watch, three months; one in the fourth watch, one month . . . while if the dream occurs at sunrise, immediate fulfillment will result.[39]

Like the pre-Islamic Arabs, Mohammed was a believer in dreams; among his sayings is the following: "The truest dream is the one which you have about daybreak." [40] In view of this statement by the Prophet, it is not surprising to read that the Arabs still believe in morning-dreams: "*Les onéirocritiques arabes sont d'accord pour reconnaître comme les plus véridiques les songes que l'on a au point du jour; l'observation scientifique montre, du reste, que ce sont les songes précédant le réveil qui sont les plus nets.*" [41] The Berbers of North Africa agree about morning-dreams, but for prophetic dreams they find that the Spring is the most propitious season.[42]

The belief in the morning-dream has remained alive in Europe also.[43] We must add, however, that this belief is not, and probably never was, one of the most popular. The people who still believe in divination by dreams seem more concerned with the interpretation of what they dream than with the time when the dream occurs.

Dante, as we said, in all probability believed in the early morning-dream. In fact, not only was his belief shared by many of his contemporaries, but he found it confirmed by some of his favorite authors, and, what was even more important, it could be explained rationally:

> . . . *la mente nostra, peregrina*
> *più da la carne e men da' pensier presa,*
> *a le sue vision quasi è divina.*

Notes

1 "*Il sogno presago della madre incinta nella letteratura medievale e antica,*" *Analecta Bollandiana*, XLV (1927), 225–261. In this article I do not intend to deal with the morning-dream in as thorough a manner as Lanzoni does for the dream of the pregnant mother. In view of the richness and the complexity of the topic, the material presented here is bound to be of an elementary and introductory nature.

2 N. Busetto's long article "*Il sonno, i sogni e le visioni*" (*Giornale Dantesco*, XIII [1905], 143–155), deals mainly with "*i sogni secondo la dottrina di Dante e degli Scolastici,*" and is a psychological investigation. Some attention is devoted to morning-dreams by F. D'Ovidio in his *Nuovi Studi Danteschi. Il Purgatorio e il suo Preludio* (Milan: Hoepli, 1906), pp. 526–8. Commentators such as Scartazzini, Fraticelli, Casini, etc., because of the nature of their work, usually limit themselves to a few remarks and to the well-known quotations from Ovid and Horace.

3 *Inf.* XXVI, 7–9. Here and elsewhere I quote from *Le opere di Dante*. Testo critico della Società Dantesca Italiana (Florence: Bemporad, 1921).

4 *Inf.* XXXIII, 26–27, 37–39, 43–45.

5 *Purg.* IX, 13–19.

6 *Purg.* XIX, 1–7.

7 *Purg.* XXVII, 91–98.

8 II, 9: "*Ancora, vedemo continua esperienza de la nostra immortalitade ne le divinazioni de' nostri sogni, le quali essere non potrebbono se in noi alcuna parte immortale non fosse.*"

9 Paris, Leroux, 1879–1882, I, p. 278. Cf. also Hastings, *Encyclop. of Rel. and Ethics*, Vol. V (1920), pp. 30–32, 33–40 sub "dreams"; A. Maury, *La magie et l'astrologie dans l'antiquité et au moyen âge*, Paris, 1860, pp. 229 ff.; and Ersilia Caetani Lovatelli, "I sogni e l'ipnotismo nel mondo antico," *Nuova Antologia*, XXIV (1889), 445–464. The literature on the subject is, of course, extensive.

10 It seems that no fewer than twenty-six such handbooks on the interpretation of dreams were put together in classical antiquity: Artemidorus' work is the only one extant. Cf. J. B. Stearns, *Studies of the Dream as a Technical Device in Latin Epic and Drama* (Lancaster, 1927), Introduction. The reader is referred to Bouché-Leclercq, *op. cit.*, and to B. Büchsenschütz, *Traum und Traumdeutung im Alterthume* (Berlin, 1868).

11 A French translator of the *Onirocritica* did say something about morning-dreams which is interesting enough to quote: "Concerning the time and houre when dreams of importance appeare, I should be of Ouids opinion, that it is about the breake of day, or after midnight. For till about midnight, all the senses, and corporall powers are occupied in digesting the supper which lasteth with some more, with others lesse time according to the strength, or weaknesse, heate, or coldnesse of the stomack, and all this while, the spirit can haue no leasure to accomplish great matters, during the impediment, and trauaile of the digestion. But the digestion

being made, and the senses at rest, the Soule which alwaies watcheth, labouring more easily faigneth, fashioneth, and representeth marueilous thinges for the honour or safety of his host the body: shewing him in a mirrour, certaine forms, figures, & kindes of visions both of good, and euil, past or to come." Cf. " 'The Epistle Dedicatory' The French Translator to his friend, a gentleman of good account," in The IVDGEMENT, or exposition of Dreames, Written by Artimodorus, an Auntient and famous Author, first in Greeke, then Translated into Latin, After into French, and now into English, London, 1606.

12 Idyls ii, 1–5. Cf. Theocritus, Bion and Moschus. Rendered into English Prose by A. Lang (London: Macmillan, 1880):

To Europa, once on a time, a sweet dream was sent by Cypris, when the third watch of the night sets in, and near is the dawning; when sleep more sweet than honey rests on the eyelids, limb-loosening sleep, that binds the eyes with his soft bond, when the flock of truthful dreams fares wandering.

13 Sat. I, x, 32 f.

14 Heroides xix, 195 f.

15 II, 37. Cf. Life and Times of Apollonius of Tyana. Rendered into English from the Greek by C. P. Eells (Stanford Univ., 1923):

For this reason those men who explain dreams, whom the poets call interpreters of visions, will not attempt to explain any vision before inquiring at what time it appeared. If it was seen early in the morning, in the sleep toward dawn, their conclusion is that it was the forecast of a clarified mind.

16 De anima 48. In all probability, the only classical passage with which Dante was familiar is the one in Ovid. For Dante's knowledge of classical authors, cf. E. Moore, Studies in Dante. First Series (Oxford: Clarendon Press, 1896).

17 For several dubious references to morning-dreams in classical literature, cf. Stearns, op. cit., pp. 51 ff. Stearns (p. 68) finds the number of unmistakable references very small, and concludes that rather than being a convention the superstition was a vagary.

18 Cf. Maury, op. cit., p. 251.

19 Cf. Walter C. Curry, Chaucer and the Medieval Sciences (New York: Oxford Univ. Press, 1926), pp. 207–8. J. Passavanti devotes several pages to natural and divine dreams in his Trattato de' sogni. According to Passavanti most dreams are meaningless, and it is a sin to try to interpret them by means of magic. Divine revelations, on the other hand, and some natural dreams are clearly meaningful, and they can safely be interpreted. Cf. his Lo specchio della vera penitenza (Florence: Le Monnier, 1856), pp. 325 ff.

20 Job, xxxiii, 15, 16.

21 Summa theologica, II, ii, 95–6. It has been pointed out (Busetto, op. cit., p. 150, note) that in the De divin. per somnium St. Thomas retains with Aristotle that dreams are not of divine origin, and are prophetic only accidentally. One must not forget, however, that in the De divin. St. Thomas does not do much else than elucidate the meaning of Aristotle's text. In all likelihood, St. Thomas had in mind the somnium naturale in the De divin., and the somnium coeleste in the Summa.

22 De somno et vigilia, III, i, 2. Cf. Lynn Thorndike, A History of Magic and Experimental Science (New York, 1929), II, 576–7. Albertus

Magnus believed that dreams (probably those not coming from God) are caused by the motion of stars, acting upon the bodies of men (*op. cit.*, III, ii, 6).

23 *De apprehens.* part IV, n. 9. From Busetto, *op. cit.*, p. 152.

24 In connection with Dante's expression *"peregrina più da la carne"* E. Moore (*Contrib. to the Textual Crit. of the Div. Comedy*, Cambridge, 1889, p. 386), gives two interesting quotations from Cicero's *De senectute* sec. 80: "nec vero tum animum esse insipientem quum ex insipienti corpore evasisset, sed quum *omni admixtione corporis liberatus* purus et integer esse coepisset, tum esse sapientem" and "Atqui dormientium animi maxime declarant divinitatem suam: multa enim, quum remissi et liberi sunt, futura prospiciunt. Ex quo intelligitur quales futuri sint, quum *se plane corporis vinculis relaxaverint.*" Cicero, by the way, is quoting Xenophon, *Cyropaedia*, 8.

25 Cf. *The Dialogues of Saint Gregory, surnamed the Great. . . .* With Introduction and Notes by E. G. Gardner (London: P. L. Warner, 1911), p. 244.

26 *Republic* ix, 571C–572B, quoted by Cicero *De divin.* i. 60. Cf. Stearns, *op. cit.*, p. 68.

27 Cf. also Passavanti: *"La qualità dei cibi e del bere fa essere varietà nel sognare; chè quegli che sono leggieri e sottili, sono cagione che 'l sogno sia leggiero e chiaro; quegli che sono grossi e gravi fanno sognare cose gravi, turbe e oscure e paurose."* *Op. cit.*, p. 330.

28 *Physionomia*, cap. 45–56 (1740), pp. 280 ff. In various Dream-Books drawn up during the Middle Ages, the time of the dream is of great importance; for a discussion of these Dream-Books cf. Thorndike, *op. cit.*, II, pp. 290–302.

29 *Op. cit.*, p. 351.

30 *Trionfo della morte*, II, 1–6. I quote from Calcaterra's ed., Turin, 1927.

31 I, xvii.

32 *Teatro italiano antico* (Milan: Classici Italiani, 1808), vol. I, p. 70.

33 I, iii. Cf. also Aretino's *Il Marescalco*, I, vi.

34 Quoted from W. W. Vernon, *Readings on the Purgatorio of Dante* (London, 1907), 2 vols. Vol. I, p. 314.

35 Cf. R. Menéndez-Pidal, *La leyenda de los Infantes de Lara* (Madrid: Casa Editorial Hernando, 1934), p. 29 note, and p. 295.

36 Cf. Stearns, *op. cit.*, p. 69, and *Notes and Queries*, ser. II, vol. I, 479. Were it necessary, additional references could in all probability be found, not only in Italian, Spanish, and English literature, but in other literatures as well. For Old French literature, many references to dreams—some of which may be morning-dreams—are listed by A. J. Dickman in his thesis *Le rôle du surnaturel dans les chansons de geste* (Iowa, 1925).

37 Cf. *Notes and Queries*, loc. cit., p. 463.

38 Cf. *The Ocean of Story*, being C. H. Tawny's translation of Somadeva's *Kathā Sarit Sāgara*. Edited with notes by N. M. Penzer (London, 1927), 10 vols., vol. VIII, pp. 99 ff.

39 Cf. Penzer, *op. cit.*, *loc. cit.*, p. 100, note. We saw that Passavanti gives an equally interesting "time-table" for the Italy of the 14th century.

40 Cf. E. Westermarck, *Ritual and Belief in Morocco* (London, 1926), 2 vols., vol. I, p. 55.

41 Cf. E. Doutté, *Magie et religion dans l'Afrique du nord* (Algiers, 1909), p. 400. Passavanti also believed that the clarity of the morning-dreams may have been responsible for the rise of the belief (*op. cit.*, p. 353). In his explanation of the belief, Stearns (*op. cit.*, pp. 68–9) does not consider this point, but remarks two interesting things: (a) that *midnight* is an hour when supernatural things may occur, and hence, that it may have been considered decisive in connection with dreams, i.e., dreams before midnight (on a full stomach) were considered false, and dreams after midnight true; (b) that *dawn* is also associated with the extraordinary (ghosts leave at dawn, etc.), and that therefore this may have helped to establish the belief in the veracity of morning-dreams.

42 Cf. W. R. Halliday, *Greek and Roman Folklore* (New York: Longmans Green, 1927), pp. 64–5. A belief shared by the people of classical antiquity, cf. Tertullian, *De anima* 48. For other references, cf. W. S. Messer, *The Dream in Homer and Greek Tragedy* (New York: Columbia Univ. Press, 1918), p. 12, note 38.

43 Cf. John Aubrey, *Remains of Gentilisme and Judaisme* (London: Folk-Lore Society, 1881), vol. IV, p. 57. Cf. also Stearns, *op. cit.*, p. 69, note 148. E. Rostagno (cf. his review of E. Moore's *Studies in Dante. First Series*, in *Bull. della soc. dant. ital.*, V [1897], 2) claims having heard this belief expressed by "*donnucce di paese.*"

V. Literary Criticism

15·Modern Literary Scholarship as Reflected in Dante Criticism

THE SIGNIFICANT scholarship concerned with the *Divine Comedy* since 1921, year of the celebration of the six hundredth anniversary of Dante's death, should be of interest even to the non-specialist, since it illustrates so well and so abundantly all the new trends in serious literary criticism. Actually it was in the interpretation of Dante that, for the first time in the history of literary criticism, emphasis was shifted from the study of the background to the study of the work itself, philological minutiae were made subservient to the elucidation of the poetry, the study of structure and unity became paramount, and the decisive differentiation was made between original ideas as such and common ideas originally expressed, i.e., regarded as informing the texture of the artifact. It was there that symbolism and imagery were recognized as determining the degree of poetry in a work, and its mythical proportions; language, style, and metrics were grasped in their psychological function as means of expression; and, finally, the question of intrinsic value, catharsis, poetical persuasion, and assent of the reader were discussed with a view to the problems of a *littérature engagée* versus "art for art's sake."

The shift from the background to the work occurred in the middle of the greatest monograph on the *Divine Comedy* the last generation produced. Its author, Karl Vossler,[1] believed it possible to explain the *Commedia* by fixing its geometrical

Reprinted by permission from *Comparative Literature* (III, 4, 1951).

position in a network of lines from history of religion, history of philosophy, history of ethics and politics, history of Old French fiction, Provençal lyricism, and early Italian poetry, as well as from popular, Biblical, and classical influences. But Vossler ended by acknowledging that, despite all this historicogenetic information, nothing was explained of Dante's poetry; and, when he arrived at his fourth volume, he was modest enough to avow that a line-by-line interpretation of each single canto, a translation of each poetical *terzina* into the language of aesthetic criticism, would be more helpful for the understanding than all the heavy artillery of the literary historian with which he had besieged Dante's poetical city throughout three lengthy volumes.

Since it seemed difficult, however, to find the same beauties and the same interest in all of the cantos of the three *cantiche*, it was easy to slip into the opposite error of a subjective interpretation. It was alleged that the power of Dante decreased on the way from the *Inferno* to the *Paradiso*, and that consequently no stylistic unity was maintained throughout the work. Benedetto Croce even believed that the *Commedia* could be split up into truly lyrical passages, revealing the eternal human emotions of love and hatred, joy and grief on the one hand, and, on the other, a dry theological framework, devoid of poetic value, in which no one is interested today.[2] This overstatement offered a momentous challenge to Dante scholarship. One of its worthiest representatives, M. Barbi, arguing the inacceptability of such an inconsistent compound in the *Commedia*, urged that "What really is of importance, more than anything else, is the [scholarly] understanding of Dante's poetry."[3] The commentators[4] now became aware that commenting did not mean reproducing the possible sources of this or that passage, or the century-long discussions of this or that unsolved problem; their task was rather to trace out the recurrent motifs, and the development of the character and stature of Dante the poetic wanderer, not of Dante the Florentine citizen. It now appeared with a new clarity that the commentator's task was to distinguish as sharply as possible the doctrinal and epic, didactic and descriptive, discursive and emotional intentions of the poet, the artistic meaning of allusions, similes, and comparisons, the manner of creating spiritual climates through landscapes, dialogue, grouping of persons, harmony between setting, action and speech, and the like. In other words, the creation of an analytical commentary was to be virtually the adumbration of a synthesis of Dante's art as a spontaneous expression of Dante's mind.

The preoccupation with synthesis and structure which resulted from the new orientation affected the treatment even of apparently isolated questions of philological-historical detail. Let us single out the problem of the identity of the famous *Veltro*, the Greyhound (*Inf.*, I, 101), as an example of the application of the new methods. On the principle that whatever comes from outside the text is irrelevant to its interpretation unless it is supported by some element within the text itself, the commentator now rejects all random guessing in terms of politics and biography—he rejects the idea, for example, that the expected liberator of Italy and the world symbolized by the greyhound might be the German emperor, or a spiritually minded pope, or the Ghibelline leader Uguccione della Faggiuola,[5] or Dante himself, or Christ at His second coming. The modern Dante scholar does not attempt to search the mind of the historical Dante. He sees no point in declaring the *Veltro* liberator to be a cryptogram for Can Grande della Scala on the grounds that Dante might have translated *can* (dog) into *veltro* to pay homage to his erstwhile sponsor. Leonardo Olschki,[6] after a similar, weaker attempt made by Vittorio Cian, rejects the interpretation of the appended words *tra feltro e feltro* as referring to the territorial boundaries of this provincial lord, situated between Feltre and Montefeltro, and refuses therefore to change *feltro* into *feltre* since the grounds for doing so would be wholly arbitrary. It is indeed said of the symbolic *veltro*, whose poetic task is to hunt the *lupa* (she-wolf), "e sua nazion sarà tra feltro e feltro" (*Inf.*, I, 105). This line in Dante's language can only mean, "And his birth will occur between felt and felt." The astrologically minded Dante can imagine a liberator, whoever he may be, only as born under the most favorable constellation. This is provided by the two influential stars which were identified with the felt-capped Dioscuri, Castor and Pollux, ancient symbols of liberty, i.e., by the constellation Gemini which occurs in May and June, the one *feltro* following (*tra*) the other. This newest interpretation starts from the text, the context, and the oldest commentaries; it is reasonable, and it remains close to Dante's way of thinking; and, what is most important, it does not destroy the poetical symbolism, and it leaves the way open for other liberator-symbols occurring in the *Divine Comedy* to be identified with the same *veltro*. The new interpretation is the product of a philology in the exclusive service of poetics and structural analysis, unwilling to sacrifice objective controls to preconceived speculations.

Structure became the great attraction in Dante studies after structural psychology [7] discovered that everywhere, and in artifacts particularly, there are textures in which what is happening in the whole cannot be explained by how the single parts are put together; on the contrary, if something happens in a single part, this something is informed by laws of the inner structure of the whole. With this principle in mind, the three apparently different styles of Dante in *Inferno*, *Purgatorio*, and *Paradiso* were seen as only one style varied to conform to the different spirit of each realm and to the gradually purified eyes of Dante. To Dante, Hell appears as a distorted earth [8] in a corporeal vision, Purgatory as a landscape hovering poetically and theologically between earth and Heaven as though it were an imaginary vision; and Paradise with its brilliant and refulgent spirits reveals itself in the most subtle theological speculations as an intellectual vision for Dante's raptured contemplation. The progression and change of style appears to Ulrich Leo [9] to be a highly successful achievement of conscious, voluntary, artistic design.

This dynamic progression, however, is further kept in order by the mathematical and geometrical construction of the otherworldly realms, which are in themselves static. The dynamic and the static elements together produce the structural unity of the eschatological atmosphere. It is this transcendental poetical atmosphere that gives unity to the lyrical elements, which according to Mario Rossi [10] would be rather vain if taken apart from their context. Only in their context do they serve emotionally to re-enforce the seriousness of Dante's imagination by giving the improbable a character of verisimilitude, if not of persuasive certitude.[11] This persuasion is achieved especially by the reportorial style of the traveler to the other world after his return to earth.[12] It is Dante the reporter's voice that vibrates with compassion for Francesca, with contempt for Filippo Argenti, with admiration for daring Ulysses, and even for the stoic suicide of Cato. But the unifying element in all these lyrical passages is considered by Pietrobono to be Dante's unswerving, objective orientation toward the dogma of the Church.[13]

Besides this general concern with structure, smaller structural probings have been made, for instance, of the probability that the seventeenth canto of *Purgatorio*, the numerically central song of the *Commedia*, would reveal also the central problem of the whole.[14] Examination did disclose a structural centrality in this canto, where Vergil explains the nature of love at a moment when it becomes clear to the travelers that all types of sinners have mistaken its nature. Those in the circles behind them decidedly loved evil, those in the circles before them were either inordinately attached to creatures or loved the Creator increasingly by becoming detached from creatures. This type of careful structure never turns out to be so pedantically exact that a topographical chart of its details would be possible.[15] The reason is that the deeper structure has been found to be not architectonic but musical. The great leitmotifs of love and the stars moved by love appear, at regular distances, as the quintessence of the unity of Dante's theological-astronomical concept of the cosmos; and they coalesce, in passages where one would not expect them, in the double motif of that love which moves the heavens and all the stars. Thus even Dante's paraphrase of the Credo must contain the central motif of the mover of the heavens who acts out of love: "Io credo in un Iddio Solo ed eterno che tutto il ciel move." [16]

The understanding of the unifying elements in the *Commedia* led to an examination of the structural unity of the *Vita Nuova*, supposed to be a chaotic work in which earlier poems were loosely linked together by prose texts to produce a mystifying Platonic love story. But the chaos was disclosed to be a most complex and refined organism, a carefully composed little work of art. And the starting point for the understanding of this unity was the correct concept of the *Vita Nuova* as "renewed life" in the religious sense, and not as "youthful life" in the amorous and Provençal sense.[17]

These structural preoccupations have brought new order also into the world of Dante's ideas, making it possible for the first time to separate two problems hitherto not distinguished. First, what were the philosophical convictions of Dante the thinker? For a thinker he certainly wanted to be in his writings on philosophy and politics, the *Convivio* and the *Monarchia*. Second, what were his particular ideas on the philosophy of love and on theology which, given poetical garb in the *Divine Comedy*, inform its symbolism and therefore are more difficult to penetrate than his plainly developed reflections in discursive language? The results of the most careful investigations may be summarized as follows: In his central approach Dante is a scholastic philosopher, not exclusively a follower of St. Thomas, but also, as Martin Grabmann was able to prove,[18] of St. Albert the Great, St. Bonaventure, Petrus de Tarantasia, and Aegidius de Roma. His Thomism, which he learned from a direct pupil of St. Thomas, Fra Remigio de' Girolami, can only be proved in cases where St. Thomas offers an individual teaching different from the common scholasticism of his time. Dante particularly liked St. Thomas' teaching on the fundamental difference between the substance and the faculties of the soul, on spiritual essences existing as pure form without matter, on the pre-eminence of the intellect over the will, and on the beatific vision as the primary and essential element of heavenly glory. Dante's intellectual relations, not only with the Dominicans of Santa Maria Novella (*Convivio*, II, 2) but probably also with the Franciscan Spirituals of Santa Croce and with the Augustinians of Santo Spirito in Florence, account, according to E. Buonaiuti,[19] for his particularly spiritual stressing of love and his Neoplatonic leanings (*Par.*, VII, 39–44). As a direct reader of Aristotle, however, and probably also of the commentary of Averroes, Dante developed for himself a genuine philosophy which stresses, more than that of most schoolmen, the importance of the secular life. Thus Dante became, as Gilson [20] says, the philosopher of the two beatitudes and of a world empire subordinated to the Church in rank and dignity but not in legal authority, having its own law, like the Church herself, directly from God. In a similar selective fashion, as Bruno Nardi has it,[21] he developed a philosophy of love which tries to reconcile earthly and heavenly love, the former being conducive to the latter in developing the spirit of sacrifice. This point, however, is inseparable from the problem of Beatrice, which will be dealt with later.

None of the Western philosophers and theologians, however, offered Dante a scheme of eschatology elaborate enough to furnish the outlines of his *Commedia*. It seems improbable that he could have constructed, without aid, from doctrinal hints only—the eschatological part is lacking in the *Summa Theologica*—or from poor and truncated Western folklore the whole concept of his other world. A purgatorial hill surmounted by the earthly paradise, a beloved Lady leading the lover to the Almighty, infernal guardians obstructing and persecuting the travelers, the smallness of the cosmos viewed from Heaven, the distribution of the blessed throughout the spheres, the most hellish torture by ice instead of fire—all of these imaginations seemed so distinctly Arabic-Mohammedan motifs, that Asín's hypothesis of Mussulman eschatology in Dante,[22] stressed recently by Cerulli, was adopted by serious scholars. Since, on the other hand, no truly doctrinal influence from Avicenna or Averroes could be proved, it became clear how ingeniously Dante the poet could use non-Christian material for structural and fictional purposes without thereby becoming in the slightest degree a heterodox philosopher or theologian.

His own philosophy, of course, is by design subordinated to his fiction. Dante seems little concerned with the fights of the schoolmen on earth in his poetical creation, where he assumes the character of a prophet and visionary rather than that of a philosopher. Not only St. Thomas and St. Francis are met in Heaven by Dante, but also the Averroist Siger of Brabant and Joachim of Flora (who dreamed of a merely spiritual Church). Both Siger and Joachim went to extremes in order to keep the different domains pure from undue mixtures and infringements, exactly what St. Thomas and Dante were striving for. Siger is now considered by E. Gilson to be simply a symbol, more drastic than St. Thomas himself, of the separation of philosophy from theological speculations, and Joachim a symbol, more drastic than St. Francis, of an ideal Church of poverty, aloof from the world, abstaining from political interference in the secular domain of the state, and in return unhampered by the emperor or the king of France.

Other investigations demonstrate how overwhelmingly Dante illustrates by means of fictional characters the fundamental scholastic teachings of moral philosophy. Ulysses is shown (*Inf.*, XXVI) exploring the seas with a daring spirit in order to discover new realms until one day he is shipwrecked and drawn to the depth of the sea and to Hell. The older interpretation conceived this Ulysses as a pre-Columbus, a tragic hero. The modern interpretation of Hugo Friedrich,[23] however, is this: No sinner is a tragic hero with Dante. Dante blames Ulysses in accordance with St. Augustine (*Conf.*, X, 35), "For greed of knowledge's sake do we see people sail to the uttermost boundaries of the earth," and in accordance with St. Thomas' teaching, "Curiositas non est studiositas, sed immoderata rerum cognitio" (*Summa*, II^a, II^{ae}, Qu. 166, Art. 2). The principle at issue is this: divine justice punishes the misguided will, the root of the action; the action itself may contain elements open to human pity.

The largest vistas have been opened in the reinterpretation of Dante's symbolism. To state first briefly what is at issue here, we may say that two extreme views have been entirely abandoned: the didactic theory that Dante's *Commedia* represents an allegory like the *Roman de la Rose* (and its epitome *Il Fiore*, which because of its pedestrian presentation alone, according to O. A. Schmidt, cannot be attributed to Alighieri[24]), and the mystical theory (Romano Guardini) that Dante's symbolic journey represents a real vision, a supernatural experience on the part of its author. A third interpretation takes Dante's fictional eschatological dream-vision as an analogical and implied ascetico-mystical purgation, illumination, and union.[25] This, however, raises the question whether the literal eschatological sense of the *Commedia*, now accepted by all serious Dante scholars, is still open to embellishment by further senses—either the allegorical, moral, and anagogical sense of Biblical exegesis or esoteric hidden senses which Dante might have had in mind. The answer today is this: The fourfold Biblical meaning seems out of the question to those who believe the famous letter to Can Grande to be spurious. Pietrobono has made it seem probable, for twenty good reasons, that Letter XIII to Can Grande could not have been written by Dante the theologian (with reference to St. Thomas, *Quaest. quodlibet.*, Qu. VII, Art. 16) despite its appearance in the Testo Critico.[26]

Not convinced by these reasons, Charles S. Singleton,[27] preferring the allegorical sense of the theologian as expressed in Letter XIII to the allegorical sense of the poet as discussed in the *Convivio*, solves the problem by not overstressing the metaphorical senses, by restricting them to the action rather than to the characters, and by not clinging to them pedantically.

The esoteric meanings have a chance of being admitted whenever they seem justified by the structure of the poem as well as by the literary sociology of the circle of Dante and his friends. The most important point of the modern critics, however, is that recourse to any other sense than the literal one, suggested by a spontaneous fictional event or character, can be admitted only if the situation would otherwise remain obscure and unintelligible.

The denial of strictly didactic allegories in Dante's *Divine Comedy* need not conflict with the fact that Dante himself uses allegories and explains them in his philosophical writings, as when in the *Convivio* he calls the *donna gentile* philosophy, her smile the philosophical persuasion, and her eyes the philosophical demonstrations.[28] However, to introduce such appended, accommodated allegories into the *Commedia* when confronted with Beatrice's smile and sparkling eyes would jeopardize the whole artistic understanding of the *poema sacro*. Even where in the *Divine Comedy* Dante speaks, as a poet, of piercing the veil and helping a little in the interpretation, it has been argued by A. Camilli that he is to be thoroughly mistrusted as endangering his own creation by an out-of-place and certainly feigned exegesis.[29] According to this critic it is a sound principle never to exceed the literal sense of an accepted symbol. Even in cases of dire necessity, where a character behaves in such a way that passing over to an allegorical sense becomes impera-

tive, we should return to the literal meaning as soon as possible.
During such allegorical excursions, however, one may be sure
that there is no other, literal sense involved besides the allegorical one. It is then as with the Canticle of Canticles as a
whole, according to the traditional Catholic interpretation: the
only meaning is the metaphorical one. Such a metaphorical passage, obviously, is the first canto of the *Inferno*, where the *selva
oscura* with the three animals belongs to quite another realm of
existence than Vergil, Hell, and the demons. Only recently this
metaphor was traced by J. H. Whitfield to Horace, *Satires*, II, 3:

> As in woods where often
> The wanderers by error are driven from their path.[30]

In passages where, as in the Canticle, the allegorical sense
is the literal one, the reader is even less entitled to ask extra-
textual and biographical questions, such as whether the dark
wood means heresy, or fornication, or pursuit of worldly honors
in Dante's life, or whether the leopard means Florence and the
lion Charles of Valois. These questions refer only to poten-
tialities, namely, Dante's life as raw material, and abandon the
actually achieved world of Dante's poetical symbolism. In other
words, the new Dante interpretation makes a strong point of
the fact that Dante in his poetry (not in his prose) overcomes
the usual medieval allegorism and fuses personal, theological,
political, moral, even astronomical elements into symbols of a
decidedly poetical and not didactic quality.[31] This interpretation
may go beyond the mark, but its laudable implication is clear,
namely, that whoever uses the word allegory for Dante's symbolism must keep in mind that his is an *allegoria ante rem*,
not *in re*. The serpent which threatens the poor souls before
their entrance into Purgatory in the Valley of the Princes is no
more and no less an allegory than the serpent of old, representing Satan in the earthly paradise in front of Eve. It is merely a
substitute for the *leo rugiens* of the Compline, as the souls
pray: "Te lucis ante terminum." If there is allegory, even "ex-
changed" allegory, it is primarily in Dante's Christian tradition,
not in Dante's poetic creation.

Here certainly Charles Singleton's question ought to be
asked: Was Dante capable of creating and willing to create his

own myth within the limits of the world of Christian revelation? [32] Singleton would say yes insofar as the personal symbolic creations of Dante are of the same "convincing" kind as those of Genesis. His poetry gives the awesome answer the prophet gives when the philosopher is reduced to silence. Dante as prophet, however, is identical with Plato's ideal poet who supplies myths as a means of illustrating truth, eschatological, moral, and metaphysical—a poet whose lies are true in a deeper sense. Dante's own mythical success within the frame of Christian revelation and Catholic dogma reflects that subjective effort which has become classical because every convinced Christian would create it in similar fashion, if he were a poet— a spiritual reality more real than Plato's realm of ideas.

Quite different from the question of Dante's mythical symbolism, which represents the allegory of poet and theologian in an indissoluble phenomenon, is the question whether the symbols of Dante do not contain psychological overtones, the reevocation of which means for the critic a deeper penetration of the artifact. The ascent of Mount Purgatory with its striving and hoping conveys to the reader, according to Theophil Spoerri,[33] all the trouble and thrill of mountain climbing: "effort at the outset, loftiness on the heights, heat at noon and rest at night, unrest in the mist and liberation when the view is widening." Such symbolic trimmings, however, are typical of critics who refuse to believe in the literal sense of Dante's work and have recourse from the outset to the "allegory of the poet." Actually, Spoerri believes only in the moral sense of the *Divine Comedy*.

But there remains a final question concerning Dante's symbolism. Sometimes the symbols have an allusional character. Therefore they may remain dark if one does not consider that Dante was writing for a circle of well-bred ladies and gentlemen who shared the same ideas on love and politics. This thesis is generally accepted. About the precise character of this literary circle, however, opinions differ. To some this group is simply a circle of friends who have "intelligence of love" and who, coming from the law school of Bologna, continued at Florence the troubadour cult which once spread through the castles of Provence—in a form adapted to the Italian high bourgeoisie.

To others this group seems to continue the half-fabulous French Courts of Love; to still others it appears as a sect tinged with an Albigensian type of heterodoxy and called *Fedeli d'amore*; finally by others again these Faithful of Love are restored to orthodoxy and appear as the wealthy and aristocratic-minded third order of the Knights Templar. If modern Dante scholarship takes these theories of literary sociology seriously, it is again for ergocentric reasons. They make much clearer certain stylistically obscure symbols.

Dante, for instance, is supposed to have expressed the political thought of this group that the world is going astray because the Church and the Empire have confused their domains. This he expressed, according to Luigi Valli,[34] by emblems, symbolizing the Church by the Cross and the Empire by the Eagle, as recurrent separate and joint (e.g., *Purg.*, VIII, 85) motifs in the *Commedia*. Robert L. John [35] even discovered that the Cross combined with the Eagle was the coat of arms of the great master of the Knights Templar and might have inspired the thirty symmetrical passages of the *Commedia* where this symbol is used directly or is translated into new symbols. Thus, in view of Dante's philosophy of the two beatitudes, the symbolism and structure of the *Divine Comedy* appear to the scrutinizing eye of the critic as a poetically draped syllogism of the following kind. Major: The Eagle is as necessary to earthly bliss as the Cross is to heavenly bliss. Minor: The earthly paradise is the necessary passage on the road to Heaven, as actually is the case in the architecture of the *Commedia*. Consequently: The Eagle of the World Empire is necessary in order to guarantee a maximum chance for all to reach the celestial Paradise.

The Knights Templar theory of John can solve better than any other theory certain problems of particularly obscure symbolism. Let us select three knotty ones: Geryon, the Ancient of Crete, and, most obscure of all, the number five hundred and fifteen.

When Dante with Vergil comes to the rim of the seventh circle of Hell, the wanderers find that there is no path down to the eighth. Vergil makes clear to Dante that they will use the flying monster Geryon, who must, however, be called from the depths of the abyss. Vergil takes the cord with which Dante is girded, goes a little around the circle until he comes to a group of Florentine usurers, and throws Dante's cord from this particular spot into the abyss; and immediately the monster Geryon moves to the place from which the cord has been thrown. This cord cannot be, as Dantologists have believed, the Franciscan cord, because this is always called *capestro* by Dante (*Inf.*, XXVII, 42; *Par.*, XI, 87; *Par.*, XII, 132) and not *corda*; nor can it be the Dominican *lumbare*, as Mandonnet would have it, because neither the one nor the other is a symbol of chastity, which Dante declares his cord to be. The only *corda* that is a symbol of chastity is the belt of the Knights Templar. Furthermore, Vergil throws the cord from the particular place occupied by Florentine usurers such as the Gianfigliazzi and the Obriachi (*Inf.*, XVII, 70). Geryon being one of them in kind and the most monstrous one, Fraud in person as Dante says, is attracted by the signal which appears to come from the usurers. The Florentine bankers of the fourteenth century were instrumental in the condemnation and fall of the Knights Templar, and one of them, Noffo Dei, was their main accuser. He is supposed to have been Dante's model for Geryon; he was later accused and hanged in Paris. Dante's sympathy with the Templars, therefore, has condensed this story into a whole sequence of symbols, including the fact that the cord of innocence has become an instrument in the process of killing Fraud.

More convincing still is the explanation of the Ancient of Crete (*Inf.*, XIV, 94–120). Crete was the island where Aeneas was shipwrecked when carrying the Roman Eagle and where St. Paul was stranded when carrying the Cross to Rome. Dante's statue of the Ancient of Crete, a monument of catastrophes, now turns his back to Damietta, weeping over the fall of this last bastion of the Templars, and looks toward Rome, most probably inquiring whether a spiritual pope will not arise there who will restore the Templars, suspended by Clement V at the wish of Philip the Fair of France.

Finally, the liberator who in the *Inferno* was called *Veltro*, is called in the earthly paradise "a five hundred and fifteen" (*un cinquecento diece e cinque*, *Purg.*, XXXIII, 43) in the apocalyptic style of St. John, who speaks of "a six hundred and sixty-six" (Rev. 13:18), whom the exegetes used to identify with the Roman emperor Nero. The commentators have either explained Dante's number as a cryptic riddle (DXV) which, with some shifting of its Roman characters could be read as Dux, leader, or have translated the name of Can Grande della Scala, supposed to be the Dux, into Greek characters and identified each of them with cabalistic values. Now, five hundred and fifteen, actually, is the year in which Zorobabel built the second temple in Jerusalem and consequently, Robert L. John points out, would represent a very reasonable symbol for the spiritual pope, restorer or second builder of the destroyed temple of the Order of the Knights Templar. The new interpretations of Veltro and cinquecento diece e cinque in no way contradict what was earlier said of the generally nonobscure character of Dante's symbolic language, because in both cases the texts must be cryptic and apocalyptic for stylistic reasons, since they record dark prophecies of Vergil and Beatrice, respectively.

Dantologists who until recent times seemed to be sure that Vergil was a symbol only for reason, the lumen rationale, human wisdom, philosophy, the natural means towards happiness or metaphysical knowledge,[36] overlooked the point that Aristotle, "the master of those who know," would have enacted this role with far more proper credentials. Those who said that Vergil is Dante's guide mainly in language and style were not aware that Vergil's ideal of style is just the opposite of Dante's;[37] furthermore, Dante's imitations of Vergil, whenever they occur, smack a little of the medieval Aeneid commentary of Bernardus Silvestris and the Poetics of John of Garland.[38] Those who stressed the patriotic connotations of Dante the Italian, who feels himself a Roman and sees himself in an uninterrupted line with Vergil, were wrong in coloring their interpretation with considerations of race, nation, and national state.

Vergil is for Dante, as the recent investigations of Whitfield underscore, the prophet of the birth of Christ in his fourth eclogue, and the singer of the Roman Eagle at a moment when the Cross is about to sanctify it. In his time all things seemed to converge toward an eternal Pax Romana and toward a vaguely envisioned Church protected by the might of imperial

Rome. Vergil, therefore, as a guide, orients Dante mainly in reconducting the Empire to the ideal balance which Vergil had dimly foreseen, which was realized for a short time under Constantine, and which was destroyed by the Donation of Constantine. This, Whitfield thinks, is the main reason why Vergil is entitled to guide Dante to the earthly paradise.

As for the much more difficult problem of Beatrice, no appreciable contribution can be said to have been made by the so-called realists who saw in Beatrice the transfigured Florentine lady, Beatrice Portinari, who died in 1290 at twenty-four as the wife of Simone de' Bardi, or by the symbolists who saw in her divine wisdom and grace. The new Beatrice, a poetical myth like Vergil, is according to her name the one who leads to happiness, *la donna salutifera*; she has an existence of importance only in poetry, not in life.

It is significant that the early commentators, on whom the new Dantologists rely so much, do not mention the name of Portinari. The critics of today try to discard, as a fact, Dante's meeting with the nine-year-old girl, as described in the *Vita Nuova*, while they would admit as a maximum concession a troubadour-like but rejected homage on the part of Dante to the wife of Simone de' Bardi.[39] The connotation of Bardi's wife, however, proves to be detrimental to any function of Beatrice in the *Divine Comedy*.[40] Charles S. Singleton's [41] newest interpretation pertinently starts from the structure of the *Vita Nuova*. Here Dante tried to solve the old problem of the troubadours as to whether carnal love is compatible with Christian charity and can lead to God. The classical troubadours, having made the lady herself a goddess, usually recanted in their later years the sinful love they had sung. Guido Cavalcanti and his circle tried to make of their lady the angelic creature, *la donna angelicata*, who had to be platonically and tragically renounced because she was unattainable.

Dante changed the pattern. His Beatrice first makes him happy with her greeting. He enjoys the slightest token of earthly love. When this creature who bestows happiness refuses to greet him again, the great lover continues none the less to sing her praise like the other troubadours, but without their note of wailing and self-pity. He is on the way to a higher love which has sacrificial elements because it makes one forget self. Then comes the tremendous blow. Beatrice dies, and her lover sees the way free to give his love direction toward God alone. His love has become charity. Beatrice is thus revealed retrospectively as a kind of charity incarnate, an analogy of proportion to Christ Himself, the way to Him in the order of rightness which does not need recantation—a Beatrice who by slight but painful detours leads to God, not by the impracticable devices of an impossible Platonism, but in the radical Christian sense. She gives the taste for sacrificial love and steps aside. When the *Commedia* opens she shows Dante, who had relapsed, the horrors of sin (horrible because destructive of charity), procures for him illumination by the visions of glory, leads him to the master of contemplation, St. Bernard, steps aside again, and has him conducted by the real pattern of created charity, Mary, to Christ and to the Holy Trinity. Singleton's concept of Beatrice solves all the difficulties of interpretation. One of his predecessors, Umberto Cianciolo,[42] pointed out that before Beatrice's final disappearance she was eclipsed twice when the direct radiance of God's loving light made Dante forget her presence, once in the sphere of the sun where the refulgent group of saintly theologians outshines the light of Beatrice, and once in the highest sphere when Dante looks at the overwhelming charity of the disciple of love, St. John.

Thus the new Beatrice is a Christlike charity incarnate. Designate her as you will—revealed truth, faith, supernatural order, spiritual church, sanctifying grace, theology, perfection, sanctity, or any other element in Dante's poetical-theological system—she remains the beloved woman of a poem, primarily love, but supernatural love which is the culmination of Christianity, the virtue which remains in eternity, the union between God and man.

In close conjunction with this new interpretation of Beatrice has come a solution of the so-called problem of the *dolce stil nuovo*. Not one of Dante's predecessors, not even Guinicelli or Cavalcanti,[43] but Dante himself is the inventor of this style,[44] the man who disentangled the knot, as Bonagiunta da Lucca [45] says. Being a spirit in Purgatory, Bonagiunta knows what the true *intelletto d'amore* (*Purg.*, XXIV) is. This sweet new style is considered by recent scholars not as a rhetorical mannerism but the very heart of Christian love poetry. Charles Singleton has seen still more clearly what Bonagiunta's words mean:

> *Io veggio ben come le vostre penne*
> *Diretro al dittator sen vanno strette.*
>
> (*Purg.*, XXIV, 58, 59)

> Clearly I see how closely do your pens
> Follow on him who dictates from within you.
>
> (Lawrence Grant White)

Again this dictator is not Amore, the pagan Cupid, but un-created Caritas, the Holy Spirit, infusing the spirit of love into the truly Christian love poets. Dante actually copied a passage from the mystic, Richard of Saint Victor: "Solus digne loquitur qui secundum quod cor dictat verba componit." [46] The impli-cation is that Dante, conversing with Bonagiunta, feigns to be hearing for the first time about his decisive poetic achievement —continuing his assumed role from the *Vita Nuova*, the role of a glosser on providential events worked out by God, who made of him also an instrument of His praise, a praise con-densed in Beatrice, *loda di dio, beata, benedetta, gloriosa,* heavenly love hidden in the garb of troubadour love. Singleton's contribution to the solution of the problem seems conclusive.

That Dante was conscious of technical stylistic problems has not been overlooked in this age of investigation of style. Examination of the problems of structure and symbol and the new concept of Beatrice have naturally shed new light on Dante's vocabulary. To keep Dante's symbolic rivers in line with his symbolic woods and hills, it had to be pointed out that his *fiumana ove 'l mar non ha vanto* (*Inf.*, II, 108) is the same "geography" as St. Augustine's *fluctus concupiscentiae* and Hugh of St. Victor's *lacus cordis*.[47] But *fonte, fontana, fiume, rio, saluto, salute, pietra, sasso, marmo, tempio, amore, cor gentil, morte, vita, fiore, rosa* also receive different meanings under the impact of the new theories.[48] Dante's verbal creation was brought into the limelight by T. Spoerri,[49] who stressed his impressive word formations—*inurbarsi, insemprarsi, inluiarsi, imparadisarsi*—but much more so by Malagoli,[50] who discovered a nominal principle in Dante's manner of using suggestive words and locutions which create by themselves visualization, space, and relief (*frontalità*).

Passionate scenes, it has been observed, are stylistically framed by Dante's anaphorical habit of repeating words and phrases at the beginning of consecutive tercets.[51] Curtius [52] has discovered that the Middle Latin use of serious wordplay, the so-called *annominatio* and *figura etymologica* of the type, *Cred'io ch'ei credette ch' io credesse* (*Inf.*, XIII, 25), was used by Dante with measure and in such an inconspicuous way that it appears only like a thin ornament—whereas the metonymical allusions of the type, *L'infamia di Creti* (*Inf.*, XII, 12), for the Minotaur appear on every page as periphrases of dignity and sublimity and as a means of communion, of sophisticated connivance, with the cultured reader who knows so much about rhetoric, antiquity, history, and mythology. The *raison d'être* of Dante's other figures of speech is under investigation,[53] particularly the fusing of troubadour elements and liturgical patterns of the type, *La gloria di colui che tutto move*,[54] and his superior imitation of earlier eulogies.[55]

As far as speech styles are concerned, Spitzer [56] has seen that the plant-man Pier della Vigna (*Inf.*, XIII) not only speaks the stilted language of a courtier but also that of an amphibious being, and that farcical elements in the grotesque scenes of *Inf.*, XXI–XXIII inform speech, movement, gestures, and names of devils alike.[57] We have learned [58] that, when Dante is embarrassed, as with Farinata and Cavalcanti's father in the circle of the heresiarchs, Tuscanisms escape him as an expression of this embarrassment before he can find the correct literary term. When Cavalcanti, the father, uses (*Inf.*, X, 69) an unusual form *lome* for *lume*, he does not do so, as has been shown by H. Kuen [59] (refuting Meyer-Lübke), because Dante was in need of an adequate rime, but because this very form occurs in one of the famous poems of Cavalcanti, the son, whose memory he wants to honor. When the dignity of the interlocutor demands the sublime, high, and tragic style of address, Vergil does the talking instead of Dante.[60] Introductory formulas to direct speeches in the *Commedia* have been compared to those in the *Aeneid* and found to be much richer, although patterned on the *Aeneid*.[61]

Leitmotifs which hitherto had escaped notice have been singled out. Such is the motif of light in Purgatory which, during the quest for peace and protection, becomes stronger and stronger with the cleansing of the heart.[62] Leitmotifs have been studied also in their musical arrangement from their first *intonazione*, through their *ripresa*, to their final appearance, as in the case of the resounding water of the eighth circle of the *Inferno*.[63] Metaphors for hunger and thirst have been recognized as a systematic ladder conducting to the heavenly food of the angels.[64]

The stylistic reason for the vividness of Dante's descriptions is found in that tone which brings the strange and the visionary down to the level of the familiar; Dante's humble style elements are recognized as partly naturalistic. He does not shrink from presenting ugly things as ugly, as when the flatterers are described as plunged in human excrement (*Inf.*, XVIII, 113–117).[65] His more lofty realism, however, has been compared to that of Giotto for its penetration of the secrets of nature and its plastic evidence, through which glows a deep Franciscan religiosity.[66] Dante's language from a euphonic viewpoint is seen as the expression of the particular spiritual climate of the different episodes: fear is expressed by stammering, horror by purposely misplaced accents, erotic passion by labials as though they reproduced kisses, satanic malignity by the absence of soft consonants.[67] This is the contribution of the age of phonemics to Dantology. Dante's range of style is considered incomparable; it is *umile, dolce, bello, soave, alto, sublime,* classical, Biblical, abstract, veristic, mixed, according to the situation described.[68] It includes the minutest detailed elaboration of vowel combinations, accents, pause, period structure, and other syntactical patterns. We have acquired in recent years a mass of information on Dante's language and style, still scattered, however, and not united in a synthesis.

As for Dante's verse, the *endecasillabo*, its origin from the Sapphic meter has been established.[69] Precisely this origin has suggested that there are different metrical overtones, according to the circumstances, hovering above the regular architecture of the *cantus firmus* of the iambic succession of unstressed and stressed syllables. Such an alternative principle is the basis of any type of Romance verse. It was Martha Amrein-Widmer [70] who discovered the psychological meaning of these hovering meters. The iambic, monotonous regularity itself is used in its military correctness when orderly marching is expressed:

Poi fummo fatti soli procedendo
∪ — ∪ — ∪ — ∪ — ∪ — ∪

The harassing and hurrying disturbance of one-syllable words marks the plight of the sinners of the flesh driven around eternally by the storm of their passion like leaves by a tempest:

Di qua, di là, di giù, di su li mena.

Liturgical solemnity characterizes the prayer which actually reproduces the cursus of the *orationes* under the guise of the Sapphic meter:

O padre nostro che nei cieli stai
∪ — ∪ — ∪ / ∪ ∪ — ∪ —
Vergine madre, figlia del tuo figlio
— ∪ ∪ — ∪ / — ∪ ∪ ∪ — ∪

A long caesura suggests a bliss to be retained and tasted:

Io son Beatrice // che ti faccio andare.

Hundreds of these psychological-metrical variations have been analyzed. One is even inclined to believe that Dante worked out all these patterns consciously.[71]

The detailed imagery of Dante, as distinct from his general symbolism, has undergone the deepest probing. His images are no longer considered mere replicas of Homeric-Vergilian similes. Their function is not simply to provide small islands of rest in the stream of epic events. Dante's simile plays various parts, epic, lyric, didactic, but has its particular fundamental structure. F. Olivero [72] has established the fact that the image appears gradually, but once shaped unfolds in various ways. It is either narrowed down to one precise aspect which has to be made clear; or it is enlarged in a vague and lyrical fashion; or comparisons are accumulated to stress an idea. Sometimes images become poetic by multiplication. Sacchetti [73] has added nothing new to Olivero's analysis. Whitfield [74] has noted that in Dante's similes a theoretical statement is illuminated by picturesque examples from nature, life, the poet's own experience, and that the reader comes under the spell of something strange yet almost familiar. For instance, Dante intimates that metamorphoses of snakes into men and of men into snakes could be a normal and quasi-biological process for the punishment of sin. Therefore he asks his reader whether he has ever seen how burning paper gradually browns around the edge. If so, he will have no difficulty in understanding how the white limbs of a sinner set afire by the bite of dismal snakes in the other world become brown and take on by this very process the color of the snake before assuming step by step the shape of its body. Thus established in a region of normality beyond strangeness, the reader is fascinated by a Dante truly "trattando l'ombre come cosa salda" (*Purg.*, XXI, 136).

T. S. Eliot [75] has pointed out, moreover, that this magic realism is further enhanced by everyday notions of the kind exemplified when in the dimness of Hell the shades glance at Dante, the living man, in the way an old tailor peers at his needle's eye in order to thread it—or, as Whitfield has noted, the flames on the soles of the simonists' feet move along only on the outer husk, as happens with greasy objects.[76] This method of making the unfamiliar homely has been extended by Dante to the purely psychological realm, as Whitfield has shown. Thus the burning love in St. Peter and St. James makes them behave on meeting one another like two billing and cooing doves (*Par.*, XXV, 18–20); and the blessed surging upward after Mary (*Par.*, XXIII, 121 ff.) have the gesture and the smile of a baby who instinctively turns to its mother's breast, full of gratitude after receiving the nourishing milk. After such reinterpretations of Dante's similes it will be difficult to maintain Santayana's interpretation: "No smack of life, but of somnambulism." [77]

A critical re-evaluation of Dante seems the logical consequence of this considerable amount of new analytical work. It came, indeed, with the anti-Crocean assent to the *Commedia* as a whole, not to selected parts.[78] This assent, certainly, is based on human empathy and poetical catharsis, which are open to any prepared reader. It is identical with an ease and comfort of response,[79] different from an artificial assimilation. This response is, however, certainly tinged by the general attitude towards Dante's Christian message; it may be a pure aesthetical reaction or a mixed, i.e., a relevant and vital reaction.[80] The most astonishing fact, however, is that those who believe they respond only aesthetically are caught by this eschatological-mystical tension between sin and the highest spirituality much more strongly than by great tragedy,[81] so that even the aesthetical catharsis reaches here the borderline of grace.[82] The general belief seems to be that this coincidence between the aesthetical and the existential catharsis can occur only because Dante's intuition of the Mysterious Reality is offered by an overwhelming (i.e., convincing) symbolism,[83] an irresistible symbolism. Irresistible it may truly be called, since all kinds of Dante readers strive to adapt it to their own views rather than to ignore it.[84]

It may be well to repeat that the new trends in Dante scholarship which have here been chosen for emphasis and exemplification concern only major questions of general interest. There remains a phalanx of minutiae, duly listed in the recent biographies by N. D. Evola, H. Wieruszowski, Michele Barbi, Umberto Cosmo, Angelina La Piana, and Aldo Vallone.[85]

Notes

1 Karl Vossler, *Die göttliche Komödie. Entwicklungsgeschichte und Erklärung*, 4 vols. (Heidelberg, 1907–10).

2 Benedetto Croce, *La poesia di Dante* (Bari, 1921).

3 Michele Barbi, "Nuovi problemi della critica Dantesca," *Studi Danteschi*, XXIII (1938), 5–77.

4 *La Divina Commedia di Dante Alighieri*, commentata da Attilio Momigliano (Florence, 1946). Cf. also the new commentaries by Rivalta (Florence, 1946); Castellino (Turin, Ed. Palatine, 1946); and Liborio Giuffrè, "Esame critico dei commenti alla *Divina Commedia* e proposta d'un nuovo," in his *Nuovi studi danteschi* (Palermo, 1941), pp. 121–144.

5 Andrea Gustarelli, *Dizionario Dantesco* (Milano, 1946).

6 Leonardo Olschki, *The Myth of Felt* (Berkeley, 1949), and Vittorio Cian, *Oltre l' enigma dantesco del veltro* (Turin, 1944).

7 M. Wertheimer, *Über Gestalttheorie* (Erlangen, 1925).

8 Erich Auerbach, *Dante als Dichter der irdischen Welt* (Berlin, 1929).

9 Ulrich Leo, "Sehen und Schauen bei Dante," *Deutsches Dante-Jahrbuch*, XI (1929), 183–221. Luigi Tonelli, *Dante e la poesia dell'ineffabile* (Florence, 1934).

10 Mario Rossi, *Gusto filologico e gusto poetico. Questioni di critica Dantesca* (Bari, 1942).

11 Leo Ferrero, *Appunti sul metodo della Divina Commedia, del dramma, dell'arte classica e decadente* (Capolago, 1940).

12 R. Palgen, "Die göttliche Komödie als Ich-Erzählung," *Germanisch-romanische Monatsschrift,* XXVII (1937), 50–67.

13 Luigi Pietrobono, "Struttura, allegoria e poesia nella Divina Commedia," *Giornale Dantesco,* XLIII (1940), 9–45.

14 Hans Rheinfelder, "Der Zentralgesang des Purgatorio und der ganzen Divina Commedia," *Deutsches Dante-Jahrbuch,* XXIII (1941), 86–105.

15 Allan H. Gilbert, "Can Dante's Inferno be Exactly Charted?" *PMLA,* LX (1945), 289–306.

16 Niccolò Gallo, "Intorno all'unità poetica della Divina Commedia," *Giornale Dantesco,* XXXVIII (1935), 151–168.

17 J. E. Shaw, *Essays on the Vita Nuova* (Princeton, 1929).

18 Martin Grabmann, "Die Wege von Thomas von Aquin zu Dante. Fra Remigio de' Girolami, O.P.," *Deutsches Dante-Jahrbuch,* IX (1925), 1 ff.; and "Thomas von Aquin und die Dante-Auslegung," *ibid.,* XXV (1943), 4–24.

19 E. Buonaiuti, *Dante come profeta* (Modena, 1936).

20 Etienne Gilson, *Dante the Philosopher* (London, 1948).

21 Bruno Nardi, *Dante e la cultura medievale* (Bari, 1942).

22 Miguel Asín Palacios, *La escatología musulmana en la Divina Comedia seguida de la historia y crítica de una polémica* (Madrid-Granada, 1943). Asín's thesis was corroborated by Enrico Cerulli, *Il "Libro della Scala" e la questione delle fonti arabo-spagnuole della Divina Commedia* (Città del Vaticano, 1949). See also Leonardo Olschki, "Mohammedan Eschatology and Dante's Other World," *CL,* III (1951), 1–17.

23 Hugo Friedrich, *Die Rechtsmetaphysik der göttlichen Komödie* (Frankfurt, 1942).

24 Otto A. Schmidt, "Ein neues Argument in der Fiore Frage," *Deutsches Dante-Jahrbuch,* XIX (1937), 27–28.

25 M. Grace Monahan, "Dante's Perception of the Soul's Purgation," *Ursuline Tradition and Progress,* IV (1944), 23–40.

26 Luigi Pietrobono, "L'epistola a Can Grande," *Giornale Dantesco,* XL (1937), 1–51.

27 C. S. Singleton, "Dante's Allegory," *Speculum,* XXV (1950), 78–86 (see pp. 91–103 above).

28 Bruno Nardi, *Nel mondo di Dante* (Rome, 1944).

29 A. Camilli, "Le figurazioni allegoriche," *Studi Danteschi,* XXVIII (1949), 197–215, summarizing his earlier studies on this subject.

30 J. H. Whitfield, *Dante and Virgil* (Oxford, 1949), p. 74.

31 Luigi Pietrobono, "Allegoria o arte?," *Giornale Dantesco,* XXXVII (1936), 95–134, and "L'allegorismo e Dante," *ibid.,* XXXVIII (1937), 85–102, versus Tommaso Ventura, *Nuovi orrizzonti della Divina Commedia* (Rome, 1907, 2nd ed., 1941); and T. Lucrezio Rizzo, *Allegoria, allegorismo e poesia nella Divina Commedia* (Milan, 1941).

32 Charles S. Singleton, "Dante and Myth," *Journal of the History of Ideas,* X (1949), 482–502

33 Theophil Spoerri, *Einführung in die göttliche Komödie* (Zürich, 1946).

34 Luigi Valli, *Il segreto della Croce e dell'Aquila* (Bologna, 1922);

Il linguaggio segreto di Dante e dei 'Fedeli d'Amore,' 2 vols. (Rome, 1928–30); and Francesco Egidi, "Guittone d'Arezzo, i Frati Gaudenti e i 'Fedeli d'Amore,' " *Nuova rivista storica,* XXI (1937), 158–195.

35 Robert L. John, *Dante* (Vienna, 1946). See also Ernst Robert Curtius, "Neue Dante Studien," *Romanische Forschungen,* LX (1947), 237–289.

36 G. Galassi Paluzzi, "Perchè Dante scelse Virgilio a sua guida," *Giornale Dantesco,* XXXIX (1936), 287–307; and Mario Casella, *Le guide di Dante nella Divina Commedia* (Florence, 1944).

37 J. H. Whitfield, *op. cit.*

38 E. R. Curtius, *op. cit.,* pp. 247 and 256.

39 Rudolph Borchardt, *Epilegomena zu Dante,* I. *Einleitung in die Vita Nuova* (Berlin, 1923).

40 Michele Barbi, "La questione di Beatrice," *Problemi di critica dantesca,* first series (Florence, 1934), pp. 113–139; and Luigi Pietrobono, "Realità e idealità nella 'Vita nuova,' " *Giornale Dantesco,* XLII (1939), 107–118; and Luigi Valli, *Il linguaggio segreto,* p. 411.

41 Charles S. Singleton, *An Essay on the Vita Nuova* (Cambridge, Mass., 1949); see also his "Dante's Comedy: The Pattern at the Center," *Romanic Review,* XLII (1951), 169–177.

42 Umberto Cianciolo, "La carità dottrinale di Dante," *Giornale Dantesco,* XL (1937), 125–139.

43 Francesco Biondolillo, *Dante creatore del dolce stil nuovo* (Palermo, 1937).

44 Ruggero M. Ruggieri, "Dante e il dolce stil nuovo," *Giornale Dantesco,* XXXIX (1936), 181–196.

45 J. E. Shaw, "Dante and Bonagiunta," *Report of the Dante Society* (Cambridge, Mass., Apr. 1936).

46 Singleton, *An Essay on the Vita Nuova,* pp. 90 ff:

47 Charles S. Singleton, "Sulla fiumana ove 'l mar non ha vanto," *Romanic Review,* XXXIX (1948), 269–277.

48 Luigi Valli, *Linguaggio segreto,* p. 423.

49 Spoerri, *op. cit.,* pp. 298 f.

50 Luigi Malagoli, *Linguaggio e poesia nella Divina Commedia* (Genoa, 1949).

51 O. M. Johnston, "Repetition of Words and Phrases at the Beginning of Consecutive Tercets in Dante's Divine Comedy," *PMLA,* XXIX (1919), 448 ff.

52 Curtius, *op. cit.,* pp. 264, 272.

53 T. A. Fitzgerald, "Dante's Figures of Speech," *Italica,* XVIII (1941), 120–123; and F. Maggini, "Associazioni etimologiche nelle imagini di Dante," *Lingua nostra,* VI (1944–45), 25–28.

54 Helmut Hatzfeld, "Das Heilige im dichterischen Sprachausdruck des *Paradiso,*" *Deutsches Dante-Jahrbuch,* XII (1930), 41–70; and Erich Staedler, "Analekten zur römischen Messliturgie in der Divina Commedia," *ibid.,* XXIV (1942), 131–158.

55 E. Auerbach, "Dante's Prayer to the Virgin and Earlier Eulogies," *Romance Philology,* III (1949), 1–26.

56 Leo Spitzer, "Speech and Language in *Inferno* XIII," *Italica,* XXIX (1942), 81–104.

57 Leo Spitzer, "The Farcical Elements in *Inferno* XXI–XXIII," *MLN,* LIX (1944), 83–88.

58 Whitfield, *op. cit.*, p. 86.

59 H. Kuen, "Dante in Reimnot," *Germanisch-romanische Monatsschrift*, XXX (1940), 305–314.

60 Angelo Lipari, "Parla tu, questi è Latino," *Italica*, XXIII (1946), 73–81.

61 Erich Staedler, "Die Wendungen zur Einführung der direkten Rede in der *Divina Commedia* und ihre klassischen Vorbilder," *Deutsches Dante-Jahrbuch*, XXV (1943), 106–124.

62 Spoerri, *op. cit.*, p. 192.

63 A. Momigliano, *Edizione commentata della Divina Commedia*, I, 117.

64 Walter Naumann, "Hunger und Durst als Metaphern bei Dante," *Romanische Forschungen*, LIV (1940), 12–36.

65 Whitfield, *op. cit.*, p. 84.

66 Achille Bertoni Calosso, "Giotto e lo stil nuovo," *Rassegna Italiana*, XX (1937).

67 Spoerri, *op. cit.*, pp. 53, 56, 76, 134.

68 Curtius, *op. cit.* p. 250; and E. Auerbach, *Mimesis* (Bern, 1949), *passim*, and pp. 171–195.

69 Spoerri, *op. cit.*, pp. 361–388.

70 Martha Amrein-Widmer, *Rhythmus als Ausdruck inneren Erlebens in Dantes Divina Commedia* (Zürich, 1932).

71 Gianfranco Contini, *Le Rime di Dante* (Turin, 1939), and Curtius, *op. cit.*, p. 247.

72 F. Olivero, *The Representation of the Image in Dante* (Turin, 1936).

73 A. Sacchetti, *Il gioco delle imagini in Dante* (Florence, 1947).

74 Whitfield, *op. cit.*, pp. 85–86.

75 T. S. Eliot, *Dante* (London, 1929), p. 24.

76 Whitfield, *op. cit.*, p. 85.

77 Angelina La Piana, *Dante's American Pilgrimage* (New Haven, 1948), p. 242, quoting Santayana, *Three Philosophical Poets* (Cambridge, Mass., 1927).

78 Eliot, *op. cit.*

79 William Joseph Rooney, *The Problem of "Poetry and Belief" in Contemporary Criticism* (Washington, 1949), p. 115, note 53.

80 *Ibid.*, p. 121.

81 Robert de Luppé, *Délivrance par la littérature* (Paris, 1946).

82 Charles G. Osgood, *Poetry as a Means of Grace* (Princeton, 1941), pp. 25–52.

83 L. Sturzo, "Modern Aesthetics and the Poetry of the Divina Commedia," *Thought*, XVII (1942), 412–432.

84 Georges Méautis, *Dante. L'Antépurgatoire. Essai d'une explication* (Geneva, 1944).

85 N. D. Evola, *Bibliografia Dantesca 1920–1930* (Geneva, 1932); H. Wieruszowski, "Bibliografia Dantesca 1931–1937," *Giornale Dantesco*, XXXIX (1938); Michele Barbi, "Un cinquantennio di studi danteschi," *Un Cinquantennio di studi sulla letteratura italiana* (Florence, 1937), I, 111–135; Umberto Cosmo, *Guida a Dante* (Turin, 1947), translated as *A Handbook of Dante Studies* by David Moore (Oxford, 1950); Angelina La Piana, *Dante's American Pilgrimage* (New Haven, 1948); Aldo Vallone, *Gli studi danteschi dal 1940 al 1949* (Florence, 1950).

VI. Influence

16 · Dante After Seven Centuries

EXACTLY THIRTY YEARS AGO, when I was a student in Piazza San Marco, I met at a reception of the *podestà* the leonine Giovanni Papini, whose *Dante vivo* was by then as well known in America as in Italy. At that time I was doing a thesis on Dante and Marguerite de Navarre for Auguste Renaudet of Bordeaux. I approached the great antischolarly scholar and asked if he really felt, as he expressed it in *Dante vivo*, that one could not understand the Trecento poet unless he were a Florentine, a poet, and a Catholic. He replied guardedly that he would have to adhere to his written word.

—Alas, I replied, I am but an American, at best a *prosatore*, and a descendant of Huguenots.

Now, three decades later, I realize that there was more truth in his claim than I care to admit. Indeed, if at that time I felt a sense of inadequacy about embarking on such a minuscule topic as Dante and Marguerite d'Angoulême, a subject on which the genial Carlo Pellegrini had shed first light, think of my feelings today presuming to give this distinguished international company a few modest thoughts on my assigned topic, "Dante nel mondo." It seems a greater presumption here at this Congress, since an authoritative volume bearing that very

This is the author's own translation of an address delivered at Ravenna on April 27, 1965, under the title *Dante nel mondo*, as part of the *Congresso internazionale di studi Danteschi* organized to celebrate the seventh centenary of Dante's birth. It appears here by permission of the *Comitato nazionale per le celebrazioni del VII centenario della nascita di Dante*.

title is being distributed to us today through the courtesy of its editors Vittore Branca and Ettore Caccia.

In assessing the importance of Dante to our heterogeneous world of the late twentieth century, it is easy to slip into easy assurances and platitudes. A poet now available to us in the world's major languages, read in all schools, gracing monuments and postage stamps, how could one pretend that he is not just as alive today and indeed more universal than he was in his own time? That Dante is as alive as ever can scarcely be doubted and the point need not be labored. More difficult to assess is the influence the poet exercises in a world so different from his own. Indeed, one might ask whether the influence of Dante—as opposed to his fame—can do other than decrease as the world changes form and content over the centuries. (Does not the *Ramayana*, for example, gain more potential readers every year than any other of the world's masterpieces?) In our brief census we should like to examine the influence of Dante today on contemporary politics, society, law, science, and religion, pausing over certain points at which his thought seems compatible with or at odds with modern thinking. We should also like to review briefly his impact on the intervening centuries, thus setting into clearer perspective his role in our own age.

Dante anniversaries are no monopoly of any one century. There were attempts to assess the modernity of Dante in 1865 (when Victor Hugo wrote his *Centenaire de Dante*) and in 1921. Most of them ended up by stating that Dante's importance to modern times is that he was a summation and synthesis of medieval thought—that his contribution, as Symonds saw it, was to give a vigorous reaffirmation of a complex of medieval thinking which was exhausting itself and was on its way out. In 1921 the French scholar Henri Hauvette was called upon to stress the modernity of Dante's thought. He did not minimize the enormity of the task assigned to him. "C'est donc par ses qualités morales—après son art—que nous sentons très près de nous ce poète formé à l'école du XIIIe siècle. Par sa pensée proprement dite, Dante nous apparaît aujourd'hui dans un lointain irrévocable: et l'indice le plus certain de l'éloignement auquel il est voué pour nous est le fait qu'il a placé son idéal dans le passé et non dans l'avenir. L'idée de progrès semble lui être restée étrangère: il n'a vu autour de lui que décadence et désorganisation."

My purpose here, in the face of Hauvette's conclusions, becomes not to overstate the modernity of Dante's thought, but to affirm the value and applicability of that markedly medieval thought for the present century. Can we, in these terms, claim Dante as a man of our own time, a claim made by many in the nineteenth century?

There is an additional complication, immediately apparent, which makes Dante more difficult of understanding to our world. Of the greatest authors of the past, Dante is the least accessible. Dante's aesthetic was one of obscurantism. He grudgingly challenged us to get not only one, but four meanings, from his poetry. Leaning on an obscurantist tradition going back to Clement of Alexandria and others, he claimed to have enclosed in his canticles, if not also in his canti, the levels of sense described in the students' jingle of his day:

Littera *gesta docet*	The letter teaches deeds (facts)
Quid credas allegoría	Allegory what you should believe
Moralis *quid agas*	The moral meaning what you should do
Quo tendas anagogía.	The anagoge whither you're headed.

It is true that prejudices against poetry pushed him—as discretion pushed the troubadour poets—toward obscurity. Dante was a poet, and thus under attack from the four categories of antipoets arraigned in the epilogue of Boccaccio's *Decameron*: churchmen, pedants, philosophers, and historians. Petrarch, who shared in the defense and compared poetry to allegory and theology, would have added a fifth category: the medicoes.

Dante knew that to his own generation his *Commedia* would be hard going and apparently wished it so. In the second canto of *Paradiso*, he warns many of his readers that they are in water too deep and should give up the reading. He advises only a few to pursue to its conclusion their reading of the vast allegory:

> Ye other few . . .
> Ye may indeed commit your vessel to the deep
> Keeping my furrow, in advance of the water
> That is falling back to its level. (I, 3–6)

It would seem that Dante, with his excessive disdain for the average reader, cared even less about what you and I should thing of him after seven centuries. Yet, like Petrarch, he was not without a sense of obligation toward posterity. In the *Convito* he admitted to a sense of duty toward making posterity understand the lessons and accomplishments of the past. This he viewed as the principal duty of all men. Suiting the action to the conviction, Dante took many of his materials from recent Italian history and reworked them for posterity. Was Dante not thinking of future generations (his own being a prisoner of its own rumors and prejudices) when he set the record straight about so many people of his and the previous age? He thus whitewashed the reputation of Francesca da Rimini, re-affirmed the loyalty of Piero della Vigna, and so on. In his righteous wrath he also adjusted the record on Boniface VIII and managed to tax with sodomy a former master whose writings specifically condemned this crime against nature. Dante, for that matter, admitted this whitewashing intention of his poem, for he promises Count Ugolino in hell that he will rehabilitate him: "nel mondo suso ancora io te ne cangi" ("I shall set things straight about you in the world above").

Dante chose to be less than comprehensible in other than allegorical practices. He chose as symbols of virtue and of vice the most remote, local characters. Professor Bergin has shown that of 164 identifiable characters in the *Inferno*, 80 are of Dante's own society, including 64 from Italy itself. (As Dante himself notes, Florence's name "expands throughout hell" [*Inf.*, XXVI, 3]). All this promises obscurity for the modern reader. Homer dealt with figures so universally recognizable that they were easily converted into symbols. Achilles or Ajax is wrath. Penelope is chastity. Ulysses is Everyman in his quest. Vergil, more civil and elegant, is more available to us because we are acquainted with the orderly world he depicted. Removed as they are, Homer and Vergil present us figures and incidents which do not require a cluster of footnotes and identifications at the foot of each page. As Voltaire complained in his *Lettres philosophiques*, "On ne lit plus le Dante dans l'Europe, parce que tout y est allusion à des faits ignorés." The values of clarity which Aristotle saw in Homer (in addition to those other virtues by which Aristotle saw him surpassing all other poets: diction, thought, pathos, etc.) allow one to read through his two epics without feeling the constant need of an exegete. In Dante, we must know as much as possible about even the most minor figures to understand the nature, intent, and punishments associated with their crimes. Indeed, the exegetes themselves sometimes fail, and one reads such notes as: "Nothing is known about this anonymous Florentine suicide of Inferno XIII" or this "anzian di santa Zita of XXI."

Why, in sum, did Dante elect so often to cast as major symbols compatriots and contemporaries almost unknown even to readers of his own country and age? With such a panoply of historical examples of lust—for example, Helen of Troy, Berenice, Cleopatra, and Dido—why did he choose an unknown young wife from Verona? Was it merely to settle a personal account of gratitude? Was it a desire to rival Homer, Vergil, Suetonius, Plutarch, and others in creating out of nothing a comparable tragic heroine? (It must be acknowledged that he achieved just this. In Germany alone, Francesca has inspired 46 dramas, 42 novels, and more than 70 short stories [Zoozmann].) Or was it because her very anonymity made Francesca a more fitting selection to conform to his medieval addiction to hermeticism?

Dante even had recourse to acrostics and the aid of metrics and versification in his desire to be less available. As a numerologist, many numbers were sacred to him. According to Curtius and others, Dante used cabalistic numbers to give added meaning to his groupings: a "decad" of the violent against neighbors, a heptad of sodomites, and an "ennéad" of lustful sinners. Innumerable systems and traditions are called upon to explain his arcane passages. According to Cobourg, the *Comedy* could be best explained through rites of freemasonry. However, since Dante hoped to bequeath to his homeland a new vernacular, he found himself in a dilemma, for it would not do to leave a language without the clarity of an illustrious, courtly, cardinal, and curial means of expression. Whereas modern poets, working with a sophisticated and supple language, yet still under the influence of the Symbolists, endeavor to use a clear language to write obscurely, Dante, sharing the medieval ideal of crypto-

poetry, had to keep his language a clear legacy even while giving
his message obscurely. He succeeded in this curious task, be-
queathing a concrete vernacular, with Tuscan forthrightness, to
his country—even though his *Comedy* was translated into Latin
around 1381 and in 1417. It was not an easy success. I am struck
by the fact that one has usually attributed only to sculpture his
Michelangelesque verses:

> . . . the form accordeth not
> With the intentions of art
> Because the material is dull to respond. . . .
>   (*Par.* I, 127–9)

It seems that their obvious personal meaning to Dante concerned
the disaccord between intention and language as he constructed
his allegory out of the lugubrious first-stage of Italian. Indeed,
93 times he found the right word missing and according to
I. A. Fay's *Concordance* had to invent a new term.

  Dante, then, as a result of a view of poetry which had
prevailed for several centuries before him and was about to die
out, as a result of a personal preference for hermeticism, tended
to alienate himself from the readers of the succeeding centuries.
Yet the very subject matters he dealt with tended in their
medieval phase to be foreign to the reader of today.

  Dante's view of government is certainly an alien one, even
though supported by idealism and logic. It has been nicely observed that Dante's quest for a universal government is compatible with the ideals of our United Nations organization,
that the Greek *Monarchia* means after all not monarchy, but
single rule. Yet Dante was of his time in believing that the
political body should be an empire, that the empire is of divine
establishment, that its divinity is attested by the birth of the
Savior within its precincts, and that the state is inferior to the
Church. He is modern only in believing that the state, while
inferior to, remains independent of the Church. He even states
in *De Monarchia* that the state reflects the Church as the moon
is a satellite of the sun.

  Dante fell into the error, as sometimes happens in our
times, of expecting great things from a man on a horse. His

enthusiasm for Henry VII, who was to plummet and die of
summer fevers, is reminiscent of Petrarch's initial enthusiasm
for Cola di Rienzo. An unsophisticated modern Italian wonders
how Dante selected for Italy a candidate from that barbaric
horde which had overrun Italy at least three times. He cannot
reconcile Dante's judgment with the secular attitude which
led Giusti to cry out in his refrain, "E non vogliam Tedeschi!"
His *Monarchia* is an apology for a *veltro*, a greyhound who
might come and unify Italy. In modern times we have seen
these political condottieri who rise to power on the ground
swell of a frustrated nationalism. In any case, Boccaccio tells
us that Dante wrote his *Monarchia* around 1311–12, when
hopes rose high for Henry. Indeed, Dante reserves a place in
Paradiso for Henry, who thus enjoys a more blissful eternity
than most modern autocrats. It was my old master Giuseppe
Borgese who wrote: "As the imperial authority was more and
more on the wane, Dante more resolutely sided with it, a reac-
tionary captured in the tangles of the past." This is more accurate than Frederick Engels's claim in the Italian edition of the
Communist Manifesto that Dante was the last poet of the
Middle Ages and the first of the modern era, accurate in only
the first of its two premises.

In the turbulent Middle Ages it was easier to assume that
empire was the appropriate form of government for Western
Europe. Despite the obvious social disparities under feudalism,
monarchy was supported as the best regime for all classes. Yet
the idea of a Christian monarchy or empire, with its possibilities
for unifying and conciliating various ethnic groups, is a concept
hard to understand today, when almost all Western nations
save Spain have broken away from a state religion to the extent
that even a concordat with a church seems foreign to us. Furthermore, we can no longer believe that states are founded
under a divine dispensation, as did Dante, who in the *Convito*
found it providential that Aeneas came to establish the Roman
Empire at the very time when King David, progenitor of
Christ's mother, was born.

It was Machiavelli, whose *Discourses on Livy* reveal an
intimate knowledge of *De Monarchia*, who looked at Dante's

system with a modern eye and saw what was wrong with it. There was simply no chance for a protocol of equality between Pope and Veltro. Especially was there no chance of the armed lord accepting to be a vassal of the unarmed pope, as was implied in Dante's line of the *Monarchia:* "Let Caesar, then, show toward Peter the reverence which a first-born son shows his father." Machiavelli was eventually proved right by his alleged student, the dictator of Italy, after the Concordat of 1929. No, the balance of power which was needed to restrain the Veltro was not the Church. It was, as Montesquieu wisely discovered in the eighteenth century, co-equal legislative and judicial branches of a government.

It might be wise, however, to try to justify Dante on the grounds of his time and the deplorable condition of his homeland, just as one nowadays justifies Machiavelli's cynical preachments by the weak and divided condition of Italy at the end of the Quattrocento. Did Dante have any presentiment by 1321 that a scant two hundred years later half of Europe would start to withhold from Peter the reverence which a first-born son shows his father? Had he no notion that the VELTRO which would serve as a counterweight to papal authority would be, as the anagram showed, LVTERO? So far as we know, his studies of history and his observation of weaknesses in Rome never let him foresee the convulsion which would split Christendom in twain so shortly after his death.

In the intervening years Christianity has changed, Europe has changed, political and social thinking have changed. But Italy is still there and the influence of Dante, despite the rejection of his political theorizing, is a political influence. Throughout the centuries Dante has served as a symbol and ideal of Italian unity and nationhood when no such nation existed and when Metternich was dismissing Italy as a "geographical expression." In the 1840's Russia was more advanced as a nation during the reign of Nicholas I than was Italy, but one recalls the conclusion of Carlyle's lecture on "The Hero as Poet" (1840). Even while dismembered and scattered, he claimed, "Italy is actually one . . . The nation that has a Dante is bound together as no dumb Russia can be." Hugo put it more simply, "L'Italie s'incarne en Dante Alighieri."

How close to us is Dante in his thinking on social issues? Except for his modern premise that the welfare of the individual depends on that of his society, Dante's social ideas are frequently at odds with our own. It has been stated by someone that the problems of the thirteenth century were problems of thought rather than conduct, that, for example, Christians knew that they could fight wars, but had to reconcile this with the Sermon on the Mount, whose pacifism was approved by Aquinas. On the issue of war, Dante could be theoretical or concrete. He has been hailed as a great conscientious objector to war. Viscount Bryce wrote that the call for peace and for some authority to enforce peace came from Dante first among laymen, to be taken up by great spirits in later ages, such as Erasmus at the beginning and Henry IV of France at the end of the sixteenth century, Grotius and Leibnitz in the seventeenth, and Kant in the eighteenth. It is true that Dante wanted a peaceful City of God based on the principles of St. Augustus and Aquinas, and assumed that just warfare might be needed to accomplish this ideal. When, however, wars were started over other issues, or out of pride, usurpation, or ambition, then Dante could dismiss them as foolhardy, just as in *Paradiso* XIX he deplored the warfare of Philip IV and of the bellicose English and Scotsmen ("lo Scotto e l'Inglese folle"). Yet Dante does not mention the greatest pacifist of his century, the Friar Giovanni di Vicenza, whose League of Peace after 1233 almost abolished wars in northern Italy, even if he had to impose peace through threat of military action. Dante evidently preferred the methods of Saint Francis to those of Friar Giovanni.

Dante's economic thinking occasionally departs from modern concepts. He was just as concerned as we are today about deflated currency. When Philip the Fair debased the coinage to one-third its value in 1302 (to carry on his Flemish military campaign) Dante noted the hardships this brought about:

> There one sees the harm he brings on
> Along the Seine, falsifying money. . . .
> (*Par.* XIX, 122–3)

Dante thus equates the devaluating of money with the sin of counterfeiting so severely punished in *Inferno* XXIX.

Condemnation of usurers was certainly to be expected. To debate whether usury meant moneylending or charging exorbitant interest on loans is begging the question. In the Biblical and Christian view, any rate of interest was wrong. The modern view came in with the Renaissance, which approved moneylending at a decent interest. As early as the *Essays* of Bacon this interest was set at 7½ per cent, or 6 per cent if property is offered as collateral. Bacon's view parallels that of the Puritans, vigorous proponents of capitalism, a system which Dante, as Borgese observed, condemned through Vergil's words on usury in *Inferno* XI, 94–111. It might be noted, however, that Dante merely let Vergil quote Aristotle and Scripture. His condemnation is most cautious, merely affirming that one who earns money from another's toil seems to offend the plan of nature or God, a general truth which is shared by many today and has given Wall Street such a bad name around the world. Nor does Dante show us any famous usurers suffering in his hell. He seems to be less censorious than Chaucer in the anti-Semitic *Prioress's Tale*, more severe than the Canonists themselves.

Dante went much further than we in his concern over avarice and prodigality, which are no less than sins to him. The rise of the bourgeoisie and bourgeois values after Dante, of industry, of Puritanism—all tended to support for a while Dante's condemnation of these two contrasting frailties. In modern times a totally new element has entered the picture: the graduated income tax, universally levied. This social levy, which the Puritans viewed as illegitimate, has leveled incomes and made it more difficult for the individual to be avaricious or even prodigal. The tithe of one's income which the medieval Christian owed to his Church was a modest levy compared to the taxation, direct and indirect, imposed on modern man. In any case, Dante felt that avarice and prodigality were moral rather than civil sins. He places these sinners not too deep in hell, even though the punishment, borrowed from the example of Sisyphus, is by modern standards much too severe. It would almost seem that Dante, under Franciscan influence, invokes these sins merely as a weapon against the clergy, for no lay examples from history or legend are recalled—only a few tonsured clerics, unnamed and indeed unidentifiable in the gloom of hell.

Yet in the seventh canto of the *Inferno* Dante has not had his complete say about prodigality, for deeper in hell he places wasters of their own or their family property, rent by wild dogs. Wasting one's patrimony, deplorable as it may be, is hardly viewed as a mortal sin nowadays, although Sartre amusingly included one of these spendthrifts of the *bien familial* in the hell of his *Jeux sont faits*, pursued not by angry dogs but by angrier ancestors. In Dante's *Inferno* the squanderers Jacomo da Sant'Andrea and the Sienese Lanno were at least wasting their own money, rather than that of the Church, and were thus violent to themselves, and so punished to the same degree as suicides.

Was Dante in advance of his time in his view of women? The Middle Ages, through its clerical writers, tended to view women as subjected to man, as dangers to man's morals and peace of mind. St. Thomas hedged in his *Summa Theologica:* "The image of God . . . is found in both man and woman. But in a secondary sense the image of God is found in man and not in woman." The double standard was thus preserved. As Louis IX (Saint Louis) advised his daughter, Isabelle, Queen of Navarre, "Obey your husband humbly." The antifeminine strain epitomized by the second part of the *Roman de la Rose* and the *Corbaccio* erupted everywhere. Even Dante, as Bede Jarrett suggests, furnished materials for criticism of woman: perhaps thinking of Caccaguida's mother (*Par.* XV) or of Piccarda (*Par.* III), Franco Sacchetti complains of modern women who do not calm and restrain their husbands "but encourage them to fight for their factions and have thus brought much evil into the world."

Dante's view of women departed from the realism of Tuscan poetry, represented by Cecco Angiolieri, toward a more idealized view, conditioned by the Sweet New Style. Since Dante's own wife and mother of his children did not apparently fit into his ideal world of poetry, he never mentioned her. Since Beatrice's marriage does not fit into his ideal scheme, he mentions in Earthly Paradise (*Purg.* XXXIII, 7) Beatrice "with the other virgins." In general Dante tended to idealize women (only 24 did he find in the total realm of hell) and it is certainly true that vastly more women populate his Paradiso than his Inferno, a fact curiously and unconsciously corroborated by illustrators of the *Comedy*.

Dante's science is probably the area which most alienates him from the world today. Indeed, science itself was not yet secularized, with St. Thomas declaring that theology is the universal science. The poverty of medieval science was due in part to a willingness at the time to rely on such ancient authorities as Aristotle, Galen, Ptolemy, Pliny the Elder, and Scripture. We are told of the medieval student who discovered spots on the sun and reported them to his priest, only to be told, "My son, I have read Aristotle many times and I assure you that the spots you have seen are in your eyes and not on the sun." Dante, believing the Stagirite the "master of those who know," was another who accepted the "dead hand" of Aristotle. Dante was continually absorbed with science and sought to popularize it, his popularization being, as the historian Carl Stephenson puts it, "the best the age afforded." He has been optimistically viewed as foreseeing discoveries of modern science, such as the circulation of the blood (*Inferno*, I, 20: "lago del core") and the value of experimental science (*Paradiso* II, 95: "Esperienza . . . ch'esser suol fonte ai rivi di vostr'arte" ["Experiment, which is the source of the rivers of your arts"]); here Beatrice discourses like Roger Bacon. In 1921 the Russian mathematician Florenskij theorized that Dante's geometry and physics surpassed Euclid and anticipated contemporary theories on mass, matter, and light.

Hauvette showed that Dante made an effort to stay up-to-date in the field of science and cites as example Dante's remarks not on sunspots, but blemishes on the moon. In his *Convito* he had explained their origins, apparently after Averroese. Then, after having found a different explanation in Albertus Magnus, he hastened in *Paradiso* II to give them corrected origins. A similar example concerns his classifying of the angelic hierarchies. At first, in the *Convito*, he had accepted those propounded by Brunetto Latini. Then, after accepting rather those indicated by Dionysius Areopagiticus, he warns his reader not to fall into the error of St. Gregory, who recognized his mistake once installed in Paradise and "laughed at himself": (*Paradiso* XXVIII).

With medieval science setting scholastic logic so high over empiricism and the above mentioned experimentation, Dante has been credited with a modern skepticism concerning the syllogism, whose unreliability he attacked more than once. In *De Monarchia*, II, 5, he wrote: "Nam ex falsis [syllogismis] verum quodam modo concluditur, hoc est per accidens." "For if truth is sometimes reached through false syllogisms, this is purely accidental." And in *Paradiso* (XI, 1–2) he deplores the "senseless concern of mortals for defective syllogisms." But Dante was not alone. Others, too, were questioning syllogistic reasoning, and such insoluble posers as that of Buridean's ass, theoretically starving and dying of thirst midway between a bale of hay and a bucket of water were destroying faith in the syllogism.

The one episode which everyone adduces to demonstrate Dante's modernity and courageous spirit of scientific inquiry is that of Ulysses, ancestor of the modern astronauts. Says Hauvette, "Dans l'Ulysse dantesque nous ne pouvons voir que le glorificateur de l'énergie virile et de l'esprit de sacrifice, mis au service de la science." Man, says Ulysses, is made to follow "virtute e conoscenza." And so he sails out onto the uncharted ocean to extend man's knowledge of his world. Yet the example is not clear. This may still be wily Ulysses, the false counselor mocking the challenges of science, or it may be Dante counseling against bold scientism. For Poseidon (in the absence of a recognized Christian God at the time) took offense at this hybris and managed to engulf Ulysses and his men. If Dante had suppressed the final seven verses of the Ulysses passage, the Ithacan vagrant might indeed have served as the symbol of the modern scientist, and justified Tennyson's interpretation of his function:

> To follow knowledge like a sinking star
> Beyond the utmost bounds of human thought.

One of the writers of a standard history of Italian literature has declared that "Dante's life and work and hope are all an assiduous battle for the triumph of justice among men. Even his penitents and saints have this thirst for justice on earth" (Donadoni). Since the endless search for justice among men is as relentless now as it was in the Trecento, it would seem that Dante's ideas of crime and punishment would draw him close to modern man. However, it is not that simple. The reader of the *Inferno* and *Purgatory* may, of course, share Dante's self-righteousness as he personally judges so many of his predecessors and contemporaries. This tremendous assumption of authority is comparable only to the concept of the *Last Judgment*. Dante seemed to fear that on Judgment Day many would be claiming salvation who did not deserve it:

> But look thou: Many cry Christ, Christ!
> Who will be far less near him at the Judgement,
> Than such as know not Christ.
>
> (*Par*. XIX, 106–8)

In his *Commedia* he simplifies somewhat by an initial screening of the more obvious cases the tremendous task of judgment which lies before Christ. The authority vested in the Prince of Peace was shared by Dante, so that, as someone has written, the medieval maxim "Quod principi placuit legis habet vigorem" is modified to "poetae placuit."

If many of Dante's ethical and moral evaluations are shared by modern man, it is hardly surprising that some are not. For Dante's system of crime and punishment is not always in accord with contemporary law, or even ethics and taste. The body of law at his disposal was somewhat improvised. As late as 1148 the Tuscan Gratian (from Chiusi) published his *Concordia discordantium canonum*, trying to bring order to an accumulation of Biblical precepts, papal decretals, accounts of councils, tribal laws, court precedents, and personal opinions of learned men. This *Decretum Gratiani* brought together canon and civil laws, and forms the first part of the *Corpus juris canonici*. Dante hails this synthesis on encountering Gratian in the tenth canto of *Paradiso*:

> That other glow exists from the smile of Gratian
> Who helped the one and the other court
> So that he is popular in Paradise.
>
> (*Par*. X, 103–5)

This *Corpus Juris Canonici* was then one of the two traditions Dante had to choose from, the other being the Roman tradition of Justinian's *Corpus Juris Civilis*, the lay or civil tradition dating from the sixth century. Justinian is mentioned in both the *Purgatorio* and the *Paradiso*. In Purgatory Dante asks of what avail is Roman law since none is there now to enforce it:

> What avails [Italy] that Justinian refitted the reins on thee
> If the saddle is empty? Without that
> The shame were less.
>
> (*Purg.* VI, 88–90)

The criticism is of course not of Justinian's code, but of those plunderers and opportunists in Italy who would invalidate it. Canto VI of *Paradiso* is the only canto in the entire *Commedia* that is spoken by a single figure. Here Justinian justifies his civil law by explaining that the entire concept of empire is of God's making. Thus, a Christian God himself informs civil law. With such a clear conviction of the synthesis of canon and civil law, Dante in effect becomes a lawgiver himself, comparable, as Bede Jarrett has said, to Niccolò Roselli (1314–62), or St. Antonino (1389–1459).

As we noted above, modern taste, as well as modern law, has inevitably drawn away from Dante's definition and gradation of sin or of crime. Let us review several instances of crime and punishment from the *Inferno*. Sexual mores are a convenient example. The lustful today are not so much the object of opprobrium as of statistics. Reports on sexual behavior stress that chastity and even constancy are not the norm. As Professor Carl Friedrich of Harvard once said, "If all the extant laws against sexual misconduct in this country were actually applied, two-thirds of the population would be in jail." Literature, art, films, advertising, all emphasize the cult of the flesh. Dante placed Cleopatra in the fifth circle of Hell, but the film industry put her on billboards and made millions out of her peccadilloes. In modern times Francesca da Rimini could have demanded a compatibility test before being married to Gianciotto, thus avoiding the triple criminality to which this misalliance finally led. In any case, Dante (possibly under Vergil's influence) was most indulgent to sexual sinners, letting them at least spend eternity with their paramours. He is less than modern in attributing Francesca's downfall to the reading of a book. The modern disinclination to blame literature for adultery is exemplified by the scornful remark of a former mayor of New York when opposing a censorship bill being debated in the state legislature of New York: "Gentlemen, did you really ever know a woman who was ruined by a *book?*"

Homosexuality, more punished than heterosexuality in the literary tribunal of Dante Alighieri, was so deprecated in the Middle Ages that it sufficed (as Professor Benjamin Nelson has shown) to encumber a legitimate charge of usury with a false charge of sodomy to assure a condemnation in medieval courts. True, Renaissance Platonism produced a new attitude of permissiveness toward such sexual deviation. However, only the twentieth century (leaving aside the axe of Hitler) flaunts this practice openly. Indeed, our present world, where everything is collectivized and organized and pyramided in social entities, establishes societies of homosexuals, publishing their own journals, monopolizing radio wave lengths and television channels, a veritable Agitprop for self-protective legislation. In modern times, the families of Francesco d'Accorso or Andrea de' Mozzi could sue a Dante for libel. Dante, who makes no acknowledgement of the comparable practice of Sapphism, retains a medieval scorn for sodomy, calling its practitioners (in Brunetto's words) *tigna*, or scurf. Indeed, whereas the encounter with Ser Brunetto is sometimes viewed as a high point of pathos and indulgence in the *Inferno*, I should stress rather the elements of ridicule or low comedy which mark the meeting and leave-taking in this canto:

> They puckered their brows on us
> Like an old tailor on the eye of his needle
> (Inf. XV, 20–1)

> Then he turned about and seemed like one of those
> That run for the green cloth on the field at Verona
> (Inf. XV, 121–3)

Let us look at the final sin of incontinence, that of sullenness or anger. Dante's treatment of anger is a special one. His own anger at Filippo Argenti is either an indication that righteous wrath is pardonable and perhaps even commendable, as

Vergil's ire and approval of his own would demonstrate. Or perhaps it is an illustration that anger is bad because it communicates and stirs up reciprocal wrath in others. Dante is, however, wrathful on many occasions during his great vision. Modern psychology has become quite sophisticated about emotions, more interested in explaining than condemning them. By the modern James-Lange theory of emotions, the legend that Filippo Argenti once slapped Dante because he was angry, would have to be restated as: Filippo Argenti once was angry because he slapped Dante. Or again, as Borgese put it in his essay in *Speculum* on Dante's wrath, with particular reference to the Argenti episode: "A physician of our time would say, perhaps, that a powerful release of adrenalin had balanced a morbid personality and completed its frame."

Modern law and attitudes are more indulgent toward anger, and crimes resulting therefrom are viewed more flexibly as "unpremeditated." In the Middle Ages wrath was a sin. In modern times wrath is a sin only when it converts itself into commission of a crime. Dante never lets us know to what acts Filippo Argenti was driven by his wrath. Nor does he extract any other example of iracund murder or harm from the hundreds of cases available to him from Achilles, Ajax—nay, from Cain—down to his time. Indeed, we only hear Cain's voice, like a transient thunderclap, high up on the Mount of Purgatory.

One may conclude from an observation of all of Dante's cases of incontinence that modern society is increasingly permissive about these human foibles unless they lead on to a more recognizable crime.

It is curious that as Dante turns to the graver sins of malice and bestiality, the very first is one which has no clear universal meaning or civil status in the modern world: heresy. In the *Convivio* (II, 9, 55–8) Dante defines heresy as the greatest of all bestialities. Whereas Catholicism has more adherents than any other religion in the world, Catholics number only one-sixth of the total population associated with the great living religions. These other religions have their own orthodoxy, and hence their own heresy. We no longer condemn revivals of ancient faiths such as that of the Epicureans, enclosed in flaming sepulchers by Dante but highly respected and copied since the days of Pater and Wilde. Indeed, after the Reformation, Christianity found itself with several orthodoxies, and there was at least one pope who placed Dante's name on the *Index of Forbidden Books*.

Excepting the word's meaning to the papal Curia and College of Cardinals, it might be alleged that the word *heresy* has now a more notorious meaning in the political than the religious sense. Unfortunately, a few countries still exist in the world where political heresy, that is denial of orthodoxy and authority, could bring punishment comparable to that meted out to Cavalcante Cavalcanti. Dante foresaw this. In choosing the example of the Ghibelline leader Farinata, Dante anticipates the fact that renegade or defeated politicians become heretics. Indeed, a majority of the heretics mentioned, Cavalcanti, Cardinal Ottaviano, and Emperor Frederick II, are civil rather than religious *figurae*. Only Pope Anastasius among these is a heretic in a truly religious sense, even though Dante follows a Church legend rather than historical fact.

Modern law will scarcely quarrel with Dante's condemnation of violence enacted upon one's neighbors, especially when the poet punishes warmongers, tyrants, and highwaymen. As for those violent against themselves, modern society is more indulgent toward squanderers and toward suicides. Suicides were placed by Dante lower in Hell than was the evil Attila, boiling in the previous canto. To modern society suicide is more deplored than condemned, even though there are statutes against it and even though great precautions are taken lest even criminals condemned to death resort to it. In Dante, suicides (he shrinks from even using the word) not only suffer a cruel punishment, but worse yet, unlike other souls, they may never be reclothed on the Day of Judgment. If one could assign a time when suicide lost its moral and social stigma, it was surely during Romanticism, when it became, in the satirical words of Daumier, "une idée romantique." Even though the dead Werther was refused Christian burial, most of the Romantic writers preached a new understanding of suicides, including the very Catholic Chateaubriand in his *Atala*.

Crimes against God do not constitute a legal category in modern law. Thus, in our essentially lay society, blasphemy (an archaic practice at best) has lost its status as a sin and has become rather an offense against taste. In fact, in an age encouraging great tolerance of one's neighbor's religion, it is in worse taste to blaspheme the God of another man's religion than one's own. Dante seemed to foresee this trend, for those who shout defiance of God on the burning sands of Canto XIV are Capaneus and the giants of Phlegra, defiers of the Greek Zeus. The defier of the Hebrew-Christian God, Adam, Dante places curiously in *Paradiso* XXVI.

Panders in Dante's codex of law are curiously paired with seducers, a grouping which modern society and legal powers do not accept. Both are scourged by devils in the *Commedia*. In Rome today all prostitutes are required to have a pander for their own protection. Even so, the sin of Venedico Caccianemico and all those Bolognese panders is considered much greater today than that of Jason, the Don Giovanni who seduced Hypsipyle and Medea. Modern psychiatry has made Don Juanism or priapism one of its most frenetic objects of study. (Priapus somehow escaped Dante's attention.) Modern psychiatry could easily exonerate Jason: Jason resented his father Aeson, his uncle Pelias, and Medea's pretensions as a sorceress; he was no doubt dominated by his mother; he needed to reassert his virility to avoid a castration complex; and so on. Dante's attitude toward seducers was to prevail for four centuries. Chaucer, Tirso de Molina, Molière, Mozart, and others have made a special effort to make Don Juan despicable, Mozart even going so far as to make him a jewel thief. Dante could not foresee the eventual exoneration of Don Juanism, but he was sufficiently modern—or had such respect for Vergil—that the seducer of Dido won his praise as the "righteous son of Anchises," even as the seduced Dido is condemned to the circle of carnal sinners.

Barrators exist in governments everywhere today. What was once called traffic of authority is now known as "influence peddling." Authoritarian governments quietly thrived on it, whereas in democratic republics it can topple governments. Influence peddling is frowned upon for practical as well as ethical or moral reasons, and a Congressional investigation of this practice in the United States was suspended until after the national elections. From Dante's description of the barratry practiced in the neighboring Tuscan town of Lucca, it would seem that neither in the Orient nor in South America has the institution of the bite or bribe become so widespread.

Dante's scorn for hypocrites stems particularly from his hatred of Tartuffes within the Church. His special targets in the "wretched college of hypocrites" are understandably the Frati Gaudenti. That the context of his condemnation of hypocrisy is mainly ecclesiastical is further demonstrated by the costumes of these sinners, heavy leaden mantles patterned, as he puts it, on the habits of the monks of Cologne. Whether in Molière or in Sinclair Lewis, the *faux dévot* today is more the subject of ridicule than indignation. Here it should be pointed out how frequently Dante reinforces his condemnation of human failings by setting them into a Church rather than lay setting. Even such a patently reprehensible sin as thievery is so presented. With all the notorious thieves of history and legend at his command, Dante condemns thievery through the relatively obscure symbol of Vanni Fucci, who robbed the treasure of San Zeno Church in Pistoia.

Deep in hell are the evil-counselors, wicked strategists, causers of dissension, counterfeiters, and liars—all of them, of course, unrepentant. Like thieves and hypocrites, sowers of discord are placed disadvantageously in a Church setting, and Fra Dolcino, head of the Order of the Apostolic Brothers (a sect abolished by Clement V in 1305), thus makes this vice almost equal to heresy. Among these sinners there is one who is almost twentieth-century in his guilt, evoking the war-guilt trials of Nuremburg. This is Guido da Montefeltro explaining that he had no idea that Pope Boniface was intending to break the cold-war truce which he, Guido, was counseling, so that Palestrina, the stronghold of the Pope's enemies, was subsequently destroyed. Though Guido's suggested stratagems would have made Machiavelli blush, he now insists that he acted under duress.

It is curious that alchemists, impersonators, counterfeiters, and liars are all punished by recognizable physical maladies: leprosy, madness, dropsy, and high fever. Dante's moral opprobrium concerning false impersonation has not been successfully communicated to modern times, for following centuries have been most sympathetic to that lovable scoundrel, Gianni Schicchi. As Professor Altrocchi has shown, Cademosto, Granucci, Regnard, Alfred Meissner, Thomas Roscoe, Charles Lever, Mary Roberts Rinehart (not to forget Puccini) have removed all moral indignation from this wonderful tale. Nor has anyone ever rebuked the Hauptmann von Köpenick, the greatest false impersonator of German literature, even though falsification of identity on a passport or visa is still a severe crime today. As is, of course, counterfeiting, the crime of Master Adam of Brescia and of Hitler, who printed up thousands of British pounds as a stratagem of war.

Whereas the modern world will not quarrel with Dante that betrayals of family, fatherland, redeemer, emperor, and benefactors are in principle worthy of harsh punishment, the concept of fatherland is now modified by a superstructured factionalism between a Communist and so-called free world, more worldwide than the Guelf-Ghibelline or White-Black dissensions of Dante's time. Thus traitors in the United States were heroes in Stalinist Russia. Indeed, the question of betrayal becomes less clear in modern times. Modern sophistication even questions the guilt of Brutus, Cassius, and Judas, as the archsinners of all humanity. The guilt of Brutus and Cassius, questioned as early as Donato Giannotti in Italy itself, is still in doubt today. As for Judas, Kazantzakis has his Christ feel a deep compassion for the unfortunate apostle selected by God to execute the unhappy betrayal for which he will suffer universal and eternal disgrace, but which is necessary for the redemption of mankind.

Finally, Dante's adaptation of the ancient legal principle of making the punishment fit the crime alienates him from modern times, for his is a poetic rather than a logical adaptation. It leads him to depict sinners enduring punishments suggesting or prolonging their earthly lives, or else enacting penances reminiscent of their weaknesses as men, such as misers struggling with heavy weights. Poetry sometimes takes Dante to the extreme opposite of logic, as when Satan chews on the three archsinners, and all analogy is lost with the nature of their crimes. Dante's classification of crime, elucidated in *Inferno* XI,

a bold and sincere attempt of a scholastic mind, has little meaning in the modern world. No longer do we use such classifica-
tions as incontinence, violence, and deceit, both the last two
subdivided, as I see it, into crimes against fellow man, crimes
against oneself, crimes against God. This scholastic approach
leads to such illogicalities as equating hypocrisy with theft in
the Eighth Circle. The modern principle of penology which
insists that there are two phases of criminality—intention and
tort—is not consistently followed in Dante's system. Francesca
is no less guilty even though she and Paolo fell "senza sospetto"
(unsuspecting) into their sin.

In a world which is slowly turning against capital punishment, to the extent that mobs will congregate at prisons or
embassies to protest the death sentence of even the most con-
spicuous murderers, Dante's Inferno stands as a symbol of
capital punishment. The alternative, imprisonment in a penitentiary, where repentance and penance may occur, is represented by Dante's Purgatory. In Dante a criminal may be
damned or saved via Purgatory through the mere fact of death-
bed repentance, and identical sins are represented in both
Hell and Purgatory. Whereas actual repentance of crime has
no validity in modern criminology, Dante's dual system has a
curious parallel in the fact that of two criminals sentenced for
an identical crime in different areas of the United States, one
may be sentenced to death and the other to repentance.

To leave the subject of Dante's crime and punishment,
modern man is troubled by its alien concepts. Vergil's Tartarus
is more compatible and reasonable to us, for when we read of
Aeneas hearing the screams of the wicked being punished, we
can easily graft onto the *Aeneid* our own codes of crime and
punishment and thus find no inconsistency or foreign values
in it.

Dante's role in the modern world must be assayed briefly
on one final score: his religion. Dante was the poet of the
world's greatest religion. Naturally Dante was most quickly
translated in the Catholic countries: Spain, 1428; Catalonia,
1429; France, ca. 1550; whereas the Reformational countries
Germany and England published translations in 1767 and 1785.

With 572 million Catholics in today's world, Dante is still the poet of the greatest Church. However, emerging peoples are accompanied by emerging religions. As we stated above, Catholicism makes up only one-sixth of the population of today's believers in one of the great religions. The second greatest religion of the world today is the Moslem, with 446 million adherents, a religion spread from North Africa to the Philippines and destined to a probable future penetration deep into Africa. Although Palacios and other Arabists claimed that Dante adapted Mussulman eschatology and symbolisms, leaning on al-Ma'arri's *Epistle of Pardon* and the legend of Mohammed's trip through paradise, this did not prevent Dante from vilifying the Prophet. What are Moslems to do with a book which describes their messiah in the following indecorous way:

> Even a cask, through loss of middle piece or cant,
> Yawns not so wide as one I saw, ripped from the chin
> Down to the part that utters vilest sound.
>   Between the legs the entrails hung;
> The pluck appeared, and the wretched sack
> That makes excrement of what it has swallowed.
>   (*Inf.* XXVIII, 22–27)

and has him passing eternity in hell? Is it any wonder that the *Comedy* was not translated into Arabic until this century? That it has not even now been completely and accurately translated? The standard Arabic translations by Hasan 'Uthmān and by Abbūd Ali Rāshid omit the reference to their Prophet and are almost as offended over Dante's handling of Saladin.

The Church which Dante represents is very aware of these emerging peoples. It is possible that the Church will make modifications and concessions to their ways and beliefs just as the Jesuit missionaries let North, Central, and South American Indians inculcate Christianity with indigenous symbols and practices. Till now, the tenacity and orthodoxy of this Church of Peter, almost as immovable as the rock on which it was founded, has kept Dante more meaningful for our age. A believer in Providence might even feel that it was ordained for Dante to be born within the confines of the medieval theocracy for the same reason that Dante supposed Christ born in the outer marches of the Roman Empire: in order that his message be sustained and propagated throughout the geographical extent and temporal duration of the Church. It is axiomatic that as the Church moves toward *aggiornamento* it will move away from Dante. In a volume summarizing the debates of Vatican Council II (First Session), I do not find the name of Dante.

Dante's religion, in sum, was of a totality and intensity foreign to the religious mood prevailing in the West today. It must be admitted, however, that medieval faith and religiosity were qualities whose disappearance could be regretted now. Was it not Cardinal Newman who wrote: "There would be a gain to this country were it vastly more superstitious, more bigoted, more gloomy, more fierce in its religion than at present it shows itself to be."

As we prepare some final considerations of the influence of Dante in this twentieth century, let us review briefly the intervening historical periods and assess his influence on them before summarizing our thoughts about our own age. Unlike other medieval and scholastic writers, Dante never underwent an eclipse in the Renaissance. Never was there a human being the equal of Dante, wrote Michelangelo in a sonnet, and praised him for teaching us about hell and purgatory. The artists kept his memory green as much as anyone. Michelangelo illustrated a volume of the *Comedy*, unfortunately lost from a ship off Livorno. Raphael painted Dante as both a great philosopher and theologian. Botticelli executed delicate impressions of the Dantean vision. Indeed, one remembers Cornelius' remark to Hermann Grimm: "Betrachten Sie die italienische Kunst; der Verfall beginnt, wo die Maler aufhören, Dante in sich zu tragen." ("Consider Italian art; its decay begins the moment the painters cease to carry the image of Dante within themselves.") In France, Luigi Alamanni was teaching classes on Dante at the very court of Francis I. In England, the fame of Dante continued unabated after Chaucer retold the Ugolino episode and adapted the prayer of St. Bernard. English and German translations of the *De Monarchia*, came out, but these countries, caught up in the Reformation, did not yet translate the *Comedy* into the vernacular. The current proverb in anti-Papist Britain—"Inglese italianizzato, diavolo incarnato"—

marks an anti-Italian prejudice, but by its very existence reveals the extent of Italianism in England, that phenomenon which has lasted until our day. Certainly the rise of the Reformation reduced Dante's influence as a teacher and theologian, although every writer in every country was citing Dante to prove that a great literature could be couched in a vernacular language. The Jesuits, in their great Counterreformational drive, did not make an implement of Dante's great work.

The seventeenth century, in fact, launched a three-pronged attack against the *Divine Comedy*. The Jesuits, then dominating political and educational institutions in the Catholic countries, began their unremitting attack on Dante which was to continue through later centuries. *De Monarchia* had been on the Index since the blacklist's very year of birth, 1564. It has been stated that only five editions of Dante appeared in 1600–1750, and no commentaries whatsoever. A second criticism of Dante was on grounds of style. He wrote in crude taste and worked in genres which Aristotle had not approved. Finally, his subject matter was viewed as indecorous if not atrocious. The seventeenth century distinctly preferred Arcadian or Euphuistic literature, emphasizing pastorals, romances, and other anodyne genres which did not trouble the established social order. In the century of decorum, Dante was a bit too much. His influence was thus negligible, except on such stray writers as Milton.

The eighteenth century, with its new interest in history, also found literary history crowded with primitives of genius who strove to compete with men of obviously greater civility, reason, and orderliness. There was this new discovery, Shakespeare, crude but brilliant, who did not quite equal in stature the refined Racine. There was Dante, primitive but a genius in his way, as Vico viewed him. However, did Dante manage to boast to Vergil: "Tu se' solo colui da cui io tolsi / Lo bello stile che m'ha fatto onore"? What presumption! Among his many detractors, there was Dante's countryman, Saverio Bettinelli, who reproached him for "la stranezza della locuzione e soprattutto la transgressione nelle regole dell'epica." There was Voltaire, who found the *Comedy* "d'un goût bizarre" and dismissed it as a "plaisanterie en vers," although Dante did have the courage to place Popes in hell and call the Church a harlot. As Counson explains Voltaire's attitude: "Dante avait le tort immense de ne rentrer dans aucune catégorie définie, de ne ressembler à rien." Later Vossler solved this by inventing a new genre, the *Danteid*. Finally, there was Goethe. Long before his *Faust*, in 1787, Goethe found the *Inferno* detestable, the *Purgatory* ambiguous, and the *Paradiso* boring. In the century which was perfecting the microscope, compiling the *Encyclopédie*, rejecting God for deism, rejecting faith for reason, the influence of Dante's thought was limited.

It was the ninteteenth century which saw the greatness of Dante and was most influenced in a number of ways. Two factors favored this. First was the Gothic Romanticism. The Romantics all turn to Dante and write on the poet directly or on themes of his works: A. W. Schelling, Schlegel, Keller, Lamartine, Hunt, Coleridge, Wordsworth, Foscolo, Byron, and the others. The second factor was the development of modern philology, the greatest advance in literary scholarship since humanism. The text of the *Commedia* was further studied, translations became more accurate, the first Dante lexicon appeared (1852), commentaries multiplied. Even to translate Dante became a consummate honor. Cary's tomb in Westminster Abbey carries the simple identification he preferred: "Translator of Dante." Dante even led some (like Schlegel and Novalis) back to the Church of Rome.

Naturally, the painters were influenced by Dante, in more ways than one might suspect. Of the many praises of Dante by Blake, Rossetti, Doré, and the rest, I should like to quote merely one little-known passage on mimesis in Delacroix's journal of May 9, 1824, two years after his *Barque de Dante*. One should remember that Delacroix, a Sunday poet himself, was an articulate critic of literature. "Le Dante est vraiment le premier des poètes. On frissonne avec lui, comme devant la chose. Supérieur en cela à Michel-Ange, ou plutôt différent. Car il est sublime autrement, pas par la vérité. 'Come colombe adunate alle pasture,' 'Come si sta a gracidar la rana,' 'Come il villanello' etc. C'est cela que j'ai toujours rêvé sans le définir. Sois en peinture précisément cela. C'est une carrière unique. . . . Ne pense qu'à Dante."

Dante came into his own in the nineteenth century. He was not only popular, he was influential. Striking is this insistence of nineteenth-century writers on his modernity. He was made into a Romantic by the Romantics, and he talks like one in Byron's *Prophecy of Dante*. When Lamartine was making his *Discours de réception* at the French Academy, he declared "Dante semble le poète de notre époque." In his *Defense of Poetry*, Shelley sensed that Dante was not only more modern than realized, but with time his influence would be even greater; he found many of Dante's words "pregnant with a lightning that has as yet found no conductor."

In the twentieth century it is more difficult to embrace Dante in this way as a contemporary. For example, our literature and thought are constantly exposed to and conditioned by the four influences of Marx, Darwin, Einstein, and Freud, none of them Catholic and three of the race described by Dante as "la gente, a cui il mar s'aperse."

Although Marx almost never mentioned Dante in his writings, we know from his biographers that he knew Shakespeare, Dante, and Hegel "from his youth on" (Nicholson) and that he admired Dante as one of those "whose creations also mirrored their epoch" (Mehring). He compared to Dante's Inferno both the sulphur baths of Argenteuil and the phosphorous-match factories which employed child labor. But no acceptance of Dante as a contemporary here. Marxist critics have seen Dante more often as a supporter of fascism (Balaci) than as a voice of the working classes (Ivashenko). The Marxist view of society could hardly be more alien to that of Dante. However, I submit that his fellow-exile Dante did have his influence on Karl Marx, and perhaps a deeper one than hitherto suspected. The Marxist critic Bystrianskij in 1921 declared that both the Communist leader and the Florentine exile "had drunk deep of the chalice of hatred prepared by a class-conscious society." Always at war with society and engaged in violent polemics, Marx was buoyed up by a personal motto. He placed it in 1867 at the end of the preface to Volume I of his *Kapital*. This motto was none other than the Dantean "Segui il tuo corso, e lascia dir le genti."

We find no mention of Dante in Darwin. Nor can we

reconcile his evolutionary view of man's history with Dante's view of Genesis. Man did not evolve, but was made in God's image, as Dante reminds us in *Monarchia*. "Propter quid dictum est: faciamus hominem ad imaginem et similitudinem nostram." Dante attests this belief in the literal meanings of Genesis in *Inferno* XI, 107, *Monarchia* I, 8; I, 13; III, 4; III, 5; *De vulgare eloquio* I, 4, and elsewhere. The encroachments of Darwinism in modern times can only be at the expense of any Dantean influence.

Einstein, who paved the way for new sources of power, has shown that man can face more terrible spectacles than ever pictured in Dante's hell. His biographers tell us he had read Dante, but he does not write of him. Even if Dante's imagination anticipated our century by placing a man on the moon (burdened by thorns rather than a survival kit), Dante and Einstein are incompatible. M. Luccio's attempts to make Dante a precursor of Einstein (*Scientia*, 1960) have not convinced scientists. Dante, still dependent on what Einstein has called the "organismic science" derived from Aristotle, becomes more and more remote as an influence as physics, chemistry, and biology—in a new saltation—correspondingly accelerate Dante's withdrawal into the past.

Freudianism is also a force combatting the contemporary influence of Dante. Dante's great contribution was classifying kinds and degrees of guilt, whereas Freud questioned the very existence of guilt, explaining rather than reproving the *Schuldcomplex*. Since almost no author ever offered so much material for Freudian interpretation—the *Vita Nuova* with its Freudian dreams, the *Divine Comedy* with its colossal sublimation of a guilty love—it is curious that Freud almost never mentioned Dante. There is a casual comparison (1898) of the caves of St. Cangian with Dante's Inferno; there is a passing explanation (1919) of why Dante's shades are not scary: "So long as they remain within their setting of poetic reality, such figures (ghosts of the dead) lose their uncanniness. The souls in Dante's *Inferno* may be gloomy and terrible enough, but they are really no more uncanny than Homer's jovial world of the Gods." Freud's only reference to Dante as a psychologist was his statement that "the theme of unsatisfied revenge and inevitable punishment

[was] represented by Dante as continuing through all eternity" (letter to Wilhelm Fliess, August 20, 1898). There are also mentions in Freud's *Leonardo* and his *Moses and Monotheism*. Freud's disinclination to exercise his craft on Dante was shared by his disciples. One momentary exception is a passage in Jung's classic book on the interpretation of dreams which accepts Dante's vision of the Celestial Rose as a variant of a standard dream during which a shooting star traces the outline of a flower in the vast firmament. It is just as well that Freudian probings of Dante have been held in abeyance, although Professor Soichi Nogami tells us that it is currently popular in Japan to explain Dante's love for Beatrice as a pathological psychiatric phenomenon. Yet the fact that this fruitful field of analysis has been neglected is perhaps earnest of the diminished influence of Dante on contemporary thought.

It is not possible then to share the nineteenth-century acceptance of Dante as a contemporary. We have relegated Dante back to his own century, to a Middle Ages not only Christian, but Greco-Roman and Hebraic. In the centenary year 1921 Viscount Bryce heralded this new view. "He is so intensely interested in the problems of his own time that he makes alive and real to us, living six centuries away, things which the dust of oblivion would have otherwise long since covered. Hardly any poet whom all ages have valued was so much concerned with his own." This is no mean compliment! This is the importance of Dante which no fluctuations of taste or science can take away. It is in this role as the consummate voice of the Middle Ages that Dante transcends all ages and indeed nationalities. Whether or not Shakespeare is German, as the Germans claim, Dante now holds an international passport. *Civis mundi.* No one could have been more wrong than those fascists who came here to Ravenna from Bologna and Ferrara to add their bit to the commemoration of September, 1921. They managed to cudgel a few who refused to accept their view of Dante as a precursor of Italian fascism and nationalism. Fortunately, today we can reject this view without running such risks.

Far into the future scholars will foregather here in Italy, as we have, and the same question will be posed. What does Dante

mean to us in 2064, 2121, 2164, and after? We have been
assuming that with the broadening bridge of time Dante risks
becoming more and more an outsider to the brave new world
of the coming centuries. Could the opposite prove true? As
man changes, as taste and morals evolve, as science careens
forward, might there be social attitudes, ethic convictions, and
personal prejudices which—according to the Nietzschean theory
of cyclical history—may bring Dante closer to posterity than
he is to us? Even that major difficulty of Dante of which Voltaire complained—the wealth of local references and historical
figures—will diminish as figures on the stage of history and
literature become crowded almost beyond recognition, and
Dante's Boniface VIII or Ezzelino III will be no more unfamiliar to new readers of future centuries than will be Shakespeare's Richard III, Tolstoy's Alexander I, or Hugo's Napoleon
III.

    In sum, what is the value of Dante to us today? It is as an
artist, a poet, a visionary, a hero, and a man. Eliot and others
have so viewed him in our time. He is not just a medieval theologian, as a modern trend of American scholarship has tended
to see him. To this trend one must object in Borgese's words
that "too many people feel as if Dante had been a Dante
scholar." Perhaps it is the modern poets imbued with Dante
and Dantean images—Eliot, Pound, D'Annunzio, Claudel,
Akhmatova, and so many others—who have allayed the concern expressed by Borgese. We now know that the greatest value
of Dante is rather a personal than a social one. Ask just as easily,
what is the value of a medieval cathedral, with its stone demons
threatening hell and its rose-windows promising heaven? I do
not of course invent the analogy, but I find it satisfying and
relevant. One can say of a cathedral what Quinet has said of
Dante, that his influence on society was nil, but his influence on
individuals was immense. One can go further. Dante remains
in the hearts and consciences of millions. The tremendous personal impact of the *Comedy* can be compared best with the
feeling which overpowers one as he stands alone in the glowing
gloom of a Chartres Cathedral. It was Longfellow who captured
in Dantean tercets, quoted earlier by Professor Wilkins, this
experience transmitted alike by Dante's book and by a medieval

basilica, its statuary and stained glasses promising that Love which moves the sun and the other stars.

> So, as I enter here from day to day,
> And leave my burden at this minster gate,
> Kneeling in prayer and not afraid to pray,
> The tumult of the time disconsolate
> To inarticulate murmurs dies away,
> While the eternal ages watch and wait.